The Official History of Colonial Development

VOLUME 4

CHANGES IN BRITISH AID POLICY, 1951–1970

The author has been given full access to
official documents. He alone is
responsible for the statements made
and the views expressed.

The Official History of Colonial Development

VOLUME 4

CHANGES IN BRITISH AID POLICY, 1951–1970

D. J. Morgan

First published 1980 by
THE MACMILLAN PRESS LTD
London and Basingstoke
Associated companies in Delhi
Dublin Hong Kong Johannesburg Lagos
Melbourne New York Singapore Tokyo

Printed in Great Britain by
Unwin Brothers Ltd,
The Gresham Press, Woking Surrey

British Library Cataloguing in Publication Data

Morgan, David John
 The official history of colonial development
 Vol. 4: Changes in British aid policy, 1951–1970
 1. Great Britain – Colonies – Economic policy
 2. Economic assistance, British
 I. Title II. Changes in British aid policy,
 1951–1970
 338.91'171'241041   HC259

ISBN 0–333–26233–6
ISBN 0–333–28800–9 (5 volume set)

Contents

List of Tables

Preface

My interest in the field of Colonial and Commonwealth economic policy was aroused in 1941 when, on joining the staff of Dr Arnold J. Toynbee's Foreign Research and Press Service in Oxford, I was required to prepare a study of the economic background and implications of the Ottawa Trade Agreements, 1932. Over the following years – at the University of Liverpool, the London School of Economics, the University of the West Indies, the University of Manchester, the Overseas Development Institute, and the Institute of Commonwealth Studies of the University of London – I extended my interest beyond trade policy to the problems of development and aid. This was enormously assisted in the first place by my residence in Jamaica over the years 1955–1959 whilst I was Head of the Department of Economics at the University College. During those years I was able to gain first-hand knowledge of the economies and economic problems of the Caribbean area: Mexico and Central America, Venezuela and Guyana, the British, French and Dutch islands, Cuba, Haiti and Puerto Rico. It was assisted in the second place by the privileged access to the files of the Colonial Office in order to prepare a short history of the origins and nature of British aid to developing countries, which was published by the Overseas Development Institute in 1964 under the title of *Colonial Development*. In the third place, there were study-visits to the New Commonwealth. In 1964 a Houblon-Norman award enabled me to renew my acquaintance with the West Indies, beginning with Bermuda and the Bahamas, in order to study banking developments and aid problems. A Hayter grant in 1966 and a Leverhulme award in 1969 enabled me to become acquainted with the economies and economic problems of East and Central Africa, Ethiopia and Egypt. In particular, I studied the working of joint ventures between local and expatriate interests, including among the former the local development corporations and among the latter both the Commonwealth Development Corporation and the Commonwealth Development Finance Company. I was fortunate to meet Governors, Ministers and officials, Governors of Central Banks, staffs of local development corporations, banks and businesses of many kinds, economists in the Universities and Research Institutes, and the Regional Controllers and staffs of the CDC, who gave me the benefit of their experience.

The invitation to prepare a full-scale study of Colonial Development in the new Peacetime Series of Official Histories was exciting and challenging. Because of the sheer mass of official documentation made available, it was also daunting. Thus, for one fairly self-contained episode, namely the East African Groundnuts Project over the years 1946–51, when it was the responsibility of the Ministry of Food, between 600 and 700 files were 'put by' by that Ministry, while the Lord President's Office, the Cabinet Office, the Treasury, the Foreign Office, the Commonwealth Relations Office and the Colonial Office added an assortment of complementary files. In order to decide on a firm outline for the whole History, I began by reading through the Cabinet Conclusions for the years 1935–65, so that the topics which engaged the attention of Ministers in the broad field of Colonial Development were known in the context of the concerns and decisions of the time. Topics were then followed, in turn, through Cabinet Committees to departmental files, where internal and inter-departmental discussions led up to Briefs for Ministers. In the Treasury, the Chancellor of the Exchequer customarily awaited on an agreed draft from his senior officials before he was prepared to discuss even with his Cabinet colleagues. Once Ministers have come to their decisions, matters are returned to officials for implementation. The more general the decision – and Cabinet decisions are necessarily often in somewhat general terms – the more discretion there is in implementation. Officials might even feel justified in providing favoured treatment in cases where Ministers deny any preference, as happened over the allocations to the Overseas Food Corporation discussed in Volume 2, Chapter 5, Section xii. Without the ready assistance of experienced records officers, the whole operation would have been imperilled. It is a pleasure to thank those in the Departments concerned, namely the Foreign and Commonwealth Office, the Cabinet Office, the Treasury, the Ministry of Agriculture, Fisheries and Food, and the Ministry of Overseas Development. Many others, particularly in the Historical Section of the Cabinet Office, did much over the years to facilitate the study and deserve my gratitude. I have acknowledged at the appropriate places in the text my indebtedness to those with whom I discussed while the study was being prepared.

In the course of his announcement of the Peacetime Series (H. of C. Deb., Vol. 793, cols 411–12, 18 December 1969), the Prime Minister,

Mr Harold Wilson, stated that the Series 'would enable important periods in our history to be recorded in comprehensive and authoritative narratives, written while the official records could still be supplemented by reference to the personal recollections of the public men who were involved'. In accordance with this intention, the following persons have kindly commented on the part of the draft where they had first-hand knowledge: Sir William Gorell Barnes, the Viscount Boyd of Merton, Sir Sydney Caine, Mrs E. M. Chilver, the Lord Greenwood of Rossendale, Sir Stephen Luke, the Rt Hon. Malcolm MacDonald, Sir Leslie Monson, the Lord Ogmore, the Earl of Perth, Sir David Pitblado, Sir Hilton Poynton, Sir Philip Rogers, Sir David Serpell, Sir John Winnifrith.

I am grateful to them for their kindness in reading the draft and discussing it with me; additions to and other improvements of the text resulted. I should like also gratefully to acknowledge the interest in the History shown by Mr Harold Macmillan at a critical time.

Finally, my wife Eleanor took a keen interest in the whole project from beginning to end and many improvements in the text were suggested by her: I am happy to acknowledge her assistance. As always, the remaining shortcomings and blemishes, great and small, are entirely the responsibility of the author.

D. J. Morgan

21 April 1978

List of Abbreviations

AACC	Anglo-American Caribbean Commission
CAO	Central African Office
CCD	Committee on Colonial Development
CCED	Committee on Commonwealth Economic Development
CDAC	Colonial Development Advisory Committee
CDC	Colonial Development Corporation (1948–1963) then Commonwealth Development Corporation
CDF	Colonial Development Fund
CD & W	Colonial Development and Welfare
CDWAC	Colonial Development and Welfare Advisory Committee
CDWP	Colonial Development Working Party
CEAC	Colonial Economic Advisory Committee
CEDC	Colonial Economic and Development Council
CEPS	Central Economic Planning Staff (Treasury)
CPC	Colonial Policy Committee (Cabinet)
CRO	Commonwealth Relations Office
DTC	Department of Technical Co-operation
D & W Organisation	Development and Welfare Organisation (Barbados)
ECA	Economic Co-operation Administration (United States)
EEC	European Economic Community
EFTA	European Free Trade Association
EPC	Economic Policy Committee (Cabinet)
ERP	Economic Recovery Programme (United States)
GATT	General Agreement on Tariffs & Trade
HMOCS	Her Majesty's Oversea Civil Service
IBRD	International Bank for Reconstruction and Development

ODM	Ministry of Overseas Development
OFC	Overseas Food Corporation
ORD Acts	Overseas Resources Development Acts
REC	Regional Economic Committee (West Indies)
SCAC	Standing Closer Association Committee
SEAF	Committee on Food Supplies from South-East Asia
UAC	United Africa Company
WFS	Ministerial Committee on World Food Supplies

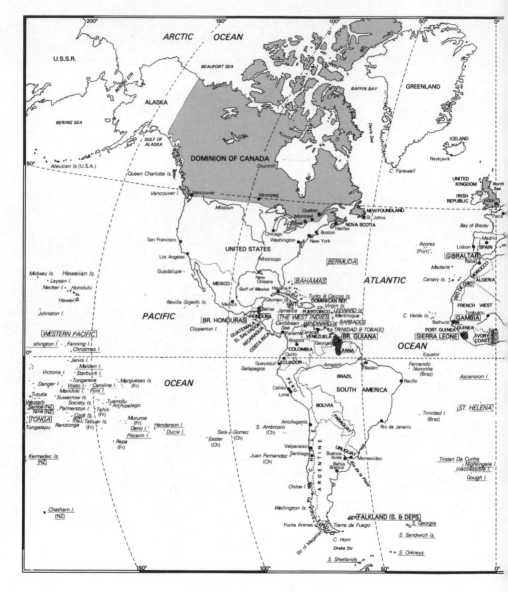

The Commonwealth, 1960

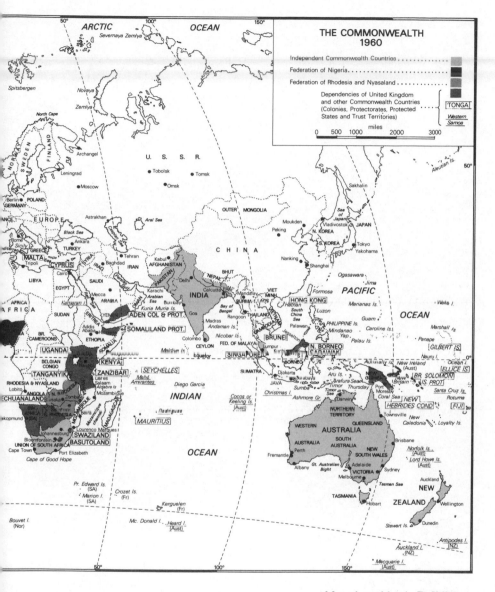

Map planned by A. E. Kelleway,
Historical Section, Cabinet Office.

1 The Contribution of Colonial Development and Welfare, 1940–1970

With the expiry on 31 March 1970 of the Overseas Development and Service Act, 1965, the CD & W system came formally to an end. In 1965, the year of the Overseas Development and Service Act, the Secretary of State for the Colonies was responsible for thirty-two territories, excluding the British Antarctic Territory which had no permanent inhabitants. The list was as in Table 1.1.[1]

TABLE 1.1 British Dependent Territories and their Populations, November 1965

Territory	Population (latest estimates)
Aden and the Protectorate of South Arabia	1,100,000
Antigua	60,000
Bahamas	134,000
Barbados	242,000
Basutoland	733,000
Bechuanaland Protectorate	548,000
Bermuda	48,000
British Guiana	630,000
British Honduras	103,000
British Indian Ocean Territory[1]	1,400
British Solomon Islands Protectorate	137,000
British Virgin Islands	8,500
Cayman Islands	8,853
Dominica	64,000
Falkland Islands and Dependencies	2,117
Fiji	449,000
Gibraltar	24,386
Gilbert and Ellice Islands	50,000
Grenada	93,000
Hong Kong	3,692,000
Mauritius	741,000

TABLE 1.1 *(cont.)*

Territory	Population (latest estimates)
Montserrat	13,500
New Hebrides[2]	66,000
Pitcairn	86
St Christopher–Nevis–Anguilla	59,000
St Helena and Dependencies[3]	5,170
St Lucia	94,000
St Vincent	85,000
Seychelles	46,000
Swaziland	285,000
Tonga[4]	71,000
Turks and Caicos Islands	6,272

[1] This territory consists of the Chagos Archipelago (formerly part of Mauritius) and Aldabra, Farquhar and Desroches Islands (formerly part of Seychelles).
[2] This is an Anglo-French Condominium. Authority is exercised jointly by British and French Resident Commissioners under the 1914 Protocol.
[3] The dependencies are Ascension Island and Tristan da Cunha.
[4] Britain was responsible for external affairs, defence, banking currency and exchange under a Treaty of Friendship.

By 31 March 1970 the three High Commission Territories were independent: Basutoland as Lesotho (4 October 1966), the Bechuanaland Protectorate as Botswana (30 September 1966) and Swaziland, which retained its original name (6 September 1968). So also were Barbados (on 30 November 1966), British Guiana as Guyana (on 23 February 1970), and Mauritius (on 12 March 1968). Fiji was to follow later that year (10 October 1970).

Additionally, and more significantly, there had been time to integrate the system of Colonial assistance within the system of overseas aid. As shown in previous volumes, this had not been the case in 1965. A White Paper entitled *Colonial Development and Welfare Acts, 1929–70: A Brief Review* was published in 1971 'to mark 40 years of aid under the Colonial Development and Welfare Acts and the transformation of an imperial obligation into an international undertaking'.[2] Of course British Government assistance for economic, social and educational advance in the Colonies and dependencies has a long history stretching back to the nineteenth century. From the first its development and extension was not easy; it was usually a target for criticism and opposition. Sir Leslie Monson mentioned to the author a statement which Gladstone made to a Parliamentary Committee in 1862 to the effect that all British Colonies were destined, sooner or later, to become independent of Britain, and that it was therefore wrong to provide them with services at the expense of the British Exchequer which they could not finance from their own resources. In an investigation Sir Leslie made for the Foreign and Commonwealth Office in 1973, he came across a direction in 1892 that no contribution from Imperial funds should be made to the cost of administering certain islands over which a British Protectorate had just been established and that the administration should, therefore, be such as they could support from their own resources. The administration consisted, in fact, of one expatriate officer, a local policeman and an interpreter! This direction was written in a minute by the Marquess of Ripon, Secretary of State for the Colonies in Gladstone's Cabinet of the time. It is a piquant contrast with the fact that in the 1960s some Colonial territories became independent and still continued to receive budgetary aid from HMG. Dame Margery Perham's *Life of Lugard*, Volume II, shows the limits that were imposed on Joseph Chamberlain by his unwillingness to run against Parliamentary hostility to expenditure on the Colonies. This hostility was increased, and his position was correspondingly weakened, by the considerable expenditure incurred in the Anglo-Boer War. Only railways and, to some extent, what would now be called economic infrastructure were the exceptions to the predominantly *laissez-faire* conception of Colonial development. Railways had for long been exceptional for they were not only financed by governments, but in many cases constructed by governments. Girouard, who succeeded Lugard in Northern Nigeria, was expressly appointed with railway construction in mind and was himself, by previous experience in South Africa and Egypt, a railwayman rather than an administrator. Yet the fundamental assumption was that there should be no more than a degree of responsibility by the governments for the provision of the economic infrastructure, without which private enterprise would not be willing and could not be expected in general to operate. Chamberlain managed to do little more than that in the West Indies, but in Africa it is hard to discern any deviation from this outlook.

The early *ad hoc* assistance became formalised in time by the legislation of 1929 and 1940, when assistance became less a matter of emergency aid to particular territories because of natural disasters or of finance for some major capital projects, and rather a result of systematic examination of schemes put forward by overseas governments on the invitation of HMG. The 1929 Act created the machinery for the examination of projects on their individual merit, and the machinery worked well. But it was no more than a halfway stage. The requirement that projects should both aid and develop agriculture and industry in the Colonies, and thereby promote 'commerce with or industry in the United Kingdom', was not seriously restrictive in practice, but the exclusion of education, though not health or general research, was. Also, the sharp distinction between capital expenditure and recurrent expenditure inevitably favoured richer Colonies, which found it easy to finance maintenance costs, as against poorer Colonies, which did not. Increasingly, as the decade of the 1929 Act passed by, it came to be felt that schemes should be assessed as part of comprehensive development plans rather than singly.

Yet the basic philosophy of the economic relationship between HMG and the Colonies precluded any meaningful discussion of the feasibility of any new financial relationship. Thus HMG might, for example, have taken responsibility for, say, educational expenditure throughout the aided territories, and so have relieved Colonial budgets of an increasing burden and improved the ability of poor Colonies to provide recurrent finance in other fields. France did just that in her Empire; it was one of the major differences between the aid systems of the two countries.

The 1940 Act corrected the deficiencies of the system that had been tried over the previous ten years. It voted more funds. It widened the purposes of 'schemes' to cover 'any purpose likely to promote the resources of any Colony or the welfare of its people', and explicitly included expenditure on education. It required comprehensive development plans to be submitted. It discontinued the statutory Advisory Committee procedure. The sums available were allocated on the basis of need for finance, on the one hand, and ability to find and use finance, on the other hand. Part of the funds voted were reserved for central schemes, usually concerned with research, higher education and training, which benefited more than one territory. This was a valuable innovation, and possibly the first systematic attempt to deal with general problems of growth in Colonial territories. With the benefit of hindsight, it is to be regretted that the central allocation was not made a larger feature of the 1940 system from the outset, even if it had to be in part at the expense of the territorial allocations.

In 1955 an attempt was made to alter the territorial allocations in the light of the potential for development, on the one side, and the ability to finance developments, on the other. However praiseworthy the purpose, the exercise was found to make little difference in practice as funds could not, for political reasons, be denied to territories with little potential for development. Indeed, the exercise of 1955 did much to highlight the real nature of the problems of development and development assistance. An influential architect of the 1940 system summed up the position as he saw it in 1957 in these words:

> Probably the net effect of the Colonial Development and Welfare System has been to increase the total sums available for development expenditure; to increase rather less the actual amounts spent on such development, the balance going to the increase of Colonial reserves; but to make comparatively little difference to the kind of project undertaken except in the field dealt with by central schemes. To some extent the system has come to be a rather complex method of general supplementation of Colonial reserves.[3]

This is a sustainable thesis. The complexity of the method was unpopular with recipients, while the 'general supplementation' was an unavoidable, rather than an intentional, outcome of the process of administering the funds. The system for approving schemes was cumbersome and tended to be biased against novelty. Yet it must be recognised that the personal accountability of permanent heads of departments explains to a significant extent the caution. A notable example is provided by the Mona reservoir scheme in Jamaica. The original estimate of £382,000 was approved in December 1942. A further £80,900 was granted in 1945 to meet increases in cost, bringing the total to £462,900 in loans which were free of interest for the construction period and whose terms of repayment or, alternatively, conversion, in whole or part, into free grants was to be considered after completion. In 1946 the reservoir was completed but there was a drought and the reservoir was later found not to be watertight. Consulting engineers recommended that work costing £100,000 was required and in January 1954 a further loan of that amount was approved. In 1955 the Committee of Public Accounts of the House of Commons very thoroughly investigated the matter. It was found that the site engineer, who had meantime died, had a discretion concerning the advice on siting made by the consulting engineers and had chosen to proceed otherwise than they had advised. The PAC recommended a closer supervision of schemes to ensure that expert advice was in all cases implemented.[4] Anyone reading the discussion of this scheme in the Report is certain henceforth to sympathise with those civil servants who avoid novel schemes and risky projects. (The Governor of Jamaica at the time of the enquiry, Sir Hugh Foot, later Lord Caradon, told the author that the words 'Mona reservoir' would be found written on his heart when he died!)

Apart from such meticulous enquiries into some of the breakdowns, there was never any system for assessing schemes other than the regular accounting procedures, which were concerned solely to ensure that funds had been used for the purposes prescribed and in the authorised manner. Whether the contribution of a scheme exceeded, equalled or fell short of the expectations stated when the scheme was put forward for approval was never a matter for official assessment. Naturally, officials often came by some indication of the general usefulness of certain kinds of schemes in the course of their correspondence with Colonial governments and their occasional visits overseas. But this was incidental and qualitative rather than regular and quantitative. Certainly, it must be acknowledged that, given the smallness of so many of the individual schemes, combined with the fact that much of the benefit was longer-term and widely diffused rather than immediate and narrowly concentrated, there would be limits to any meaningful assessment in very many cases. Nor, as has been seen, was CD & W allocated with strict regard to economic potential. There was a strong political element and, as the then Chancellor of the Exchequer admitted in 1944, an underlying moral basis to the system. Even so, it is to be regretted that some effort was not made to do more than certify that funds had been spent in a proper manner.

The valedictory White Paper of 1971 reviewed (1) the initiating role of Parliament and legislation, (2) the administration of the successive Acts from 1929 to 1965, and (3) how the funds were spent. It then described five major projects, namely (i) overseas geodetic and topographical surveys to provide reliable maps, which are an essential prerequisite for intelligent development projects; (ii) air communications in the Eastern Caribbean; (iii) broadcasting development; (iv) University education; and (v) the development of African agriculture in Kenya. Aspects of each of these projects have been dealt with at various stages in this History. The White Paper brought the information together and then, in its fifth and final chapter, considered the contribution to research made, at first *ad hoc* and then systematically, under CD & W by HMG.

Among the various appendices in the White Paper, there is a table which divides the total issues of grants and loans to benefiting territories by class of scheme, other than research schemes, for the period 1946–70. Total issues, excluding research, came to £324.4 million. In all, twenty-one kinds of scheme are separately shown. From the table, it is possible to see how the money was spent. The territorial distribution was as follows: 45 per cent to Africa; 22 per cent to the Caribbean area; 8 per cent to the Mediterranean Colonies, chiefly to Malta; 7 per cent to the Western Pacific; 6 per cent to South-East Asia and a similar percentage on services in Britain, mainly survey work and student training. The remaining 5–6 per cent was spread over a number of small, usually island, territories from Hong Kong to the Falklands. The countries which received the largest grants were Nigeria (£40 million), Kenya (£23 million), Malta (£20 million), Tanganyika (£14 million), British Honduras (£13 million) and British Guiana (£12 million). Education claimed 21 per cent of total expenditure, with primary and secondary education accounting for 10.5 per cent, technical and vocational for 3.4 per cent and higher education for 7.1 per cent. Roads claimed 17 per cent, medical and health services 9.2 per cent, water supplies 6.2 per cent, housing and town planning 4.4 per cent. Expenditure on the major sectors in Africa was approximately two-and-a-half times that in the Caribbean, where the presumed bias of expenditure on social services is not confirmed by the figures. Special needs caused local variations in the general pattern. Thus, 84 per cent of expenditure on land settlement was made in Africa, and half of it in Kenya on the settlement schemes of the Swynnerton Plan, (the five-year 'Plan to intensify the development of African Agriculture in Kenya' which was started in April 1954), while 43 per cent of the money allocated to civil aviation was spent in the Caribbean, mostly on airfields in the smaller islands, compared with 22 per cent for the whole of Africa. The balance was also affected by heavy expenditure in certain sector on the smaller territories. Thus, 75 per cent of expenditure under the head of industrial development was made in Malta, while 19 and 25 per cent of the housing and town planning expenditure was made in Gibraltar and British Honduras, respectively.

But there are few Colonial territories where one would not find a new hospital or a new road or new schools or new water works which have been provided by the generosity of the United Kingdom peoples through the Colonial Development and Welfare system. In some of the poorest – for instance, in some of the smaller West Indian islands – it is hardly an exaggeration to say that all new public works in the last decade or two have been financed by Colonial Development and Welfare funds.[5]

These expenditure figures have been obtained by aggregating expenditure for each of the financial years 1946 to 1970 made (i) in each territory, and (ii) for each kind of scheme. Yet it is obvious that the real value, in terms of goods and services, of a £ changed substantially over the thirty years that the system operated. Ideally, a real value index should be calculated to show the material contribution to each

TABLE 1.2 CD & W Scheme Aid as a Percentage of Gross Domestic Product at Factor Cost, 1950–1970

SOURCES – Aid: calendar year estimates derived from ODA financial year data.
GDP: UK *National Accounts Statistics 1957–1970*, Vols I and II.

	1950	1951	1952	1953	1954	1955	1956	1957	1958
Aden									
Federation of Arabia									
Antigua	2.786			3.417	6.048	3.792	3.375	7.257	6.722
Bahamas									
Barbados	1.974	1.070	0.120	0.135	0.318	0.564	0.776	1.174	0.485
Basutoland (Lesotho)									
Bachuanaland (Botswana)									
British Guiana (Guyana)	1.171	0.586	1.640	1.260	1.478	2.491	1.748	3.150	1.291
British Honduras					5.792	5.446	4.672	5.391	9.97.
British Solomon Islands									
Cayman Islands									
Cyprus	0.579	0.429	0.418	0.455	0.114	0.190	0.041	0.039	0.198
Dominica	5.118								
East Africa High Comm.									
Falkland Islands									
Fiji	0.119			0.327				0.326	
The Gambia									
Gibraltar									
Gilbert and Ellice Isles									
Gold Coast (Ghana)							0.286	0.072	
Grenada						0.860	3.891	5.061	1.32.
Hong Kong					0.033				
Jamaica	0.632	0.871	0.642	0.669	0.348	0.334	0.331	0.293	0.33.
Kenya	0.886	0.684	0.587	0.456	0.388	0.845	1.114	0.648	0.649
Leeward Islands									
Malaya						0.056		0.025	
Malta						1.029	1,447	0.821	0.30.
Mauritius	0.383	0.437	0.811	1.205	0.484	0.334	0.528	0.546	0.14.
Montserrat				4.200	4.200	10.000	11.200	8.333	9.33.
New Hebrides									
Nigeria	0.439	0.637	0.390	0.288	0.382	0.284	0.236	0.322	0.33
N. Borneo (Sabah)									
Northern Cameroons									
Northern Rhodesia (Zambia)					0.357	0.137	0.043	0.010	0.10.
Nyasaland (Malawi)					1.533	2.179	1.129	1.055	0.96.
Federation of Rhodesia and Nyasaland						0.042	0.024	0.034	0.01.
Palestine (Israel)									
Pitcairn Islands									
St Helena									
St Kitts, Nevis and Anguilla	1.211			1.571	1.138	1.333	0.500	1.412	3.17.
St Lucia	9.895								
St Vincent									
Sarawak									
Seychelles									
Sierra Leone									

1959	1960	1961	1962	1963	1964	1965	1966	1967	1968	1969	1970
					0.041	0.122	0.210				
2.610	4.619	5.045	3.872	2.789	2.154	2.483	3.661	6.410	3.381	6.000	1.162
.545	0.386	0.496	0.910	0.579	0.157	0.699	0.391	0.046			
					1.942	3.257	1.874	0.388			
					4.761	5.849	3.171	0.364			
4.845	2.506	1.947	1.256	1.202	0.615	0.605	0.165				
2.382	6.355		1.000	2.336	4.603						
.568	0.023	0.007									
.263	5.116	10.023	3.619	4.467	2.269	3.463	6.895	2.810	6.034	9.339	0.969
			1.027	0.072	1.472	0.599	0.749	0.689	0.882		
		4.355	7.179	5.369	3.551						
	0.006	0.001									
4.618	1.672	1.424	0.787	1.639	1.750	2.145	2.920	5.154	3.827	3.422	0.477
	0.003	0.025									
0.678	0.213	0.054	0.104	0.072	0.004	0.004					
.473	0.572	0.795	1.487	1.107	0.092						
	0.008	0.004									
3.851	7.714	3.820	3.472	4.648	2.591	0.165					
.154	0.548	1.316	0.745	0.150	0.368	0.257	0.242	1.418	0.252		
3.500	6.000	3.429	0.625	0.750	3.667	4.083	7.000	13.286	6.000	19.857	1.467
.305	0.177	0.063	0.041	0.018	0.007						
.193	0.150	0.162	0.241	0.053	0.101	0.029					
.702	1.739	3.002	1.996	1.202	0.568	0.011					
.018	0.015	0.007	0.002								
.053	5.179	3.756	5.756	3.476	0.341	0.089	8.229	4.880	0.679	2.049	1.111
	2.294	3.509	5.655	4.656	2.077	0.592	2.791	4.255	3.409	6.027	1.769
		3.490	1.302	1.784	2.528	3.018	5.169	5.328	3.906		

TABLE 1.2 (*Cont.*)

	1950	1951	1952	1953	1954	1955	1956	1957	1958
Singapore									
Somaliland									
Southern Cameroons									
Swaziland									
Tanganykia (Tanzania)									
Tonga									
Trans-Jordan (Jordan)									
Tristan da Cunha									
Trinidad		0.120	0.263	0.263	0.208	0.121	0.097	0.071	0.027
Turks and Caicos Islands									
Uganda	0.846	0.438	0.407	0.378	0.422	0.044	0.021	0.003	0.014
Virgin Islands								11.667	6.000
West Indies Federation									
Zanzibar									

CD & W Aid given as at % of GDP at factor cost

	1950	1951	1952	1953	1954	1955	1956	1957	1958
United Kingdom	1.026	0.947	0.816	0.834	0.869	0.860	0.835	0.834	0.741

SOURCE: Central Statistical Office, 9 Nov 1972.

economy. The necessary information, involving appropriate deflators for price changes and details of the split between receipt of goods and of technical assistance services, where costs might have varied relatively to one another, is not sufficiently available to make the exercise feasible. So there is no alternative to the usual adding together of 1940 £s and £s in later years, however meaningless in real terms the sum happens to be. A caveat must be entered. [The White Paper, *New Policies for Public Spending* (Cmnd 4515, October 1970), expressed the overseas aid programme for the first time in constant prices net of capital repayments as well as in gross cash terms, so as to be comparable with other items. It was stated in the White Paper (para. 5, p. 6) that: 'The economic aid programme, which for 1971–72 will be £245 million in gross cash terms, will be maintained at the levels forecast in Cmnd. 4234, rising to £300 million in 1973–74, and there will be a further increase to £340 million in 1974–75. At constant prices and net of repayments of loans, the total provision for overseas aid, i.e. including items additional to the economic aid programme, will rise from £213 million in 1971–72 to £256 million in 1974–75.']

One exercise that has proved to be possible is to show CD & W scheme aid as a percentage of Gross Domestic Product at factor cost. Here data on GDP are not sufficiently available for the 1940s, so the exercise can only be for the last twenty-one years of the

1959	1960	1961	1962	1963	1964	1965	1966	1967	1968	1969	1970
	0.006	0.006	0.003	0.011	0.003						
						4.669	3.588	2.931			
0.668	0.870	0.863	0.062	0.030	0.088	0.033					
0.201	0.180	0.020	0.050	0.016							
0.285	0.769	0.881	0.397	0.059	0.008	0.005					
11.000	9.200	5.857	8.500	3.333	4.667	13.778	12.400				
0.933	0.994	0.872	0.666	0.466	0.351	0.300	0.340	0.296	0.215	0.237	0.031

system, i.e. 1950–1970. The results are given in Table 1.2. An inspection of these figures shows that (i) only in 1950 was CD & W aid in excess of 1 per cent of the United Kingdom's GDP, though as late as 1960 it was 0.994 per cent, falling thereafter with the fall in the size of the Colonial Empire; (ii) only for the small territories and for the grant-aided territories in the Caribbean does the percentage stay significantly above 1 per cent, with the exceptions of Nyasaland and the Southern Cameroons; (iii) whereas Nigeria received the largest absolute sum, as a percentage of GDP the contribution of CD & W to Kenya, Tanganyika and Uganda was greater than that to Nigeria.

Comparisons with Colonial capital formation have been made for the ten years ending 31 March 1956, when CD & W expenditure was almost £120 million. It came to under 4 per cent of total Colonial capital formation.[6] Consequently, both claims for the CD & W system of assistance and expectations of its real contribution should be made only in the light of these figures.

SOURCES

1. H. of C. Deb., Vol. 720, col. 86, 17 Nov 1965: Written Answer by the Secretary of State for the Colonies, Mr A. Greenwood.
2. Cmnd 4677, 9 June 1971, p. 5.

3. 'Colonial Development: A British Contribution to World Progress' by Sir Sydney Caine: *Progress* [the Unilever magazine] Autumn 1957, pp. 80–4.

4. *First Report from the Committee of Public Accounts, Session 1955–56*, 21 June 1955 (HC 15–1).

5. 'Colonial Development', op. cit., p. 83.

6. Ibid., p. 82.

2 From the Department of Technical Co-operation to the Ministry of Overseas Development

1. OFFICIAL COMMITTEE ON THE FUTURE OF THE DTC, 1964

It was agreed at the Permanent Secretaries' Conference at Sunningdale in October 1963 that more should be done within Whitehall to examine problems of machinery of government.[1] It was considered to be an appropriate time, as the Government was about to announce its decisions on the future of the Overseas Representational Services and on the future of the Colonial Office, to begin by considering the future of the Department of Technical Co-operation (DTC). An Official Committee was constituted for the purpose. Much thought had already been given to the future of the DTC in the light of the various ideas which had been canvassed over the preceding months for a 'Ministry of Overseas Development' (ODM). Any such proposal raised problems concerning matters such as (i) the division of responsibility between the ODM on the one hand and the Overseas Departments and the Treasury on the other; (ii) the ODM's relationship with the British Council, (iii) the degree of the ODM's concern with loans and budgetary aid to the Colonies (iv) the ODM's responsibility for HMG's relations with the IBRD, WHO, UNESCO, FAO, etc. It was thought by the Director-General of DTC that, if satisfactory answers could be found to these problems, there was much to be said for establishing an ODM. Some of the arguments in favour were as follows. First, as aid had become a major activity of Government, it should be handled by a single Department responsible for formulating and putting proposals to the Treasury, whose overall responsibility was the allocation of Government expenditure as a whole. Secondly, it was not always politically acceptable for Treasury

13

Ministers to answer aid questions and Debates, nor was the Secretary for Technical Co-operation responsible for more than a small part of the aid field. A Minister who could answer for the whole field was desirable. Thirdly, many capital projects created a direct requirement for technical assistance, and it would make for better management if proposals for capital aid and technical assistance were brought together in one Department.

In a brief for the Treasury representative on the Committee, it was emphasised that the Director-General's memorandum was heavily conditioned by the fact that, as he had explained in his opening paragraph, it did not discuss the arguments in favour of establishing an ODM but rather considered what such a Ministry would have to do if it were to be set up.[2] It was this approach – apart from any desire to placate possible critics of an ODM – which was thought to have led the Director-General to underestimate the main difficulties. Officials who believed that such a Ministry could fulfil a valuable role also felt that the danger of the Director-General's approach was that some at least of the difficulties might be slurred over.[3] Discussion in the Committee should be interpreted in the light of this consideration. Thus, while it was accepted that there was probably scope for developing a more conscious aid policy, it was asked whether the creation of a Ministry which would stand between the Overseas Departments and the Treasury, both of which would continue to have a large interest in the subject, would not create a risk of the same work being done three times over in different places. Again, it was urged that it would neither lessen the time geographical Departments would have to devote to aid questions nor relieve the Treasury of interest in the balance of payments aspects or in the global total of aid and the terms on which it was given. Aid for the Colonies was held to be different in kind rather than in degree, because the Secretary of State for the Colonies was responsible for what happened inside a Colony and not only for diplomatic relations with it. Aid, both budgetary and capital, was regarded as an important instrument of policy and it seemed unlikely that the Secretary of State would wish to transfer either sort to an ODM, though it is possible that to some extent, as a Treasury official minuted, 'This difficulty over budgetary aid is of course only a symptom of the fundamental objection to a new Ministry of this kind'.[4] Furthermore, while some capital aid projects were closely linked with technical assistance problems, others were not. The amount of capital aid was sometimes linked with, dependent upon or alternative to, an amount of defence aid, which was a highly political issue and one which concerned Overseas Departments. It depended in the end, it was submitted, on which particular aspect of Government policy was taken to be dominant. For, if the essential question was the amount of United Kingdom resources which could be disbursed to less-developed countries, then the case for having an ODM could be a respectable one. But if the interest was the quality of the United Kingdom's relations with, say, India, British Guiana or Jordan, the case could fall short of conviction.

Some senior Treasury officials saw the ODM as primarily a political concept rather than an administrative one.[5] One who held this view declared: 'The truth of the matter is that at present aid is not regarded politically as a matter of the highest priority: if it were, the Treasury would be under much more constant and forceful pressure to increase the allocation of aid funds to all Overseas Departments.'[6] He proceeded thus:

This is no doubt one of the reasons – although not the only one – why the size of the aid programme is not in practice expanded as much as we had expected it to. So long as the Government does not wish to push aid as a matter of the highest priority, there are considerable advantages in retaining the present set-up, in which the Treasury occupies a relatively strong position, quite apart from the difficulties inherent in switching over to an ODM arrangement.

But he went on to say: 'If however either this Government – or a new Government in the future – were to wish to inaugurate a more active and positive aid policy, then the creation of an ODM might well be the best means of ensuring that such a policy was adopted and carried through in practice.' Yet departmental caution emerged over the greatly increased expenditure that would inevitably follow from a change of policy and the creation of an ODM. Apparently forgetting the change of priority that was implicit, he concluded: 'Whatever arguments there might be in favour of such an outcome on its own merits or at the right time, it seems very doubtful – to say the least – whether our present balance of payments situation makes the present a timely moment for thinking in such terms.'

The three Overseas Departments reacted rather differently from one another to the proposal to set up an ODM on the lines that had recently been sketched out by the Labour Party.[7] The CRO believed that, as far as Commonwealth aid was concerned, the two questions raised by the proposals were: (i) which Minister in Whitehall would negotiate with visiting Commonwealth Finance Ministers; and (ii) whether the CRO or the ODM would authorise instructions to

High Commissioners. As aid raised both political and trade issues, for instance land settlement in Kenya, defence aid in India and the treatment of local British interests in Ceylon, it involved the CRO, the Treasury and the Board of Trade as well as the ODM and, in practice, the CRO considered that it was itself more likely to take the lead in negotiations in London rather than the ODM. Technical assistance did not usually raise major policy issues, nor were most capital aid projects for the Commonwealth inextricably linked with technical assistance problems as far as the experience of the CRO was relevant.

The Foreign Office did not foresee difficulties on the scale feared by the CRO, largely because only a few foreign countries received substantial amounts of British aid and the Foreign Office was, therefore, only beginning to embark on aid as a major subject. Also, virtually all Foreign Office aid took the form of Section 3 loans which were administered by ECGD. The position was quite different again as far as the Colonial Office was concerned. There were seen to be three broad alternative ways of dividing functions between an ODM and the Colonial Office. First, the ODM could take over all aid matters, including both the capital and budgetary aid to the Colonies. This was regarded by the Colonial Office as impracticable as the budget was crucial in the management of a Colony, and the Secretary of State could not, for that reason, hand over responsibility for budgetary aid to another Ministry. Secondly, an ODM could deal with all aid for independent countries only, leaving all Colonial aid problems to the Colonial Office. This had the disadvantage that Colonial aid would be kept quite separate from the rest of aid problems, and so the Government's general philosophy on aid matters would be worked out by a Department which had no first-hand experience of the Colonies and their special problems. Thirdly, an ODM could deal with all aid to independent countries and with technical assistance and capital aid for the Colonies, leaving budgetary aid to the Colonies with the Colonial Office. This seemed the best solution, although one that was far from ideal. Accordingly, it was doubted in the Colonial Office whether the proposal for a separate ODM was a sound one. Nor was it thought that this analysis was altered by the impending amalgamation of the Colonial Office with the CRO. Though it might appear rather odd that budgetary aid to an independent country, like Zanzibar, could be dealt with by an ODM while budgetary aid to the Colonies would be dealt with by the enlarged CRO, there was, it was believed, in fact a difference in kind between HMG's relationship with Colonies and its relationship with independent countries, whether Commonwealth or non-Commonwealth.

11. MINISTERIAL DISCUSSIONS

The Secretary for Technical Co-operation, Mr Robert Carr, wrote on
11 May 1964 to the Prime Minister, Sir Alec Douglas-Home, to seek a
discussion of aid policy and administration. Although aid had been
given considerable attention by the Government, he felt that the
programme had lost impetus over the previous three years and had not
reached the levels forecast. The latter fact enabled the Labour Party to
take the initiative in a field which, he claimed, the Government had
pioneered and where it deserved 'to be on top'. He had come to feel
that our system for administering aid was 'too diffuse to obtain a
sufficiently quick and comprehensive control of policy and execution
or to make a proper impact presentationally'. The Prime Minister
called a meeting to discuss the matter.[8] The Secretary for Technical
Co-operation circulated a memorandum on aid policy and management which he raised as a political issue because, given the level of
performance over the previous three years, 'the gap between what we
have done and what we said we would do could be used against us in a
damaging way, casting reflections both on our competence and
sincerity.'[9] Consequently, he suggested nine points which might form
the basis of a concerted programme to retain the political initiative.
The last of these was the most radical. It sought a decision to set up, at
an appropriate time in the future, a single Ministry for the management of all forms of aid. It was to serve the broad policies laid down by
the Foreign Office and the CRO. This is where it differed from the
Labour Party proposals, which envisaged an autonomous Ministry.
Mr Carr felt that until there was a single Ministry of External Affairs
and while, therefore, the initiative in the control of policy came from
the Overseas Departments, only the management of aid should be
unified.

At the meeting at No. 10 Downing Street on 4 June 1964 there was
general agreement that policy decisions on aid should continue to be
made by the appropriate Oversea Department, but that there might be
a need for closer contact between the Oversea Department and the
DTC whenever technical assistance was involved. It was agreed, first,
that there was a case for considering whether aid policies were
presented to the public in the most effective way; and, secondly, that
Mr Carr's suggestions concerning the machinery of government
should be considered. The Chief Secretary to the Treasury, Mr J. A.
Boyd-Carpenter, was invited to arrange for an examination by officials
of the points raised and, in particular, the statistical points and the

desirability of another White Paper on aid in the autumn.[10]

The machinery of government points were referred to the Committee considering the note of the DTC.[11] On statistics, it was noted that Development Assistance Committee figures were published on an agreed international basis, which excluded military aid.[12] The point had been carefully considered in relation to the 1963 White Paper, *Aid to Developing Countries* (Cmnd 2147), which included a paragraph (para. 35) in which it was stated that military aid was likely to cost between £25 million and £30 million in 1963–64, and that the statistics in the White Paper were otherwise for economic aid only. As far as the publication of a further White Paper on aid was concerned, the question was considered by Treasury officials and Ministers in February 1964. In a minute of 26 February 1964 the Chief Secretary stated that 'the best thing is to produce a White Paper when, but only when, we have a story to tell. Otherwise it can be a menace.'[13] In the Treasury, a White Paper every two years was thought to be about right; annually was too frequent, while one in three years was thought to be not quite frequent enough. This pointed to the summer of 1965 as an appropriate time for the next White Paper.[14] There were no substantial recent policy decisions to be included in an aid White Paper, while it would be necessary to admit that the 1963 White Paper was overoptimistic in estimating aid expenditure in 1963–64 and, more seriously, was misleading in stating in paragraph 19 that British private investment in developing countries was approximately £150 million a year. In fact, the figure for 1962 was £72 million, although it was believed to have been substantially higher in 1963. The general question of publicity for aid was passed to the Information Officers of the Departments concerned for joint consideration and action.[15]

III. COMMITTEE FOR THE MACHINERY OF GOVERNMENT

The Secretary for Technical Co-operation presented his recommendations for an ODM to the Committee for the Machinery of Government on 16 June 1964.[16] The first paragraph clearly stated the purpose. It read as follows:

> The Secretary for Technical Co-operation has recommended to the Prime Minister that the Government should announce its decision to set up at an appropriate time in the future a single Ministry for the

management of development aid. This he believes to be necessary for the sake of efficiency in the future. But he has made clear that he is making it as a political proposal, designed as part of a concerted programme to keep the initiative on aid matters; British bilateral aid to independent countries on a considerable scale is new in the last six years, and he thinks that the Conservative Governments of these years are entitled to take full credit for it.

While the purpose was basically political, the method was essentially developmental. The argument ran as follows: aid-giving had become an important aspect of external policy, but to secure the full political value for our aid economic development must be seen to follow from it; therefore, we had to provide effective aid which, in turn, meant closely integrated, i.e. unified, management. Thus, the primary function of the new Minister was regarded as both formulating policies and taking, stimulating and co-ordinating action which would bring about economic and social development. The use of aid to further immediate political and trade interests was not to override the general purpose for which HMG had committed itself to aid-giving. For, as the Development Policy Committee believed, our political objectives were best followed by keeping in mind the long-term economic benefits to developing countries in terms of self-sustained growth, which was the object of our aid policies.[17]

In its final report,[18] the Committee on the Machinery of Government concluded, after thoroughly canvassing the arguments for and against the setting up of a new ODM, that there was room for considerable differences of opinion concerning the practical effects of setting up a new Ministry and the benefits that might flow from it. The DTC was in favour; the Foreign Office was favourably disposed; the CRO, Colonial Office and Treasury preferred to retain the existing arrangements, which might well be improved. The Overseas Departments had already arranged for technical assistance experts to be called in wherever capital aid projects were being considered. But, as the Secretary of State for Foreign Affairs, Mr R. A. Butler, indicated to the Prime Minister, Sir A. Douglas-Home,[19] what Ministers had in mind was a Ministry for Aid Management rather than, as the Labour Party had put forward, a Ministry of Overseas Development, which appeared to involve the separation of development aid from the general overseas policy of the existing Overseas Departments. He felt that there was 'a strong case for more expert and more stringent administration of our overseas aid, and it may well be that a Ministry for Aid Management is the only practical answer'.[20]

However, the Labour Party's statements about the new Department had not specified the area of policy with which it would be concerned. Thus, in the House of Commons on 6 February 1964, Mr Harold Wilson had said, during the debate on Commonwealth Trade and Technical Assistance, that he felt that what was needed was 'A full-scale Ministry of Overseas Development under a Minister of Cabinet rank, to take over all responsibility for all Commonwealth and other overseas development . . .' Yet the phrase 'a Minister of Cabinet rank' was itself vague. It could mean a member of the Cabinet; it could mean a Cabinet Minister who had charge of one of the service departments; or it could mean a Cabinet Minister who combined the charge of the new department with some general non-departmental function in the Government; or it could mean a Minister not in the Cabinet who would have charge only of the new Ministry. Again, the phrase 'all responsibility for . . . overseas development' could, at one extreme, embrace responsibility for the political philosophy underlying aid policy, the scope of our aid effort, the direction of it, the management of it and the presentation of it at home and abroad. At the other extreme, it could mean simply the co-ordination of other Ministers' policies for using aid for the purpose of their respective Departments' policies together with the management and presentation of arrangements for aid which had been negotiated by those Ministers. There was, plainly, a big difference between these two extremes and a big difficulty in drawing a line between the territories of the new Department and those of the existing Overseas Departments at some point between the two extremes. One thing was clear from the absence of any Labour Party proposal to combine the offices of Foreign Secretary and Commonwealth Secretary – namely there was no opportunity to adopt the simple and logical plan of an aid agency appended to a Department of State which the Minister in charge could use as an instrument of his policy. In these circumstances the only practicable way of attempting to judge how wide the scope of the policy issues for the new Department seemed to be to judge the likely standing of the various Ministers concerned in relation to one another.[21] However, one Treasury view was that it was not worth while setting up a Department if it was not strong enough to stand up to the Overseas Departments in devising and improving a general policy of aid.[22] It was felt to be in the widest Treasury interest that, if a Ministry were to be set up, it should be a strong one.

iv. ESTABLISHMENT OF THE ODM

Following the General Election, the new Government decided to proceed with the setting up of an ODM under a Minister, Mrs B. Castle, with a seat in the Cabinet. Following a meeting on 21 October 1964 between the main Departments concerned to discuss the functional scope of an ODM,[23] the Minister submitted a note on the function of her Ministry to the Prime Minister.[24] It argued that, 'taking into account the intentions expressed in the Labour Party Manifesto', it seemed that Ministers intended that the new Ministry should take responsibility for:

(a) The Aid Programme as a whole, and its make-up as between bilateral and multilateral aid and between capital aid and technical assistance.

(b) Terms and conditions of capital aid and the principles on which technical assistance is granted.

(c) The size and nature of the aid programme for each country.

(d) The management of capital aid and technical assistance.

(e) Relations with international aid organisations.

(f) The United Kingdom interest in United Nations programme of technical assistance.

(g) Liaison with voluntary bodies operating in the same fields.'

It was explicitly stated that the ODM accepted the necessity 'to keep in harmony with the policies of the Overseas Departments'. It was further agreed that, because of the constitutional responsibilities of the Secretary of State for the Colonies, all aid given had to be provided in detailed agreement with the Colonial Office. Yet it was stated that the new Ministry expected to play an important part in Colonial aid generally and a primary part in negotiations on development aid, though it was admitted that development aid and budgetary assistance could not always be separated one from another. It was suggested that the ODM should be given responsibility for 'the development element of capital aid', while budgetary assistance remained the responsibility of the Colonial Office.

This was the one contentious proposal in the whole submission. When the new Secretary of State for the Colonies Mr Anthony Greenwood, later Lord Greenwood of Rossendale, first met the Permanent Under-Secretary, he asked for a note on the ideas of officials as to the proper relationship between the Colonial Office and the

ODM.[25] The Permanent Under-Secretary considered it inappropriate to show his Minister the full report of the working party—at any rate, certainly not without the chairman's permission—and so a special memorandum was prepared for the purpose.[26] It was argued that, in view of his overall responsibility for the Colonies, there were strong arguments for maintaining the existing arrangements, although, in the longer term, the interests of the Colonies might suffer from their total exclusion from the concern of the ODM. Official opinion was solidly against handing over responsibility for both budgetary aid, including special assistance, and development aid. It was not seen how such a transfer could possibly work smoothly and effectively. Consequently, if a change was unavoidable, it was thought that functions should be split, the Secretary of State retaining responsibility for budgetary and most forms of special aid, while responsibility for development aid was transferred to the Ministry for Overseas Development. This was thought to be a workable solution. The DTC had taken over responsibility for the administration of aid for higher education in the Colonies and that had, it was stated, worked reasonably well. The Colonial Office had decided how much of the total CD & W allocation should be available for that purpose, and the DTC had to secure the agreement of the Colonial Office for specific projects in Colonial territories. It was suggested that, as aid for economic development played a very large part in our political relations with our dependent territories, it was essential that (i) the Secretary of State should have the final word in determining allocations of development aid as between various territories; (ii) the Colonial Office should take part in most, if not all, of the financial negotiations with delegations from the overseas territories; and (iii) the Colonial Office should be 'thoroughly and properly' consulted about the application of development aid in the various territories. The Secretary of State was advised that the split would be workable on these conditions.

When the submission by the Minister of Overseas Development was studied in the Colonial Office, officials felt that the proposed arrangement would not be workable, because on many issues that had to be resolved important political and financial questions were inextricably interwoven.[27] Thus, dissatisfaction with the way financial affairs were being conducted in the Southern African Territories had led to the sending of the Taylor/Watson Mission early in 1964. This was said to have had clear political, as well as purely financial, implications. It was asked who would be responsible for taking this kind of decision, if the Colonial Office lost responsibility to the ODM. Again, in Swaziland a financial, fiscal and economic exercise was at that time in hand. The purpose was to work out a block grant system for budgetary aid, based on an agreed tapering formula over a period of years which was intended to result in Swaziland being able to stand on her own feet. The exercise involved the raising of additional revenue, which, in turn, raised fundamental political issues in the territory. As the financial projections in the development plan had been found to be misleading, it was also necessary to redraft the plan. So three requirements were being treated: fiscal and financial proposals, the likely growth rate and the appropriate development proposals. All were said to be interconnected and inseparable from our conduct of political relations with the territory, particularly under the new constitution. The official concluded:[28]

It would be unthinkable to let the Ministry of Overseas Development assume responsibility for determining the financial and fiscal policies the territory is to adopt, unless they also accept responsibility for the conduct of our political relations with the territory. It would be difficult enough to hand over the development plan to that Ministry: we could only do so on the basis that the ultimate approval of the territory's development plan, and consequently all our assistance towards it, rested with the Secretary of State.

As a final illustration, the official mentioned that hardly any proposal for a pay or salary review in a grant-aided Colonial territory could be considered on its financial merits, for 'It is always a highly political question, involving the risks of strikes and so forth.'

The Parliamentary Under-Secretary of State, Mrs Eirene White, accepted the view that the proposals of the Minister of Overseas Development would seriously undermine the responsibility of the Secretary of State for the dependent territories.[29] It was argued that as long as the Colonial Office was responsible to Parliament for the well-being of a territory, it could not accept parallel administration in the field of economic development, other than on an agency basis. The Secretary of State wrote accordingly to the Prime Minister.[30] Apart from some specialised fields of aid, notably higher education, research, surveys and the like, which the ODM could conveniently undertake in the Colonies, he said that he felt strongly that responsibility for development aid to the Colonies should remain with him.

The Minister of Agriculture and the Minister of Education had also raised objection to other parts of the proposals of the Minister of Overseas Development, and the Prime Minister asked the Head of the

Civil Service, Sir L. Helsby, later Lord Helsby, to 'sort the matter out'.[31] It was feared that the Prime Minister would be advised that, while the Colonial Office should retain responsibility for budgetary aid, the ODM should have the responsibility for development funds, though it should be exercised in consultation with the Colonial Office. In that event, the Secretary of State was advised to insist on the following conditions: first, that he should finally approve development plans and that correspondence with Colonial Governments should emanate from the Colonial Office; secondly, that while the ODM would advise on the allocation of development aid as between the various Colonies, the final decisions would be made by him; and, thirdly, the ODM would have to consult and obtain the agreement of the Colonial Office for individual Development and Welfare projects in the Colonies.

The Prime Minister, had, it seems, started with a prejudice against the Secretary of State's proposal, before he asked the Head of the Civil Service to advise.[32] The Prime Minister was advised that he should tell the Secretary of State that, given the existence of the ODM, the conclusion to which he objected was unavoidable.[33] When they met on 29 October 1964 the Secretary of State accepted that responsibility for development aid to the Colonies should be transferred to the ODM, provided, of course, that budgetary aid remained with the Colonial Office.[34] The willingness to accept gracefully came well from a new Secretary of State in a new Government which had redeemed its promise to establish a new Ministry. It was not as easy to do so for those officials who had entered the Colonial Office two or more decades earlier and had seen and, in time, largely fashioned the successive responses of the Office to views as they emerged on Colonial policy. It is, or surely should be, understandable, therefore, that some officials were likely to be rather bitterly disappointed by the outcome. Yet it was much less to be expected that they would, in consequence, write harshly about the changes. That this happened indicates the depth of feeling and commitment on the part of those officials. On the eve of the meeting between the Prime Minister and the Secretary of State, the Head of the Civil Service received a personal minute which read:

I have long realised that the Colonial Office is nearing its end and had always hoped that it would have an honourable and dignified funeral. I must say I profoundly dislike the present trend of thinking which seems to me very like chucking a rotten carcase on the rubbish heap so that the vultures can peck its decaying flesh. After all, we have a history that can be traced back 300 years;

perhaps more closely associated with the history of Great Britain than any other single department.[35]

The Head of the Civil Service, while acknowledging that the disadvantages of the new arrangements might be more apparent to the Colonial Office than to any other department, felt that the decision to create an ODM had not been reached in any spirit of disregard for the history and significance of the Colonial Office. The Prime Minister's decision to appoint a separate Secretary of State for the Colonies was cited as proof that he was mindful of the claims of the Colonial Office. Providing the ODM and the Colonial Office found ways to co-operate tolerably with one another, the Head of the Civil Service felt that no one 'need feel unduly disappointed'.

Whether this helped to assuage the hurt feelings of those who had served the Colonies with dedication for most of their careers is not recorded in the files. Most others would be likely to accept it as fair comment on the approaching demise of a Department of State which had so largely lost the territories it had once proudly administered.

The next step was to agree a tolerable working arrangement between the two Departments. Somewhat protracted discussions took place about the future relationship between them on questions of aid. The tone of some of it might be gleaned from the following opening sentences on a minute by a Colonial Office official commenting on a letter from the ODM. They ran as follows: 'The attached letter . . . is not on the whole unreasonable, though it does display the over-sensitiveness of those of dubious parentage. The idea that an EOD Notice should show warmth of feeling strikes me as novel. . . .'[36] But eventually, a concordat was reached between the Colonial Office and the ODM.[37] Officials felt that they had safeguarded the Secretary of State's responsibilities to a greater extent than had earlier been expected, with the result that the Colonial Office had kept a tighter hand on aid matters than either the Foreign Office or the CRO.[38] The Permanent Under-Secretary, minuting 'Glory be', approved the draft of a Circular Despatch which was intended to inform Colonial Governments of the new arrangements.[39] It was as follows:[40]

CIRCULAR 207/65   The Church House
London, SW1

10 May 1965

Sir,
I have the honour to inform you that, following the establishment of the Ministry of Overseas Development, certain new procedures will

be followed in dealing in London with questions affecting development planning in dependent territories, and with applications for financial assistance from the Governments of such territories. These procedures, which are set out below and will take effect at once, have been agreed between the Minister of Overseas Development and myself as reflecting the division of responsibility for such matters between our two Departments. It may be helpful if I explain here how that responsibility is now shared.

2. The Minister of Overseas Development is responsible for development aid to Colonial territories. The Secretary of State for the Colonies remains responsible for their financial and economic policies, and, therefore, for the content and approval of the development programmes towards which aid will be given. He is also responsible for budgetary assistance, emergency assistance and reconstruction programmes arising from natural disasters, and all other forms of financial aid to Colonial Governments (e.g. military and security assistance) except development aid and technical assistance.

3. These arrangements clearly require the closest co-operation and consultation between the two Departments which will be jointly concerned in promoting development in the dependent territories. The Ministry of Overseas Development (usually abbreviated to 'O.D.M.') will naturally have a close interest in the content of development programmes, while the Colonial Office will wish to satisfy themselves that specific projects take due account of the needs of the territory and the effect on its economy and its budgetary position.

4. *Development Plans*. It is intended to maintain the requirement, which was laid down in paragraph 12 of my predecessor's Circular Despatch No. 563/63, that CD & W schemes, as well as Exchequer loans, should be approved only within the framework of approved development plans. In considering future development plans (about which separate communications will be sent to Governments in due course), the Colonial Office will consult with the O.D.M. and make full use of the latter's Economic Planning staff, professional and technical. When development plans are forwarded to me, not less than ten copies should be sent initially, so that copies may be made available to all concerned without delay.

5. *Aid allocations and approvals*. The O.D.M. are responsible for making allocations of U.K. development aid and for approving,

with the Treasury concurrence as necessary, CD & W schemes and Exchequer loans. They will act in these matters in agreement with the Colonial Office. It will be open to either the Colonial Office or the O.D.M. to initiate schemes or proposals for aid. But most schemes and proposals will no doubt continue to originate in Colonial territories, in the context of development plans. Scheme applications should continue to be sent to the Colonial Office, but two additional copies should be sent, which will be transmitted immediately to the O.D.M.

6. Other questions which remain within my responsibility, subject to consultation with the O.D.M. as may be appropriate, include:-

(*a*) Budgetary assistance.
(*b*) Military and security assistance.
(*c*) Aid following natural disasters.
(*d*) External and internal borrowing other than Exchequer loans.

Correspondence on these and similar matters should be addressed to me in the same way as in the past, but an additional copy should always be sent so that it can be transmitted, if necessary, to the O.D.M. Question of financial assistance to dependent territories from external sources other than H.M.G. will usually be of concern to both the Colonial Office and the O.D.M.; here again, correspondence should be addressed to me, with an additional copy.

7. The general effect of what is said above is that correspondence on all these matters should continue to be addressed to me, extra copies being provided as indicated. Similarly, communications to Governments on these matters will issue from the Colonial Office. However, in the case of matters on which the former Department of Technical Co-operation corresponded direct with Governments (such as technical assistance and staffing questions) the O.D.M. will also correspond direct.

8. There is also one other exception to the general rule stated above. Actual issues of money for schemes financed under Section 1 of the Colonial Development and Welfare Act, 1959, as amended, are now made from the Overseas Aid (Colonial Development and Welfare) Vote of the O.D.M.; and issues of Exchequer loans approved under Section 2 of the Colonial Development and Welfare Act, which are made from the Consolidated Fund, are also controlled by the O.D.M. Requests for such issues (including the usual quarterly

statements of CD & W expenditure and issues) should in future be addressed to the Minister of Overseas Development direct, in the same form as that in which they have hitherto been addressed to me; and the Minister will communicate direct with Governments about the making of such issues.

9. This circular is addressed to all Governors; British Government Representative, Basutoland; High Commissioners of Aden and the Protectorate of South Arabia and the Western Pacific; Resident Commissioners, Gilbert and Ellice Islands and the New Hebrides; all Administrators and the British Commissioner and Consul, Tonga.

I have the honour to be,
Sir,
Your most obedient,
humble servant,
ANTHONY GREENWOOD

It is not part of this History either to follow through the working of this concordat between the ODM and the Colonial Office or to assess the operations of the ODM. However, it might be stated that, at the time when a possible ODM was being canvassed in Whitehall and elsewhere, it would not have been difficult to have developed a strong case for not having an ODM at all. Such a case would have been based essentially on the 'grave difficulty'[41] with which the three Overseas Departments would be faced in divesting themselves of direct responsibility for matters so much within their field of interest. That argument applied *a fortiori* to the Colonial Office. But there had been some powerful arguments on the other side for creating a central organisation to deal with all forms of aid and, as has been seen, the case for doing so had prevailed. Indeed, pressures both at home and abroad had built up so much that the establishment of a new organisation to deal with aid could not, politically speaking, await the amalgamation of the Colonial Office with the CRO, and of that, in turn, with the Foreign Office to form the Foreign and Commonwealth Office (FCO). Some officials in the Treasury held the view in 1964 that, instead of a separate Ministry, what was required was a considerably streamlined aid wing of a combined External Affairs Department. In the light of experience with the ODM running in parallel to the CRO and the Foreign Office, Treasury officials came more strongly to support the establishment of a unified Department of External Affairs when the opportunity arose.[42] Officials of the ODM had reached the same conclusion after two years of the ODM's separate existence.[43] The merger did not come until 12 November 1970. The new Conservative Government announced the merger along with other important changes in the machinery of Government on 15 October 1970 in its White Paper, *The Reorganisation of Central Government* (Cmnd 4506). Paragraph 34 of the White Paper was devoted to Overseas Aid and read as follows:

> The Government have reviewed with particular care the future organisation of government in the aid field, against the background of considerable public interest at home and abroad and of the need to engage the private sector of industry, commerce and finance to a greater extent than hitherto. They have come to the conclusion that, in order to unify ministerial responsibility for overseas policy, overseas aid should become the ultimate responsibility of the Secretary of State for Foreign and Commonwealth Affairs. They recognise, however, that the management of overseas aid is a function distinct from the general conduct of foreign affairs and that it is important to maintain the valuable body of expertise and skill in aid administration which has been developed in the Ministry of Overseas Development and its predecessors. The development work of the unified department will therefore be in the charge of a Minister for Overseas Development who will have, by delegation from the Secretary of State, full charge of his functional wing of the Foreign and Commonwealth Office; his status (though not his legal position) will be equivalent to that of a Minister in charge of a separate department not represented in the Cabinet. The overseas development administration of the Foreign and Commonwealth Office will continue, like the Ministry of Overseas Development, to be staffed by home civil servants (with continuing provision for secondments in both directions with the Diplomatic Service).

By 1969 it was firmly understood in the F & CO that the concordat included the acceptance by the ODM of the principle that the reasonable needs of dependent territories had first claim on the British aid programme. While the practical importance of this understanding can be exaggerated in view of the smallness of the financial needs of the few remaining dependent territories in relation to the size of the whole aid programme and while there could hardly be a more subjective term than 'reasonable', the principle nevertheless offered a safeguard against the treatment by the ODM of dependent territories on a par with independent countries. The safeguard was effective in the occasional case where this distinction seemed likely to be overlooked.

The merger in 1970 of the ODM in the F & CO was intended to unify Ministerial responsibility for overseas policy though maintaining a coherent aid programme and the expertise to organise and service it. The ODM was, therefore, transformed, as the Overseas Development Administration (ODA), into a functional 'wing' of the F & CO, with a Minister in charge who had direct access to the Secretary of State. The merger facilitated the substitution of less cumbersome arrangements for the handling of the business concerning dependent territories in place of those embodied in the concordat. A joint division was set up to serve Ministers in both 'wings'. When the ODA was detached from the F & CO in 1974 as a Ministry of Overseas Development again, though in its latest version it ceased to have the right to a Minister of Cabinet rank, the joint division was retained to serve Ministers in both the F & CO and in the ODM when dependent territories were involved.

SOURCES

1. File EOD 386/027, Part A, 1963–1965, item 4, Committee on Machinery of Government: Future of the Department of Technical Co-operation – MG(DTC)(64), 1st Meeting on 26 Feb 1964.

2. Treasury File 2FD 244/883/03, Part A, pp. 27–9, Brief of 4 Mar 1964.

3. Ibid., pp. 30–1, minute of 4 Mar 1964 by Sir R. Harris.

4. Ibid., minute of 5 Mar 1964.

5. Ibid., pp. 33–6, Brief of 12 Mar 1964 by Sir R. Harris. At the time the Treasury referred to the new Ministry by the initials MOOD. Later this was shortened to MOD but, in order to avoid confusion with the Ministry of Defence, the initials ODM were accepted.

6. Idem.

7. H. of C. Deb., Vol. 688, col. 1382, 6 Feb 1964, speech by Mr Harold Wilson.

8. Treasury File 2FD 35/154/03, note of a meeting held at No. 10 Downing St on 4 June 1964. Apart from the Prime Minister and the Secretary for Technical Co-operation, the Foreign Secretary, the Commonwealth Secretary and the Chief Secretary to the Treasury were present.

9. Ibid., memorandum by the Secretary for Technical Co-operation, para. 7.

10. Ibid. According to a minute of 7 June 1964 by the Chief Secretary to the Treasury, the Prime Minister was anxious (i) to bring DTC earlier into the pre-decision stage, and (ii) to improve presentation, possibly with a new White Paper and by the inclusion of military aid in the published aid figures.

11. Ibid., minute of 15 June 1964.

12. Ibid., note of 15 June 1964 on the meeting of Ministers on 4 June 1964.

13. Ibid.

14. Ibid., letter of 2 July 1964.

15. Ibid., letters of 17 and 22 Sep 1964.

16. MG (DTC)(64)6, 16 June 1964: pp. 63–6 in Treasury file 2FD 244/883/03, Part A.

17. Second Report of the DPC 1963 – extract at pp. 88–9 in ibid.

18. MG (DTC)(64)9 Final, 9 July 1964 – pp. 73–87 in ibid.

19. Ibid., pp. 98–9, confidential minute ref. PM/64/90 of 7 Aug 1964 from the Secretary of State for Foreign Affairs to the Prime Minister.

20. Idem, para. 3.

21. Ibid., memorandum of 7 Oct 1964 on a Ministry of Overseas Development, para. 4.

22. Treasury File 2-MS 24/141/01, Part A, pp. 121–4, minute of 9 Oct 1964.

23. Ibid., note of a meeting held on 21 Oct 1964. Those represented were the Treasury, Foreign Office, CRO, Colonial Office, Department of Education and Science, Board of Trade, Ministry of Agriculture, Fisheries and Food, DTC, Ministry of Health, Cabinet Office and British Council.

24. Ibid., Minister of Overseas Development: Personal Minute No. PM(64)1, 21 Oct 1964, to the Prime Minister.

25. Confidential File EOD 386/027, Part A, 1963–1965, item 59, letter of 19 Oct 1964, from the Permanent Under-Secretary of State to Sir Philip Allen.

26. Ibid., item E/59.

27. Ibid., item 64, minute of 21 Oct 1964.

28. Idem.

29. Ibid., item 65, minute of 22 Oct 1964 from the Parliamentary Under-Secretary of State, Mrs Eirene White, to the Secretary of State for the Colonies, Mr A. Greenwood.

30. Ibid., minute of 22 Oct 1964 from the Secretary of State.

31. Ibid., item 68, minute of 23 Oct 1964 from the Permanent Under-Secretary of State to the Secretary of State.

32. Treasury file 2-MS 24/141/01, minute of 23 Oct 1964 to Sir L. Helsby.

33. Ibid., handwritten minute of 26 Oct 1964 by Sir L. Helsby. The Prime Minister was also advised to speak to the Minister of Agriculture in the same sense about relations with the FAO.

34. Ibid., minute of 29 Oct 1964.

35. Confidential file EOD 386/027, 1963–1965, item 78, personal minute of 28 Oct 1964 from the Permanent Under-Secretary of State for the Colonies to the Head of the Civil Service.

36. Ibid., item 125, minute of 10 Feb 1965. 'EOD' means Establishment and Organisation Department.

37. Ibid., item 130, EOD 13/65, 24 Mar 1965.

38. Ibid., minute of 4 May 1965.

39. Ibid., minute of 4 May 1965 by the Permanent Under-Secretary of State for the Colonies.

40. Ibid., item 136.

41. Confidential file EOD 386/027, Part B, 1963–1965, item 81A, personal minute of 2 Nov 1964 from the Head of the Civil Service to the Permanent Under-Secretary of State for the Colonies.

42. Confidential Treasury file 2FD 244/883/03, Part C, minutes of 20 and 30 Dec 1966 and of 30 and 31 Jan 1967.

43. Ibid., minute of 31 January 1967 by Sir William Armstrong.

3 The West Indies, 1953–1958

1. THE POLITICAL BACKGROUND TO FEDERATION

The Conference on West Indian Federation met in London on 13 April 1953. The Secretary of State, Mr Alan Lennox-Boyd, was chairman. Delegates attended from all those territories which had accepted in principle the possibility of a Federation, namely Antigua, Barbados, Dominica, Grenada, Jamaica, Montserrat, St Kitts-Nevis and Anguilla, St Lucia, St Vincent, and Trinidad and Tobago. The Legislature of British Guiana had declared itself not in favour of participation in federation and that of British Honduras had indefinitely deferred its participation. The two mainland territories were, therefore, represented only by observers. The Conference considered in detail the Consolidated Recommendations in Appendix 5 to the report of SCAC (Colonial No. 255) and agreed on certain changes. The Consolidated Recommendations, embodying the changes agreed at the Conference, were published as Cmd 8895 in July 1953. The document was the *Plan for a British Caribbean Federation*, which was presented to the Legislatures by the decision of the London Conference. By the end of 1953 the Legislatures of Grenada and St Vincent had unanimously accepted the report. While awaiting the decision of the other Legislatures on the Federal Plan, officials in the Colonial Office began to give preliminary consideration to the steps which should be taken to bring a Federation into being if agreement was forthcoming. The Comptroller was sent a lengthy memorandum for comment.[1] The proposed procedure was based largely on that employed in the Central African Federation, involving (i) the establishment of Fiscal, Civil Service and Judicial Commissions, (ii) the setting up of Working Parties of United Kingdom officials to consider the reports of the Fiscal and Public Service Commissioners while the Report of the Judicial Commissioner was passed to the Legal Department of the Colonial Office, (iii) the holding of a final

Federation Conference of West Indian plenipotentiaries, (iv) the appointment of a Governor-General and the coming into being of an interim Federal Government in whatever form was decided upon, and (v) the making of full arrangements for the holding of Federal elections. There was agreement with the Comptroller's view that it was very necessary politically to keep up the momentum of the move towards Federation once the Legislatures had voted on the principle. The Comptroller was invited to act as Chairman of the Board of Territorial Plenipotentiaries, which would be a committee of West Indian delegates, on the lines of the Regional Labour Board, to act as a pre-Federal organisation after the constitution was promulgated.

The Comptroller was surprised, and rather dismayed, to find how much remained to be done in spite of seven years' intermittent preparatory work.[2] He suggested that the terms of reference of the three Commissions should be more precisely angled to West Indian conditions, and that they might meet separately in Barbados, Jamaica and Trinidad 'in order to help in keeping interest in Federation alive'. He was doubtful of the idea of the Comptroller presiding over the pre-Federal organisation. However, the Governor of Jamaica thought it would facilitate matters if the Comptroller did so and was given a title which linked him with the Federation. This view was passed on to the Comptroller.[3] Substantial additional work was not expected to be involved as, apart from the three Commissioners, the main work would be carried out in London. The Comptroller was not enthusiastic about the suggested title of 'Commissioner for the Preparation of the Federal Organisation', but found it difficult to think of a better one.[4] So did the Colonial Office, and the title was adopted: Mr, later Sir John, S. Mordecai, Executive Secretary of the Regional Economic Committee (REC) became, in addition to his existing post, Assistant Commissioner for the Preparation of the Federal Organisation. The Comptroller's views were embodied in a revised document, which was sent to all West Indian Governors on 4 November 1954.[5] By that date, the Federal Plan was approved by the Grenada, St Vincent and St Lucia Legislatures, by the Barbados House of Assembly and by both Houses in Jamaica. It was hoped that the remainder would soon pronounce on the subject, in particular the Trinidad Legislative Council, and, if only for internal political reasons, the Barbados Legislative Council. The Trinidad Legislative Council voted on 11 December 1954 by 15 votes to 6 for a resolution accepting the Federal Plan, subject to (a) the holding of a Conference on Freedom of Movement, (b) the decision concerning a Federal site being left to the Federal Government to settle, and (c) no impediment arising from the

Federal proposals to the introduction of a new, or modified, Constitution in Trinidad.[6] It was noteworthy that no East Indians voted
for the motion, which gave grounds for the view that the Indians were
implacably opposed to Federation.[7] As the five-year term of the
Legislative Council was due to end in September 1955, it was
suggested that the three Commissioners should be appointed as soon as
possible and the crucial Conference on Freedom of Movement should
be called early in March 1955.

The Comptroller regretted that there were still laggards delaying a
proposed announcement by the Secretary of State on the next steps,
but he doubted whether it should be published until either the
Barbados Legislative Council or one or two of the Leewards had
resolved.[8] However, an announcement before 11 January 1955 was
thought to be highly desirable, because that was the date on which the
REC met in Trinidad. The Comptroller continued: 'If nothing has
been done by the United Kingdom Government by then, there may be
criticism and disappointment, since the members of the Committee are
strongly pro-Federation and eager to get to grips with their share of
pre-Federal planning.' He thought the Barbados Legislative Council
was likely to prove the stumbling-block, feeling that 'it would be
ridiculous to allow this small, wholly-nominated body to hold us up to
the point of endangering future progress'. He was prepared to convene
the Conference on Freedom of Movement if the Colonial Office and
West Indian Governments wished him to do so. He realised that failure
to reach agreement might well bring disaster to the whole scheme,
though he feared that unanimity would be difficult to obtain. He asked
the Colonial Office to give urgent study to the problem. The Governor
of Barbados advised against any announcement before the debate in
the Legislative Council and, as the United Kingdom Parliament was
not due to reassemble until the last week of January 1955, it was
decided to postpone any statement.[9] The resolution was passed by the
Legislative Council by 7 votes to 6 on 18 January 1955, whereupon the
Colonial Office asked for the approval of West Indian Governors for
the terms of an announcement to Parliament, and suggested that the
Conference on Freedom of Movement should be convened in March
1955, under the chairmanship of the Parliamentary Under-Secretary
of State, Lord Lloyd.[10] On 2 February 1955 the Secretary of State
announced that a Conference on Freedom of Movement would be
called and, in the expectation of agreement between West Indian
Governments on the control of movement of persons, HMG would
proceed with the next steps towards a Federation.[11]

The main conflict of views over the movement of people within the proposed Federation was that between the politicians in Barbados and those in Trinidad. The former insisted that no true Federation could exist unless people from any one West Indian island were free to move to any other, subject to health and security considerations. The latter were afraid that the economy of Trinidad would, in those circumstances, be swamped by workers from the over-populated islands like Barbados, and so wished unit governments to be able to restrict immigration from other islands. A compromise was thought to be possible under which there would be freedom to move, but not unrestricted freedom to settle and take up employment. It was thought that this was the position in India.[12] When the Conference met in Trinidad from 14 to 17 March 1955 it was marked, as the Report stated, 'by a conspicuous determination' to find a solution acceptable to all the territories involved.[13] The Conference unanimously recommended that (i) the Preamble to the Federal Constitution should recite, as one of the objects of Federation, that there should be the greatest possible freedom of movement for persons and goods within the Federation; and (ii) control of movement between units for reasons other than health or security should be concurrent for the first five years, after which any local legislation would require validation by resolution in the Federal Legislature.[14] During the Conference, the Government of Trinidad and Tobago demonstrated its faith in the future of Federation by making immediate relaxation in the existing restrictions on the entry of persons for employment into the Colony. The relaxations provided for the removal of 53 categories from the list of occupations to which entry was prohibited on the part of persons from outside the Colony.[15] The Conference requested HMG to proceed with the greatest possible speed with the completion of the preliminary measures to Federation.

The three Commissions had already been set up to examine the fiscal, civil service and judicial aspects of federation. The respective chairmen were Sir Sydney Caine, KCMG, Sir Hilary Blood, KCMG, and Sir Allan Chalmers Smith, MC. At the suggestion of the Governor of Jamaica, it was agreed that, after consultation with territorial members, the Chairmen only would sign the Reports.[16] This facilitated the completion of the Reports by September 1955, though they were not published until January 1956, and then as Cmd Nos 9618, 9619 and 9620 respectively. Meanwhile, detailed arrangements were being discussed in the Colonial Office for the holding of the final Conference on West Indian Federation. The Secretary of State agreed in June 1955 that the Conference should be held in London, under his chairmanship, on about 24 January 1956.[17] The officials had come to conclude that, to avoid a risk of delegates arriving at the Conference with a number of 'sticking points' – a danger pointed out by Mr A. M. Gomes of Trinidad in a recent conversation – it was better not to circulate beforehand a draft Final Federal Plan for consideration in the West Indies. So, to avoid that risk, it was thought that the Secretary of State should announce the date of the Conference, ask that plenipotentiary delegates be appointed to settle the method by which the Plan, already agreed in principle, should be implemented and to say that Conference documents would be the *Plan for a British Caribbean Federation* (Cmd 8895), the *Report of the Trinidad Conference* (Colonial 315) and the Reports of the three Commissions.[18] It was hoped in this way to minimise the risk of delegates making their agreement to the Final Plan subject to confirmation by the Legislature, 'and so starting the whole weary business over again, particularly but not exclusively with the risk that the new Trinidad Legislature might go back on the decision to join the Federation'.[19]

Complications threatened from a different direction. Both the Comptroller[20] and the Governor of Jamaica[21] wrote of Mr Manley's desire 'to go slow on Federation'. He was involved in citrus negotiations, there were two by-elections likely before the end of the year, one or two leading members of his party, in particular Mr Wills Isaacs, were opposed to Federation while others thought Jamaica's problems should come first; and, finally, it was thought better to postpone the Federal elections until after the 1957 general election in Jamaica. In a minute of 6 October 1955 by the Parliamentary Under-Secretary it is recorded that 'Mr Manley said frankly that, although he himself was in favour of Federation, the majority of his party were not in favour, since Jamaica had less to gain from Federation than any other territory in the Caribbean. . . . In his opinion, any attempt on his part to have Federal elections before 1958 would involve him in a revolution within his own party.'[22] So he was unwilling to attend a Conference in January at which delegates with plenipotentiary powers would be expected to reach conclusions on all outstanding matters.[23] The Governor and the Comptroller alike advised that the main issues of principle should be brought to finality early in 1956, while questions of implementation should be dealt with subsequently, without hurry. On 4 October 1955 the Secretary of State had a long talk with Mr N. Manley and Mr A. Gomes,[24] who were in London for the citrus negotiations. At times, they both apparently got very heated. The Secretary of State told Mr Manley that there was doubt in some people's minds, though not in his own, that he was dragging his feet in the matter. Mr Manley denied it, stating that he envisaged the first

Federal elections would take place in 1958, that he thought it imperative that the proposals finally agreed on should *not* go back again to the Legislatures and that he was still fully in favour of Federation and in no sense holding it up. But, though prepared to have short talks in London in January, he was not prepared to attend a plenipotentiary meeting. He proposed instead that there should be talks in London at which general principles should be enunciated, and these should be followed by talks in the West Indies in which the existing proposals should be reshaped in the light of these general propositions. Concurrently, he suggested, HMG should pass a short Act authorising the setting up of a Federation at a later date by Order in Council. The decision on the final form the Federation should take should, it was suggested, rest fairly and squarely with HMG after hearing the result of the talks in the West Indies. The Secretary of State added: 'The difficulties and possible impossibilities of this stand out a mile, but he wants to discuss with me urgently.' In a minute of 2 October 1955 the Parliamentary Under-Secretary of State stated that in his own opinion neither Manley nor Grantley Adams 'would be unduly depressed if Federation collapsed. On the other hand, I doubt if either will risk being saddled by public opinion with responsibility for its failure. "Thou shalt not kill but need'st not strive officiously to keep alive" may well be their motto.'[25]

Largely as a result of Mr Manley's attitude, the Colonial Office, while hoping it would be possible to avoid any further reference to Legislatures, decided not to refer to the issue of plenipotentiary delegates, but merely to invite Governments to send delegates and leave it to Governments to settle after the Conference whether or not there should be any reference back to Legislatures.[26] It was proposed to summon a Conference for the week beginning 7 February 1956.[27] However, Mr Gomes was anxious that Trinidad's delegates should have plenipotentiary powers – otherwise there would be the need to refer the decisions back to the Legislature for approval, which was a course which, he feared, might well prove disastrous so far as Trinidad's entry into the Federation was concerned.[28] In his minute of 6 October 1955 the Parliamentary Under-Secretary records that Mr Manley 'appreciated the difficult situation in Trinidad and the importance to Mr Gomes of a final clinching of the Federation issue before the Trinidad elections, and so agreed to a Conference in January, although he would prefer February'.[29] After considerable discussion in the Office and back and forth to the West Indies, the Secretary of State issued an invitation to the Conference to begin on 7 February 1956.[30] It was requested that, in order to enable the

Conference decisions to have the necessary finality, it was essential for delegates to be empowered to commit their Governments. It continued thus: 'The essential point is that the Conference should be early, final and decisive. . . . What is needed now is action.' The invitation was accepted in each Colony including British Honduras and also British Guiana, where the decision whether or not to join Federation was held over until a Legislature with elected representatives was reconstituted.[31] In moving a resolution to accept the invitation, the Chief Minister of Jamaica, Mr Manley, put forward seven propositions which were also unanimously accepted by the Jamaica House of Representatives.[32] They were that (i) Official Members be removed from the Federal Executive; (ii) the Federal Prime Minister be given sole discretion in the appointment of Federal Senators to the Executive without minimum limitation to number; (iii) the reserve powers of the Governor-General be reduced; (iv) the Federal Government be given power of regional planning and initiation and maintenance of consultative and advisory services; (v) United Kingdom financial assistance to the new Federation be reconsidered; (vi) a new method for revising the Federal Constitution be worked out; and (vii) the 1953 Conference recommendations be amended. The Governor of Jamaica explained that these points were consistent with the acceptance by both Houses in 1954 of the conclusions of the 1953 London Conference as an acceptable and workable *basis* for Federation, reserving the right to make further proposals.[33] Nor could the proposals, in his view, be regarded as objectionable or unreasonable in themselves. He felt confident that, with goodwill, there could be a compromise at the Conference between the 'getting-it-quick men' and the 'getting-it-right men'. As far as Jamaica was concerned, the Executive Council supported both the seven points made by the Chief Minister and the proposals made by the Fiscal Commissioner. The Minister for Trade, Mr Wills Isaacs, urged that no commitments on Federation should be made until a number of economic matters were considered, including future arrangements for the provision of development capital, secure markets and assistance to raise the standard of living. Without positive new assurances on such matters, he argued that Federation would seriously impede the larger and more advanced territories. However, the Chief Minister stated that it would be impossible to secure assurances on these issues at the forthcoming Conference, which he was determined should succeed.

The Conference met from 7 to 23 February 1956. Unanimous agreement was recorded on a number of major issues relating to constitutional, economic and financial, civil service and judicial matters. It was decided that the federal elections should be held as soon as practicable after 1 January 1958, and, in any event, not later than 31 March 1958. The Conference decided that the delegations in attendance should continue as a standing body, to be known as the Standing Federation Committee (SFC) which would settle the final terms of the draft federal constitution and direct the administrative work of creating the initial federal machinery. The Comptroller, in his role as Commissioner for the Preparation of the Federal Organisation, became chairman of the SFC. The report of the Conference was published as Cmd 9733 (1956). In order to resolve some particular differences between themselves the West Indian delegates withdrew for several days. The length of the private meetings caused concern to the Secretary of State, partly because of unauthorised and, as it turned out, inaccurate reports in the press.[34] Following the successful outcome of the Conference, the Secretary of State was able to introduce an Enabling Bill into Parliament so that the Federation might be created, the constitutional instruments of Federation being made by Order in Council. The British Caribbean Federation Bill received the Royal Assent on 2 August 1956. The Governor-General, the Rt Hon. Lord Hailes, GBE, was sworn in on 3 February 1958, on his arrival in Trinidad.

II. THE DEVELOPMENT AND WELFARE ORGANISATION

In January 1954 the Treasury agreed with the Colonial Office and the Comptroller that there was no question of altering the status and main functions of the Organisation until the issues on Federation were clearer.[35] The existing establishment was meantime accepted, with the proviso that, if and when a decision was taken either way on Federation, the prime policy and *raison d'être* of the Organisation would require radical review.[36] Trinidad's acceptance of the Federal scheme on 11 December 1954, made such a review necessary.

The Organisation was at the time performing in the main two functions.[37] First, there was the provision of technical assistance through a team of expert advisers and, secondly, there was the provision of machinery for regional consultation and co-operation and the co-ordination of regional services. As the Comptroller remarked in a later letter, to operate a successful agency for technical assistance 'as the Americans have found, is by no means easy'.[38] It was generally agreed that the Organisation would be wound up on the establishment of a Federal Government. That left two issues: (i) whether any changes should be made in its establishment in the intervening period; and (ii) how far, and by what authorities, the existing functions should be continued after the establishment of the Federation. The Comptroller submitted his answers in December 1954.[39] On the first issue, assuming Federation did not come about before the spring of 1956, he urged that the establishment should not be reduced. This was largely (a) for the practical reason that it was the essential machine for the carrying out of the usual tasks, for which 1955 would be an exceptionally busy year, plus whatever part it was called upon to undertake in the planning of Federation; and (b) for the political reasons that some West Indian politicians would interpret any reduction of the Organisation as the beginning of a process (of which the main component would be Federation itself) by which HMG intended to abandon the West Indies to its fate. On the establishment of a Federal Government, he suggested, (a) there would be the need for a United Kingdom High Commissioner, both to fulfil diplomatic duties and to funnel grants-in-aid and CD & W assistance already promised; (b) the Federal Government might need a body of advisers to advise units; (c) the Federal Government would take over some of the functions of the Organisation and the REC Secretariat as regional administrative organs; (d) it was desirable that technical regional conferences, hitherto arranged by the Organisation, should be continued; (e) the position of British Guiana and British Honduras would require attention, as the United Kingdom High Commissioner to the Federal Government could not conveniently succeed the Organisation as the channel for their CD & W assistance; and finally (f) the United Kingdom High Commissioner might take over British representation in the Caribbean Commission.

Consideration of these matters was urgent if the Fiscal and Civil Service Commissioners were to be briefed before they left London.[40] At an Office meeting, officials recommended that grants-in-aid should be made direct to the Federal Government, which would be the only authority able to exercise an effective check on the expenditure.[41] The Comptroller agreed.[42] The Fiscal and Civil Service Commissioners were informed of this, of the date for the disbandment of the Organisation, which was said to be about six months after the establishment of the Federation, and of the view that it would not be necessary to have a United Kingdom representative of the High Commissioner type until the stage of full independence; but that meanwhile it might prove desirable to have a Colonial Office representative to help the Governor-General with the United Kingdom grant-in-aid aspect of his work.[43]

The Treasury was at this time unable to agree to any reappointment to the post of Social Welfare Adviser on Miss Ibberson's retirement, and reserved their position on any other reappointments.[44] The Colonial Office declined to commit itself until the Comptroller had submitted his proposals.[45] The Comptroller, while not proposing to ask for replacements of the Social Welfare Adviser and the Engineering Adviser, asked for additional administrative staff so that he might fulfil the responsibilities 'implied by my new title of Commissioner for the Preparation of the Federal Organisation'.[46] In the end, following the London Conference of February 1956, there was the very modest change of up-grading one post from Senior Executive Officer to Principal.[47] The Treasury sought further economies, and the Colonial Office asked whether the Comptroller could 'find two, or even one of the Advisers who could, if absolutely necessary, be sacrificed to the dragon of economy'.[48] Without a rather tedious and time-consuming exercise, it is not possible to say whether the Treasury had got down to such minuscule economies generally, or at least at most places, both at home and overseas, or whether, for whatever reason, there was more concern with such small savings in the West Indies than in other places. In any case, a strong measure of agreement must surely be felt with the Comptroller's response when he urged that

> it would be both unjust and impolitic to allow the Organisation to run down for the sake of minor savings: unjust, because we must in all fairness transfer our operations to the Federal Government as, so to speak, a going concern; impolitic, because there are many people in the West Indies who suspect that HMG's interest in federation is inspired predominantly by hopes of shuffling off its financial responsibilities in the area, and they would interpret any premature reduction in our functions as evidence of indecent haste, and, incidentally I think, as inconsistent with the Secretary of State's announcement to the Conference regarding the orderly winding-up of the Organisation.[49]

Instead of niggling economies, the Comptroller suggested that the Organisation should be brought to a formal end by 31 March 1958, instead of six months later as was envisaged at the 1956 Conference, and his Public Relations Adviser should in future be financed from the West Indies General Allocation instead of from the Comptroller's staff sub-head of the Colonial Office Vote. The Treasury accepted these proposals.[50] Then, in August 1956 fate took a hand in damaging further the efficiency and usefulness of the Organisation as the

Economic Adviser, Professor C. G. Beasley, died, and there was, in the Comptroller's words 'no one to look to for expert economic advice and the gap will be keenly felt in our day-to-day work'.[51] It was proposed, as a result, to bring forward the appointment of an economist on the staff of the Federal Government.[52] While accepting the need, the Colonial Office feared that West Indian politicians, and Mr Manley in particular, would be likely to favour the appointment of a high-level academic economist as Economic Adviser with a small planning staff attached.[53] However, the Colonial Office, on the basis of apparently unhappy experience with academic economists at home and overseas, felt that this was not the right type of organisation. It preferred to see an administrator with an economic bias appointed as Federal Economic Adviser or, more appropriately, as Economic Secretary, with a professional economist as the immediate subordinate.

The Comptroller replied that, at his end, they were not convinced that the solution to the problem had yet been found.[54] In any case, they were increasingly preoccupied with the difficulty of finding the answer to the simple question: 'What is the Federal Government going to do? That is, what functions is it going to perform which will justify, in the public eye, the large and costly edifice of its two Houses of Legislature, its numerous Ministers and its extensive bureaucracy?'[55] It was nineteen years since the Montego Bay Conference, and yet Federation was still seen in the West Indies only as a strategem for achieving political independence. There had been little disposition to share, even less to transfer wholly, the control of economic decision-making, with the result that the powers extended by the contribution to the Federal Government were so niggardly that the Government would, it was thought, be hard put to justify its own continuance. To be regarded as successful, the Comptroller believed, quite reasonably, that the Federal Government would have to produce results during its first five years, and not merely to take over responsibility for the D & W Organisation and the REC, though they would provide a basis for further activities. In preparation for whatever the Federal Government might decide to do, it was suggested that the IBRD might be invited to advise on regional economic co-ordination and development. However, in discussions at the Colonial Office with the Comptroller, it was agreed to substitute for a general survey by the IBRD a series of expert investigations into specific problems that required a regional approach.[56] It was suggested that this should take place on the advice of the proposed Federal Economic Advisory Bureau, whose establishment should be brought forward. It was also agreed that an academic economist with knowledge of the problems of the area should be appointed to the post of Senior Economic Adviser. Mr K. H. Straw was appointed in 1957 but resigned in 1959.

III. PRECONDITIONS FOR A POLICY OF REGIONAL ECONOMIC DEVELOPMENT

Early in 1957, the Comptroller sent to the Colonial Office a memorandum by his Administrative Secretary on the problems of the area.[57] It focused attention particularly on staff matters, arguing that in some of the poorer territories the administrative and technical staffs were so 'woefully inadequate' that it was questionable whether it was right to continue providing large grants, for example in agriculture and building, unless the deficiencies of staff could be supplied. It was suggested that the CD & W money should be used to provide allowances for expatriate staff so that recruitment could be eased and to improve facilities for technical training so that more local candidates were available for posts in Government, public utilities and commercial undertakings, which was as desirable on political as on economic grounds. In his covering letter, the Comptroller expressed his agreement thus: 'It is everywhere apparent that the Man is as important as the Money. The longer I work in this area the more impressed I am by this simple fact, and by the crippling weaknesses of local Administrations.'[58] He supported the proposals made in the memorandum and heard from the Colonial Office that 'good staff is undoubtedly the crux of our development problem' and that the memorandum and letter had 'stimulated some further cerebration on this very vexed and intractable problem'.[59] While the Organisation had provided the skilled advice in the area for which it was established, the letter went on to say that it had not, and of its very nature could not, remedy fully the weakness of staff in the territorial governments themselves, although it could, and did, advise on whether such weakness should be remedied before particular CD & W applications were approved. The memorandum being commented upon and other evidence, including that of the Colonial Office team which toured the area early in 1951, suggest that much of the CD & W money had been and was still being spent despite very obvious weaknesses of staff in the various Colonies.

In a very real sense, the Comptroller's wish for early regional justification of the existence and cost of the Federal Government and his Administrative Secretary's emphasis on the inadequacy of the means to cope adequately, at least in some of the smaller territories, with measures for economic and social development, together provide the epitome of the West Indian problem. The problem was there when the West India Royal Commission reported, it was there after eighteen years of the D & W Organisation and it was there during the short life of the Federal Government. Towards the end of 1958, after the Federal Prime Minister, Sir Grantley Adams, had mentioned at a press conference in Jamaica that the Federal Government could levy income tax after it had functioned for five years and could make it retroactive to the date of Federation,[60] there was a search for a justification of Federation in 'the execution of some careful economic planning by the Federal Government in collaboration with the Units'.[61] It was a superficially attractive line of approach which, when it was examined, was seen to be nothing more than a glorious non-starter. For, within the terms of the Constitution, there were virtually no resources available to the Federal Government and no fields within which it could undertake economic planning.[62] There were, as there had always been, three prerequisites for regional economic planning, viz.: (i) an organisation to tackle problems, (ii) resources to finance the plans, such resources, though largely in the form of external assistance, being necessarily in part internal, and (iii) the existence of a customs union to make such planning as was attempted meaningful. The continued absence of these preconditions for a policy of regional economic development very largely explains the perennial nature of the West Indian problem. It also makes any assessment of the contribution of the D & W Organisation peculiarly difficult. For, besides the aspects of the Organisation already considered, including the ambiguity of its position on its establishment, the varying response of the territories to its overtures, its changing role in the area, the Treasury's persistent cheeseparing in both grant-aided territories and the Organisation itself, there was the unavoidably limited and piecemeal approach of the Organisation because of the absence of the three preconditions mentioned. The Organisation had, not infrequently, to accept second-best or even third-rate schemes because there were none others available, and Advisers were prepared to admit to the fact. Thus the Education Adviser, Mr G. S. V. Petter, readily admitted this in a conversation with the author when the Adviser visited Jamaica in January 1957 as Chairman of the Mission on Higher Technical Education. For the same reason, in reply to the Comptroller's request for suggestions for the agenda of the first meeting of the REC, the co-ordination of policy in industrialisation was proposed rather than any large-scale programme of industrialisation.[63] The arguments advanced at the time admirably illustrate the nature of the problem. The suggestion of co-ordinating policy arose because of the tendency of the territories, in particular of Jamaica and Trinidad, to compete with one another in offering tax and other concessions in order to attract external capital to establish local industries. So it seemed useful that consideration should be given to whether (i) it was not desirable to adopt a more uniform policy in such matters as legislation of the 'pioneer industries' type; and (ii) there might not be need for some form of inter-territorial machinery to ensure that, in the case of industries where there was not scope for more than one, or at the most two, factories, all the territories did not seek to attract the same industries.

An item in such specific form contrasted sharply with the general theses put forward at the time by others. The letter to the Comptroller went on to comment on two such general theses. One had been put in a letter to the Secretary of State by Mr R. L. M. Kirkwood, a member of the Jamaica Legislative Council,[64] and the other was in a report to the Caribbean Commission.[65] The first suggested that, in order to assist in the combating of unemployment and inflation, HMG should take steps to establish factories in the West Indies for the manufacture of certain types of goods, the production of which was likely to be affected in the United Kingdom by re-armament. The Secretary of State felt unable to take up such a general suggestion but invited 'any specific and practical proposals that may be put forward on behalf of the Colonial territories'.[66] The letter to the Secretary of State went on to comment on the proposal by Professor Lewis for local industrialisation, which was not regarded as practicable by Mr Kirkwood because 'the time when these BWI Colonies will be able to get together to devise rational policies for large-scale industrialisation and to bring about that Customs Union, which Professor Lewis considers to be pre-requisite to the devising of such policies, appears extremely remote'. These were, however, not the only assumptions on the basis of which the plan for industrialisation was drawn up. It was also assumed that £10 million would be found to set up a new Corporation. Thus, all three of the prerequisites for effective regional planning were assumed. So, while the plan was regarded by the Colonial Office as stimulating in itself, it was not thought to be particularly notable for its contribution to the practicable problem of implementation.[67] The Colonial Office believed that the West Indies needed, if viable industries were to be established, local enterprise, external capital in combination with external knowledge of productive techniques and export markets. The question of incentive legislation was already under study, as was the problem of marrying local knowledge with modern techniques and world markets. These were thought, in the circumstances, to be the most promising means to explore in order to increase employment through diversifying the West Indian economies. There was little response. The persistence of local, as distinct from regional, policies was at one and the same time a reflection of West Indian parochialism and, by creating further vested interests, an intensification of it. This explains the nature of the campaign against regional industrial policy that was mounted in Jamaica at the time of the Federal Conference in Trinidad in September 1959, and the considerable weakening of the Jamaica Government paper on Customs Union that was submitted to the Federation Committee soon after the Federation Conference.

iv. TRANSFERENCE OF THE FUNCTIONS OF THE ORGANISATION TO THE FEDERAL GOVERNMENT, MARCH 1958

At the London Conference in February 1956 the Secretary of State said that the D & W Organisation would be wound up within six months of the establishment of the Federal Government, and that the extent to which its advisory services should be taken over by the Federal Government would be a matter for consideration by the Standing Federation Committee (SFC) and, from time to time, by the Federal Government. The Conference subsequently agreed that an addition should be made to the exclusive legislative list for that purpose and that the Federal Government should undertake the co-ordination of CD & W schemes to the extent that this was being carried out by the Organisation. The SFC, at its first meeting in Barbados in May 1957, agreed that plans should be prepared on the basis that the Federal Government would wish to maintain intact the advisory services as they were currently performed by the D & W Organisation. The functions of the Organisation at the time were as follows: (a) to advise the Secretary of State on schemes submitted by territories involving assistance from their territorial or central CD & W allocations; (b) to administer the West Indies General Allocation provided for regional purposes; (c) to provide British Caribbean Governments with expert technical advice; (d) to prepare periodical reports on the economic and social progress of the region; (e) to provide the machinery for regional consultation and co-ordination on economic and social matters.

In addition to these functions, the Comptroller was: (i) the British co-Chairman of the Caribbean Commission, and the Organisation provided the Secretariat for the British Section of the Commission; (ii) responsible for making recommendations to the United States authorities regarding the scholarships made available under International Co-operation Administration (ICA) arrangements for the training of West Indians at Puerto Rico – this scheme was inaugurated in 1952 and involved the selection each year of some 70 trainees from the various territories; (iii) the chairman of the Regional Labour Board, which was responsible for supervising the arrangements for the administration of the BWI farm labour programme in the United States.

It was agreed that all the functions of the Organisation and the work involved in discharging them, with the exception of those relating to the Caribbean Commission, ought to be transferred to the Federal administration over the period ending 31 March 1958.[68] While the Despatch spoke of 'the gradual transfer of the responsibilities and functions of the D & W Organisation to the Federal Administration', to those on the spot it seemed more hurried. Thus, in the words of the Public Relations Adviser,

. . . though the annual cost of the Organisation was a bagatelle by any normal standards of government spending, administrative tidiness had to be preserved: the D & W Organisation had always been a bit of an anomaly. Now that a West Indian government was taking over, it would be possible to sweep it under the carpet and forget about it. So 'Operation Scuttle', as one Adviser christened it, went briskly forward, and on the administrative side it was handled with brisk efficiency.[69]

Much remained to be done once the 1956 Conference ended in agreement. As Sir Stephen Luke told the author on 1 October 1975, the task of putting flesh on the Conference's skeleton was immensely exacting both for the political membership of the Committee and for the staff of the Organisation and of the departments of the Colonial Office directly concerned. In fact, the modest administrative resources of the Organisation were stretched to the limit. Whatever the Advisers might have felt about 'Operation Scuttle', the administrative side at Hastings House was intensely preoccupied with the problems of obtaining the necessary political decisions, on the one hand, and building up as far as the available time allowed an organisation that would provide the fledgling Federation with a reasonable start in life, on the other hand.

The only incidental problem raised by the transfer concerned the non-Federating Colonies of British Honduras, British Guiana and the British Virgin Islands. The Governor, on behalf of the first two, and the Comptroller, on behalf of the third, claimed the absolute right to continue to enjoy the benefit of the West Indies General Allocation, including the services of the Federal advisory staff paid for from the Allocation, on the grounds that the Allocation was drawn up for all the territories irrespective of their attitude towards Federation.[70] These requests were accepted by the Treasury; and the Secretary of State, with the concurrence of the Governor-General, announced the division of the General Allocation that he proposed to make.[71] The relationship of the non-Federating territories to the Advisers proved less easy to settle. The Governor-General, not unnaturally, was unwilling to abrogate Federal Ministerial control over Advisers employed full-time by the Federal Government,[72] while external Governments were not prepared to correspond with Advisers through Federal Ministers.[73] Their point was that CD & W schemes prepared by non-Federated territories and the development plans of which they might form part were not the concern of Federal Ministers and might be confidential.[74] As the successor file, WIS 407/175/06 of 1960–1962, could not be located, it was necessary to consult the relevant register sheet to determine the outcome. There was a memorandum submitted to the Council of State followed by the proposal by the Governor of British Guiana that the matter be left on the understanding that, as with British Honduras and the Virgin Islands, the Governor-General would not refer matters concerning his territory to the Federal Ministers.

The Federation of the West Indies came into being with the installation of the Governor-General on 3 January 1958. A week later the Secretary of State, Mr Lennox-Boyd, in thanking the Comptroller for his contribution as Chairman of the Standing Federation Com-mittee, added: 'As Comptroller for Development and Welfare in the West Indies you have been responsible for an organisation which has played a part far beyond that originally envisaged for it in bringing representatives of the islands together and fostering a regional, rather than a purely territorial, consideration of problems common to all.'[75] The Secretary of State thus confirmed the view expressed in an editorial in *The Times* of 19 September 1947, which declared that the D & W Organisation, 'partly because it is the only institution serving the Caribbean Colonies as a whole, and partly because it alone can supply the expert direction so patently needed', had become 'the organ through which common Caribbean sentiment has found means of expression'. On the eve of the termination of the functions of the

Organisation on 31 March 1958, messages of appreciation for the ready and generous assistance provided over the years were received from all the territories it had served.[76]

The last Comptroller told the author that he regarded the Organisation's real claim to historic appreciation, and to the gratitude of the West Indies, lay in its outstandingly important work as the first Governmental machinery established in the West Indies to undertake regional functions. Its enduring monument is not – alas! – a Federation of the West Indies, but the variety of post-federal institutions created in recent years by West Indian initiative. Through the fulfilment of the duties delegated to it, and by its own conferences and training courses, it accustomed West Indians to working together and rendered possible a smooth transition from total fragmentation to at least skeletal political union. The value of the Organisation's work as an agency for technical assistance was, in his opinion, confirmed by the decision of HMG to re-create a similar body in Barbados after the collapse of the Federation.

Sir Stephen considered that it was important to recall that those who were concerned with West Indian affairs in the 1950s were fortunate in their timing. The geographical isolation of the small, scattered communities was a factor of major significance at the end of the war. The development of air travel revolutionised the situation, making it practicable, as it had never been previously, to think in terms of some measure of political and administrative centralisation.

SOURCES

1. File WIS 175/01, Part A, 1954–1956, item 11, letter and enclosure of 19 July 1954 to the Comptroller.

2. Ibid., item 14, letter of 5 Aug 1954 from the Comptroller.

3. Ibid., item 16, Confidential telegram No. 257 of 31 Aug 1954 from the Secretary of State to the Comptroller.

4. Ibid., item 17, telegram No. 304 of 2 Sep 1954 from the Comptroller.

5. Ibid., items 20–6.

6. Ibid., item 29, Confidential telegram No. 63 of 19 Nov 1954 from the Governor of Trinidad to the Secretary of State.

7. Ibid., item 43, Secret and Personal telegram No. 71 of 13 Dec 1954 from the Governor of Trinidad to the Secretary of State.

8. Ibid., item 55, letter of 13 Dec 1954 from the Comptroller.

9. Ibid., item 62, Confidential telegram of 24 Dec 1954 from the Secretary of State to the Comptroller.

10. Ibid., item 68, Secret telegram No. 17 of 22 Jan 1955 from the Secretary of State to Governors.

11. File WIS 175/942/02, Part A, 1954–1956, item 39, Confidential telegram WICIR No. 12, 1 Feb 1955, from the Secretary of State to all Governors in the West Indies.

12. Ibid., minute of 30 Dec 1954 on a meeting held on 21 Dec, when the Colonial Secretary of Trinidad, Mr Maurice Dorman, was present.

13. Colonial No. 315, 1955, para. 5.

14. Idem, para. 6.

15. Idem, para. 7.

16. File WIS 175/01, Part B, 1954–1956, items 167–72, Confidential telegram No. 55, 3 Apr 1955, from the Secretary of State to Governor of Jamaica and other Governors.

17. Ibid., item 218, minute of 27 June 1955 by the Secretary of State.

18. Ibid., item 232, letter of 9 Aug 1955 to the Comptroller.

19. Idem.

20. Ibid., item 234, Secret telegram No. 333 of 24 Aug 1955, from the Comptroller to the Secretary of State.

21. Ibid., item 236, Secret telegram No. 98 of 25 Aug 1955 from the Governor of Jamaica to the Secretary of State.

22. Ibid.

23. Ibid., item 236.

24. Ibid., item 261, minute of 5 Oct 1955 by the Secretary of State.

25. Ibid.

26. Ibid., Secret and personal letter of 24 Oct 1955 to Governors of Barbados, Jamaica, Trinidad and the Windward Islands and the Acting Governor of the Leeward Islands.

27. Idem.

28. File WIS 175/01, Part C, 1954–1956, minute of 31 Oct 1955 on a meeting two days earlier between Mr Gomes, Lord Lloyd and officials. See also the letter of 25 Oct 1955 from the Governor of Trinidad, item 278.

29. Ibid.

30. Ibid., items 291–2, Secret priority telegram No. 80 of 10 Nov 1955 from the Secretary of State to all West Indian Colonies and the Comptroller.

31. Ibid., item 351, Secret telegram No. 620 from the Governor of British Guiana to the Secretary of State.

32. Ibid., item 346, Telegram No. 801 from the Governor of Jamaica to the Secretary of State.

33. Ibid., item 360, Secret and Personal Telegram No. 5 of 9 Jan 1956 from the Governor of Jamaica to the Secretary of State.

34. Secret West Indian file WIS 175/01, Part D, 1954–1956, items 380 and 382, letter of 10 Feb 1956 from the Secretary of State, Mr Lennox-Boyd, to Mr Garnet H. Gordon, Trade Commissioner for the West Indies, and letter of 11 Feb 1956 from Mr Gordon to the Secretary of State.

35. File WIS 43/01, 1954–56, item 2, letter of 19 Mar 1954 from the Permanent Under-Secretary of State to the Comptroller.

36. Ibid., item 1, letter of 16 Jan 1954.

37. Ibid., item 9, letter of 18 Nov 1954 enclosing Colonial Office memorandum setting out the latest views of the Comptroller, with which it agreed.

38. Ibid., item 59, letter of 9 May 1956 from the Comptroller.

39. Ibid., item 12, letter of 20 Dec 1954 from the Comptroller to the Permanent Under-Secretary of State. See also an elaboration in confidential letter of 5 Jan 1955 from the Comptroller, item 15.

40. Ibid., minute of 4 Feb 1955.

41. Ibid., note of a meeting held on 22 Feb 1955, quoted in comment by Sir Charles Jeffries in a minute of 1 Mar 1955.

42. Ibid., item 20, letter of 12 Apr 1955 from the Comptroller.

43. Ibid., item 24, Confidential Note of 6 June 1955 for the information of the Fiscal and Civil Service Commissioners on the future of the D & W Organisation.

44. Ibid., item 26, letter of 16 June 1955.

45. Ibid., item 28, letter of 4 July 1955.

46. Ibid., item 31, letter of 12 July 1955 from the Comptroller.

47. Ibid., item 40, letter of 27 Feb 1956.

48. Ibid., item 54, letter of 27 Apr 1956 to the Comptroller.

49. Ibid., item 59, letter of 9 May 1956 from the Comptroller. The Conference referred to was, of course, the London Conference on West Indian Federation of February 1956.

50. Ibid., item 65, letter of 23 May 1956.

51. Ibid., item 71, letter of 14 Aug 1956 from the Comptroller.

52. File WIS 175/93/01, 1954–1956, item 1, Confidential letter of 22 Aug 1956 from the Comptroller.

53. Ibid., item 2, letter of 10 Sep 1956 to the Comptroller.

54. Ibid., item 3, letter of 20 Sep 1956 from the Comptroller.

55. Idem.

56. Ibid., item 7, letter of 28 Nov 1956.

57. D & W Confidential file 09881, 1957, item 1A, Problems of the British West Indies.

58. Ibid., item 1, personal and confidential letter of 17 Jan 1957 from the Comptroller.

59. Ibid., item 2, personal and confidential letter of 22 Jan 1957 to the Comptroller.

60. Secret West Indian file WIS 175/01, Part A, 1957–1959, item 45, telegram No. 412 of 1 Nov 1958, from the Governor of Jamaica to the Secretary of State.

61. Ibid., item 46, Secret and personal letter of 4 Nov 1958, from the Governor of Jamaica.

62. Ibid., item 55, Secret and personal letter of 19 Nov 1958 from the Governor-General.

63. West Indies file 71295/15/3, Part I, 1951 (CO 318/507), item 18, letter of 13 Feb 1951 from Sir H. Poynton to Sir G. Seel.

64. Ibid., item 16, letter of 16 Dec 1950 from Mr, later Sir Robert, Kirkwood, to the Secretary of State.

65. 'The Industrialisation of the British West Indies', by W. Arthur Lewis, in *Caribbean Economic Review*, Vol. II, No. 1, May 1950, pp. 1–61.

66. West Indies file 71295/15/3, Part I, 1951 (CO 318/507), item 17, Despatch No. 27 of 13 Feb 1951, from the Secretary of State to the OAG of Jamaica.

67. Ibid., item 18, letter of 13 Feb 1951 from Sir H. Poynton to Sir G. Seel.

68. Secret West Indian file WIS 43/02, 1957–1959, items 13–31, priority savingram of 23 Sep 1957 from the Secretary of State to all OAGs and Administrators in the West Indies.

69. The unpublished official 'History of Development and Welfare in the West Indies' by P. Hewitt-Myring, p. 165.

70. Secret West Indian file WIS 43/01, 1957–1959, items 48, 59 and 62, telegram No. 295 of 2 Nov 1957 from the Acting Governor of British Honduras; telegram No. 434 of 29 Nov 1957 from the Governor of British Guiana, and letter of 3 Dec 1957.

71. Ibid., items 63, 64–9, 82 and 85.

72. Secret West Indian file WIS 43/02, 1957–1959, item 87, Confidential savingram No. 94 of 25 Mar 1958 from the Governor-General to the Secretary of State; savingram No. 196 of 10 June 1958 from the Governor-General to the Secretary of State, item 93, and letter of 18 June 1958 from the Governor-General, item 95.

73. Ibid., items 101 and 103, savingram No. 621 of 6 Oct 1958 from the Governor of British Guiana to the Secretary of State; savingram No. 638 of 4 Nov 1958 from the Governor of British Honduras to the Secretary of State.

74. Ibid., item 127, Secret and personal letter of 16 Oct 1959 to the Governor-General.

75. Secret West Indian file WIS 175/01, Part A, 1957–1959, item 31, letter of 10 Jan 1958 from the Secretary of State to the Comptroller.

76. West Indies file WIS 43/01, 1957–1959, item 91, letter and enclosures of 31 Mar 1958 from the Comptroller to the Secretary of State.

4 Groundnuts: the Last Phase, 1951–1964

1. THE POSITION IN 1951–1952

A South African groundnuts farmer, Mr Pitout, who had provided the OFC with technical advice from time to time, visited the groundnut areas in the early months of 1951 and was so impressed by what he saw that he wrote to the leader of the Opposition, Sir Winston Churchill, to suggest that he should call off the Opposition criticism and visit the areas himself. Mr Pitout stated that the standard of farming on the OFC estates was far higher than in either Britain or South Africa, his crops in South Africa were no better than those in Kongwa, while the crops in Urambo and the Southern Province were bigger than anywhere else in the world, and that the scheme could not again go wrong.[1] When the Colonial Office received this information via the Ministry of Food,[2] the response was understandably cautious. The new Chairman, it was said, who had just returned from a first visit, had found morale and efficiency high, crops in Urambo and Nachingwea had grown well but those in Kongwa had been nearly ruined by a mid-season, drought, while prospects in Urambo were marred by the heavy and continuous rain. Yet the Colonial Office and the OFC were confident they could 'still make a success of the reduced scheme'.[3]

The high condition of the farming was commented on by Messrs Clay and Sykes when they reported on their visit of March – April 1951 to the three areas. They were quite excited by what they saw, stating that 'to see vast areas of good crops, well cultivated and clean, was indeed a stirring sight . . .'[4] Despite some critical comments, it appeared that a pattern of agriculture was emerging in all three regions which promised to be viable 'if assessed on direct farm costs and the overheads ordinarily carried by a farm'. The latter excluded the costs of a central organisation which, it was admitted, might be necessary in such a pioneer venture. They were disappointed to find several of the major recommendations of the Working Parties at

54

Kongwa and the Southern Province had not been implemented. One was the general recommendation that groundnuts should be confined to the upland red soils and that the *mbuga* soils should be restricted to maize and sorghum. Another was the suggestion that experiments in various forms of soil conservation should be instituted. A third was the organisation for fattening store cattle at Kongwa. While they registered disappointment over the decision to abolish the Operational Research Unit, they recognised that the OFC would need to economise on general agricultural research expenditure, and it was suggested that the basic soils work should be handed over to the East African Agriculture and Forestry Research Organisation (EAAFRO) at Nairobi as, in any case, the work had a wider application than to the three OFC areas.

The Board of OFC decided in February 1951 to cut expenditure on scientific research and experimental farm activities by £35,000 to £50,000.[5] The Chairman, Mr Gillett, felt that the Corporation as such was not getting value for money on its research programme.[6] For 1951–52, the first three items in the programme submitted on 31 March 1951, were (i) studies of rainfall and other climatic elements as currently studied, including the Kongwa rain grid; (ii) continuation of soil survey work at Urambo and of pedological studies in all regions – these should be completed for practical purposes by the end of 1952; and (iii) studies in the rate of precipitation and storage of moisture in soils, particularly at Kongwa.[7] Mr Gillett decided to hive off work on soils and Rosette disease to EAAFRO and work on cotton to the Empire Cotton Growing Corporation (ECGC), and thus to confine the OFC to agronomic studies. Consequently, there was no longer a need for a Chief Scientific Officer, who was to be replaced by a Chief Agronomist.[8]

In his first report, Mr Gillett stated that the overall position was satisfactory at Kongwa and the Southern Province, one farm at Kongwa producing over 700 lbs of groundnuts per acre and another 14 bags of maize per acre.[9] But a catastrophe had occurred at Urambo, where there was failure to lift between 30 and 40 per cent of the total harvestable crop. This was partly attributed to a delay in the actual harvesting operations, but mainly to the lack of efficient harvesting machinery. The Chairman was in constant touch with Messrs Massey – Harris Ltd. and hoped that a satisfactory digging and combining machine would be evolved. Otherwise, he felt that the whole question of mechanised groundnut growing in East Africa would have to be reviewed, for 'it cannot be economical for a farm to carry a heavy capitalisation on plant and machinery which is only operative for certain of the cultural operations, and for such plant and machinery to be stored for the majority of the year and the remaining operations carried out by a large, expensive and inefficient labour force.' He added: 'It is our biggest problem at the moment.' He referred to the recommendation of the Working Party at Kongwa that steers should be purchased for fattening and resale. It had been found that steers could not be bought from Africans at an economical price and so alternatives had to be found, possibly breeding rather than ranching. But meantime, he concluded, 'further knowledge of the effect of the cattle on the grazing and the grazing on the cattle should be ascertained before any large-scale policy is adopted'. Yet again, the OFC lacked basic data and the ability to procure it quickly.

The first hurdle that the new OFC had to overcome was that of the budget estimates for 1951–52, which showed an overall deficit of just over £2,750,000 as compared with an estimated deficit in the long-term plan of £2,500,000 during that year. But, as there were reasonable explanations of the increase and the Corporation still expected to cope within the total net expenditure of £6 million which Parliament had envisaged for the full seven-year experiment, both the Colonial Office and the Treasury agreed without imposing any cut, which in the nature of things would have been arbitrary. The Secretary of State, Mr J. Griffiths, minuted that his 'only concern about this is that, in a Debate, we may again be charged with beginning to overrun our estimates'.[10]

The proposed physical and financial expansion of the scheme had been outlined in Cmd 8125. Kongwa and Urambo were to have 24,000 and 60,000 acres respectively available for agriculture in 1951; the Southern Province was to have 60,000 acres available by 1954. These acreages were to be developed and farmed over a seven-year period from cash resources of approximately £6 million. When it reviewed in January 1952 the activities of the OFC in relation to this long-term plan, the Board of the OFC felt that, excepting only physical disasters, continued inflation in East Africa and general labour shortages, the plan could be achieved within the financial limits.[11]

However, the cost of surveying, clearing, levelling and conserving land ready for agriculture was thought unlikely to fall below £15 per acre for vegetation found in the Southern Province. It commented that 'no private arable farmer in East Africa would be prepared to pay this price for land, exclusive of buildings and improvements'. On the basis of existing and projected costs of clearing, farming and overheads, both Urambo and the Southern Province were expected to show a surplus of revenue over costs while Kongwa was expected to remain in deficit.

(a) Anticipated costs (in £per acre under crop) were:

	Kongwa	Urambo	Southern Province
Direct	11.0	12.3	12.0
Regional Overhead	2.75	2.75	2.75
Scheme Overhead	1.0	1.0	1.0
	14.75	16.05	15.75

(b) Revenue was expected to be £12.7, £16.6 and £19.3 per acre for the three areas Kongwa, Urambo and the Southern Province respectively. The Board's opinion on two major aspects of the scheme were, firstly, that mechanised, or partially mechanised, land clearing in the Southern Province was not economically feasible by commercial standards and, secondly, that mechanised agriculture could be made self-supporting providing there was no drastic fall in prices and the mechanical harvesting of groundnuts could be made practicable. It required at least two years of experience to test the second tentative conclusion and thus to clear the first hurdle in the long-term plan, namely, 'establishing the economics of land clearing and mechanised farming under tropical conditions'. If it was disproved, then alternative methods were to be devised as it was considered 'unthinkable that land prepared at such cost and effort should go out of production'.

The Chairman, in discussions at the Colonial Office in January 1951, said that Kongwa could be saved if it was turned into a plantation enterprise, while Urambo should, owing to the doubts about mechanised agriculture, be turned over to African settlement and farmed under central supervision rather on the lines of the Gezira scheme. While the area of greatest potential was the Southern Province, land clearing at £15 per acre was prohibitive, and so the best solution was to turn the area over to European farming rather on the lines of the European settlement scheme he had administered in Kenya. Naturally, all these ideas needed working out in consultation with the local Government. While they might appear to differ from those of Cmd 8125, the latter was, in fact, imprecise on the long-term objectives. At the same time, in the debate on the ORD Bill, 1951, both sides of the House expressed hopes that ways would be found of associating Africans with the scheme and the Secretary of State had promised to bear this in mind.[12]

The Agricultural Adviser to the Secretary of State, Sir Geoffrey Clay, felt that, while the OFC had previously not sufficiently regarded the economic aspect, there was now a tendency to jump fences. He advised caution with respect to the long-term objectives, and thought that three alternatives should be explored – sharecropping with African tenants, that combined with direct estate production, and European tenant-farming.[13] In fact, in view of past difficulties and the – admittedly vague – objectives of Cmd 8125, it was not felt that the Secretary of State should be asked to approve further proposals without much more detailed and analysed information than was currently available. However, at the meeting between the Secretary of State, Mr Griffiths, the Minister of State, Mr Dugdale, the Chairman, Mr Gillett and officials, a large measure of agreement was reached.[14] Three issues were discussed. First, there was the need to recast the financial provisions of the long-term plan in Cmd 8125 in order to clarify the Corporation's financial commitments during the seven-year term of the new scheme. The Secretary of State agreed, asking the Chairman to work it out in detail and clear it with officials at the Colonial Office and in the Treasury. Secondly, there was the importance of preparing for alternative patterns of the organisation in the separate parts of the scheme if the whole entity was to keep running for the full term within the £6 million voted by Parliament. The Chairman repeated the views expressed earlier in the Board's review of the three areas. The common factor in all three was the reduction in the number of expatriates involved, thus reducing costs. Both Ministers strongly favoured the introduction of Africans into the scheme, and the Secretary of State felt that, subject to the limitations imposed on the Corporation by their financial resources, there was no great difference of view between his Agricultural Adviser and the Chairman. The latter was asked to draw up tentative plans on the lines proposed, which Ministers would consider further when the necessity arose. Finally, there was the importance of having active and substantial backing from the Tanganyika Government in the future deployment of the scheme. The Chairman said that the Governor and his administrative staff were enthusiastic in the field but the administration at Dar-es-Salaam had adopted a wait-and-see attitude. The Chairman feared that the local administration would not be interested in land settlement experiments as there was no land hunger problem. However, at its inception, the Government of Tanganyika had looked forward to an eventual organisation along co-operative lines. Part of the problem was that the Tanganyika Government had not taken over the social services in the three areas. Superior standards in the Corporation's medical services raised an obstacle to their assimilation into the Government's Medical Department. The best solution would,

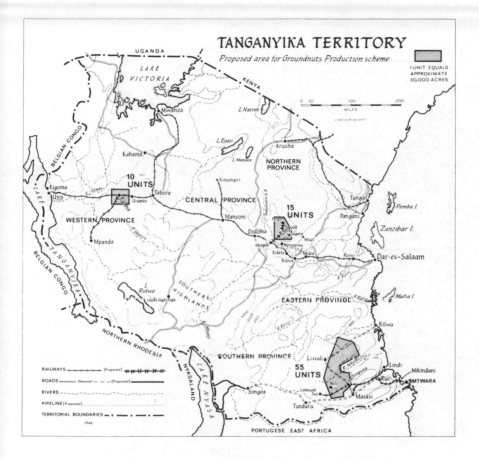

Tanganyika Territory: Proposed Areas for Groundnuts
Production Scheme

Map planned by A. E. Kelleway,
Historical Section, Cabinet Office.

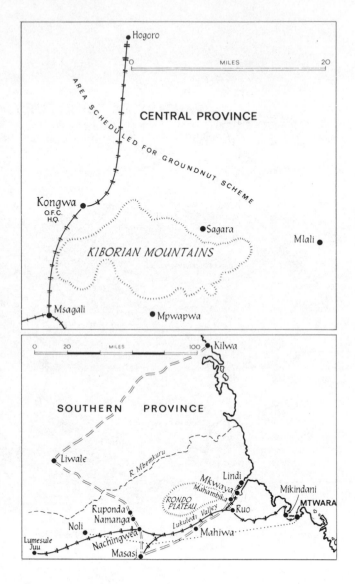

Tanganyika Territory: Sketch Maps of Central Province and
Southern Province

Map planned by A. E. Kelleway,
Historical Section, Cabinent Office.

it was thought, be for the Government to be asked to take over the services at a date in the future, and to charge for treatment given to the OFC at a rate which made the maintenance of standards possible. No extra CD & W funds could be made available for the Government to finance the services. The Secretary of State asked for a letter to be prepared for the Governor setting out the problem and urging the Government to give the Corporation its tangible support. The new Secretary of State, Mr Oliver Lyttelton, wrote accordingly to the Governor,[15] who replied in rather general terms.[16] He felt that the scheme had deviated so far from the original intentions that it was now quite different, and its aims were not clear to him. He wondered whether the Royal Commission on East Africa should include it in its enquiry. While he agreed in principle that the Government should ultimately take over the OFC Medical Services, the Standing Finance Committee had hitherto been intransigent – an attitude not helped by the grandiose plans of the OFC. For example, he stated, 'it was only last October that I opened a new magnificent hospital in the bush in the Southern Province which they are already having to cut down.' The Chairman of the OFC was opposed to a reference to the Royal Commission, both as an unsuitable topic for the kind of general enquiry being made and because further publicity for the OFC would be unhelpful.[17]

II. REVISION OF THE WHITE PAPER PLANS

In a memorandum of June 1952,[18] the Chairman stated that his experience with the scheme had convinced him 'that we know insufficient of the basic agricultural principles involved, especially in Nachingwea, in the centre of the Southern Province, and Urambo to justify the continuance of the progress laid down in Cmd. 8125'. Crop yield figures in the White Paper were not unreasonable 'for any sub-tropical area in which the pattern of agriculture has been fully developed, but, as yet, we have not attained that stage and are still pioneering to that end'. Acreages attempted over the past two years had sacrificed proper cultural practices for the sake of speed, whereas the drastic cut at Kongwa and the replanning of the area in four farms, following the recommendation of the Working Party, had had satisfactory results. But agricultural conditions in the other two areas differed significantly from those at Kongwa. At Nachingwea, he recommended a cessation of organised land clearing, and the division of the 30,000 acres already cleared into eleven farms, together with an experimental European tenant-farm and an area for African tenant-farming. Owing to the severity of the tsetse problem at Urambo, he advised that there should be no regeneration of the 65,000 acres originally cleared, and that the acreage under crops be reduced from 45,000 to between 18,000 and 20,000 acres. This acreage would be divided into eighteen farms of sizes varying from 500 to 1250 acres, with an area set aside for an African tenant-farm scheme.

At the meeting with the Secretary of State, Mr Lyttelton, the Governor, Sir Edward, later Lord, Twining, suggested that it was desirable that the transfer of control of the Corporation to the Tanganyika Government should take place sooner than had been contemplated in the White Paper and that, at the same time, the sphere of the Corporation should be extended to enable it to take on other agricultural tasks in Tanganyika.[19] He proposed that a Working Party should be set up in Tanganyika composed of representatives of the Tanganyika Government and of the Corporation to draw up detailed proposals to these ends. The Chairman supported the proposal. However, the Secretary of State felt that before a Working Party was set up it was necessary to decide whether the OFC was concerned with experimental work or whether it should seek to operate as a commercial enterprise. It was realised that, until it ascertained the most suitable basis for its operations the Corporation would have to proceed experimentally. However, the Corporation had to be self-supporting by the time the subsidy from the United Kingdom and any funds from the Tanganyika Government were expended. This was agreed by the Governor and, consequently, the Secretary of State approved in principle the proposal for a Working Party, promising early legislation to give effect to an agreed plan.

In a separate meeting with the Secretary of State, the Chairman put forward his ideas for a drastic revision of the White Paper plan,[20] which officials supported in their brief to the Secretary of State.[21] The Agricultural Adviser to the Secretary of State welcomed the proposals and the Secretary of State agreed to the new plan in principle, combining as it did 'the maximum acreage desirable for experimental purposes with the minimum from the point of view of the costs'. Neither new legislation nor a new White Paper was thought to be necessary; when a detailed scheme was approved, it would be announced publicly by the Secretary of State. The Chairman was heartened by the attitude of the Secretary of State, feeling that he could continue his policy of proving an area without being tied to any definite acreage.[22] The decision to slow down the tempo of operations, and the consequent further run-down in staff, were announced in August 1952.[23]

Qualms were expressed in the Colonial Office about the basis on which the Chairman was budgeting his new plans,[24] and he was written to accordingly.[25] He concluded his reply by saying that the scheme had been cut to rock bottom, and the next hurdle was to raise yields by improved cultural practices, but several other hurdles would follow, including conservation and utilisation of water resources, improved methods of soil conservation, land clearing with special reference to the control of tsetse, and so on.[26] It is not unfair to wonder how little relevance the experience and research over past years appeared to have to the problem of viable farm units. The Agricultural Adviser and his deputy were increasingly diffident in commenting on the Chairman's views and, when they did, were usually easily answered. For example, they readily accepted the Chairman's view, based on deep local knowledge, that their suggestion that European tenant-farming might be used in conjunction with African tenancy was liable to serious abuse.[27] Fortunately, public interest in the OFC had dwindled, and there was little real hostility towards it 'as long as it does not come into competition with the interests seeking new money grants from the Exchequer'.[28] Indeed, positive and factual information about the experiment would, it was thought, soon be generally welcomed.

III. REPORT OF THE WORKING PARTY, 1953

The terms of reference of the proposed Working Party were agreed in Dar-es-Salaam and sent for approval to the Secretary of State who, after slight amendment, agreed.[29] The Members of the Working Party were Messrs S. Gillett (Chairman), S. A. S. Leslie and then R. de Z. Hall (Acting Chief Secretary, Tanganyika), C. E. Tilney (Acting Member for Finance and Economics, Tanganyika), A. E. Trotman (Member for Agriculture and Natural Resources, Tanganyika), F. Hinds (Member of Legislative Council, Tanganyika) and Sir Charles Lockhart (OFC).

The Working Party was required:
(1) To make recommendations for the creation of a new organisation involving a closer association between the Tanganyika Government and the Overseas Food Corporation in Tanganyika. The objectives of the new organisation were to be:

(a) To bring to a successful conclusion by September 1957 the experimental agricultural scheme laid down in Cmd 8125, modified as agricultural or financial considerations might dictate from time to time, with:

(i) the primary purpose of establishing by that date, and within the financial provision available, a system, or systems, of agriculture which will enable the 180,000 acres cleared and equipped by the Corporation to be fully utilised in the self-supporting production of crops and livestock; and
(ii) the secondary purpose of contributing towards the solution of similar problems elsewhere.

(b) To enable the new organisation to participate in agricultural development and production in Tanganyika not included in Cmd 8125, on terms to be agreed in each case.

(c) To secure the co-ordination of the research work now undertaken by the Corporation with the East African Inter-Territorial, or the Tanganyika Government, Research Organisations.

(2) To make recommendations for any consequential change in the relationship of the Overseas Food Corporation to Her Majesty's Government in the United Kingdom.

(3) The report should cover the adjustments in: (i) constitution; (ii) organisation; and (iii) finance of the Overseas Food Corporation judged to be necessary in order to create a new organisation in which the Tanganyika Government could participate on terms which would be mutually acceptable.

It was recognised by the Working Party that the existing operations and finance of the OFC were not appropriate to a Public Corporation which had been constituted in the United Kingdom when its activities were conceived on a much larger and wider scale. At the same time, the responsibility to the Secretary of State inevitably tended to isolate the Corporation from the general development of Tanganyika, where its experience and expertise could be usefully employed. So it was proposed that:

(1) by legislation, in Parliament and in the Tanganyika Legislative Council, the assets, liabilities and functions of the Overseas Food Corporation in Tanganyika should be transferred as from 1 April 1954 to a Tanganyika Agricultural Development Corporation;

(2) the functions of the new Corporation should be extended to include agricultural development work in Tanganyika, either on the initiative of the Corporation with the approval of the Government or at the specific request of Government, and on terms which would fully protect the financial interests of HMG;

(3) the commitments of the Overseas Food Corporation under the tripartite agreement regarding the port and railway of the Southern Province should be assumed directly by HMG as from 1 April 1954, with an appropriate reduction in the Treasury commitment of £6 million in respect of the Overseas Food Corporation;

(4) any balance of the £6 million remaining after meeting all Overseas Food Corporation expenditure to 31 March 1954 and providing for the guarantee commitment referred to under (3) should be made available to the new Corporation for the period 1 April 1954 to 30 September 1957, subject to the existing controls;

(5) the disposal of the assets then vested in the Overseas Food Corporation and transferred to the new local Corporation, together with any further assets derived from funds provided by HMG which might be created by the new Corporation up to 30 September 1957, should continue to be subject to the control of the Secretary of State.

It was hoped that, in this way, there would be a more effective use of the Corporation's resources in both the short and the longer term.

On 14 February 1953, the Governor addressed a Confidential Despatch to the Secretary of State in which he endorsed the recommendations of the Working Party, whose Report he enclosed, and suggested that the proposed new Corporation should be 'enabled and encouraged to hand over to private enterprise any farming and other units which may be expected to be economic propositions in the hands of private enterprise'.[30]

The official reaction at the Colonial Office was favourable[31] and the Treasury was reminded that 'the Tanganyika Government is far from being an eager buyer willing to pay handsomely for the privilege of taking over the OFC', which they were under no obligation to do, and regard should be taken of Tanganyika's capacity to pay.[32] Hitherto, as the letter remarked, the Tanganyika Government had refused to take any financial stake in the Corporation, mainly because of the way in which the Corporation's predecessors consistently ignored the Government's advice, as for example against starting at Kongwa. At the same time, the Colonial Office wished to make it clear to the Tanganyika Government that HMG was not prepared to hand them all the assets of the Corporation and retain all the liabilities. The crux of the matter was the railway guarantee, which HMG was expected to take over when responsibility for the Corporation was transferred.[33] It was felt that eventually HMG would have to accept the burden. The Treasury suggested alternatives, and asked the Colonial Office to examine further how this might be handled.[34] The purpose of the ten-year commitment was to guarantee the railway and port when they handled the expected large consignments from the original scheme. HMG had no continuing interest in either port or railway under the truncated scheme of Cmd 8125. Therefore, the Treasury was, as one official minuted, likely to be sticky over the guarantee.

The proposals of the Working Party were discussed with the members of the Royal Commission on East Africa when they visited Dar-es-Salaam.[35] As the result of these discussions, it was thought important, for psychological reasons, that the designation 'Development Corporation' should be avoided, as it conjured up in the mind of the general public 'an impression of grandiose projects embarked upon with the highest hopes and financed from a bottomless purse, with eventual disillusionment and a heavy loss to the taxpayer'. So it was proposed to drop 'Development' and call the new organisation simply 'Tanganyika Agricultural Corporation'. A further suggestion was that, after taking over the assets, liabilities and functions of the OFC, as provided by the Working Party Report, each area should be hived off as a separate company as soon as it was viable. Any not viable by 1957 was to be wound up. This suggestion has a strong resemblance to the idea put forward by Professor Frankel in an addendum to the Kongwa Working Party Report. The idea was rejected by the OFC in 1950. Professor Frankel was a member of the East Africa Royal Commission. He stated at the meeting held at the Colonial Office on 8 July 1953 that what he wanted was a self-contained organisation in each area, which had its own balance sheet and stood or fell by its own results. He agreed that the Corporation's experimental work in each area should not be subordinated to the changes of fortune of each area but regarded as part of the whole.[36] A broadly similar idea had been mooted earlier. Thus, in an article in The Times (17 June 1949), Earl de la Warr suggested that, while the clearing and preparation of the land could properly be undertaken by the British Government, the actual farming should be given over to approved individuals, farming companies or African co-operative associations, with safeguards for the condition of labour, standards of husbandry, and efficient marketing. This was a modern application, with new precautions, of the well-tried way of allowing Charter Companies to develop territories in the

Empire, according to an editorial comment in the same issue of *The Times*.

To return to the discussions between the Working Party and the Royal Commission: while the first suggestion concerning the name of the new Corporation was a matter of taste, the second was less attractive once its implications came to be considered. First, there was the problem of deciding when an area was viable as a separate unit. Thus, after unusually good results in 1950–51 and 1951–52, the farmers and other staff at Kongwa firmly believed that their future was assured and were willing to take over the place on their own. Yet, in the spring of 1953, Kongwa experienced a drought of such severity that all the farms taken together produced nothing over and above the requirement of seed for the next crop.[37] It was stated that: 'Rainfall in Kongwa certainly appears to be unpredictable and, within the small area of our field of activities, the rainfall has varied from 3 inches on one farm to about 14 inches on the Experimental Farm, a distance of about 15 miles as the crow flies.' Of course, the Chairman might be able to say when a particular crop in a particular area could be taken up commercially, but that would not be the same point. In the second place, the existing purpose, as stated in Cmd 8125, was to solve the fundamental problems of tropical agriculture, which the Chairman and his three Area Managers, all from the Colonial Agricultural Service, were doing. Clearly, once the problems had been solved in an area, both in respect of food and other crops, the area might be ready for separation, although knotty questions of overhead costs might easily arise. Certainly, the suggestion could not be applied until then. Finally, it was possible that the Treasury might interpret the proposal as one for subsidising an area until it was viable and then handing it over to the local organisation, so that the British taxpayer had, at great expense, started a small series of commercial farms.[38] Indeed, the suggestion made by the Acting Governor was in line with the view of his Government that only the commercial aspect mattered. As the Chairman of the OFC commented: 'If it is envisaged that the areas are going to produce great agricultural wealth, then we are wasting our time. Had the areas offered such possibilities, they would have been cultivated by Africans or immigrant races long ago.'[39] The Chairman's conception was that

if we can show that economic crop production is feasible and, by adopting sound agricultural practices and proper land use methods, are able to (*a*) increase production, (*b*) raise the level of the African farmer above that of subsistence, (*c*) make available large tracts of previously unpopulated country to meet the demands of the ever-increasing African population, and (d) provide limited increased wealth by the production of high-priced exportable crops, then, I feel, we shall have served a purpose of considerable importance to the Colonial Empire.[40]

What started in 1947 as a matter of quasi-development largely for the benefit of the United Kingdom had become, under Mr Gillett, a genuine development project in tropical agriculture. Consideration was given to the possibility of changing one area, Urambo, from an experimental to a commercial proposition with reduced experimentation, but neither of the other two areas could be considered in that way. Urambo had grown tobacco successfully over three consecutive seasons. Professor Frankel stated that the farming of tobacco should be hived off to independent tenant-farmers who would come under the broad supervision of the Corporation which, as landlord, could supply certain extension services for payment.[41] Cmd 8125 did not contemplate a changeover of that kind; it envisaged that the experiment should continue until September 1957, when a decision would be taken regarding settlement of the cleared areas and possible further development.

iv. DECISION TO WIND UP THE OFC

Given these views and the Treasury's concern with the problem of the control of expenditure under the regime proposed by the Working Party, further thought was given in the Colonial Office to the problem of the transfer of the OFC. There were three possible courses of action. The first was to run the OFC as at the time, under direct Colonial Office control, but to allow it to use its spare capacity and, if necessary, to expand its capacity, at the expense of the Tanganyika Government for Tanganyika Government projects. It would thus be allowed to create a local subsidiary which could draw on the Corporation's physical assets, but not its financial resources, to carry out work for the local Government. The second was to adopt the proposals of the Working Party, thus converting the OFC into a local enterprise. The third was to convert the experimental plan of Cmd 8125 into a CD & W scheme under the administration of the Tanganyika Government. By legislation in the United Kingdom and Tanganyika Territory, a Tanganyika Agricultural Corporation would be established to take over the assets and liabilities of the OFC with the object of continuing the policy outlined in Cmd 8125, as modified by the Board of the OFC. The unspent balance of the £6 million as at 31 March 1954 could be added to the £140 million limit made available by the CD & W Acts, and a CD & W scheme made to provide for its issue to the Tanganyika Government on an annual budgetary basis.

The disadvantage of the first method was that it would not reinvest the Corporation's future in a statutory Tanganyika enterprise, leaving, therefore, the dangers of its running down about as great as with the OFC, while HMG would be in probably a worse position to negotiate at the winding-up stage than as matters then stood. The advantage of the second method was that it both achieved Colonial Office policy and provided the Corporation with a new local identity, which would assure its future and maintain the confidence of the staff. But, as seen earlier, such a solution met strong Treasury criticism. The third method had the advantage of the second method without the shortcomings, and was perhaps the method that should have been applied in 1951 instead of the method of Cmd 8125. The existing scheme fitted easily into the CD & W system, and so assured the Government of Tanganyika that its needs for development finance over the years 1955–60 included provision under this heading.[42]

The idea was welcomed when it was mentioned to the Governor on 16 July. It was stated in a letter to the Acting Governor on 28 July 1953,[43] by which time it was known to the Treasury, where it was welcomed not merely as a way of dealing with the accounting difficulties raised earlier but as 'a more positive and clear-cut alternative to offer to Parliament than any attempt to maintain the basis of direct control'.[44] The Colonial Office was invited to produce a paper on both the CD & W proposal and the railway guarantee for further discussion with the Treasury.

The Chairman of the OFC was anxious to have matters settled forthwith so that the new regime started with a clean bill, forgetting the past and approaching the future with a new outlook. Although £36 million had been written off, the investment had not been completely lost because, over the previous two years, the reorientation made it likely that at least two of the three areas could be utilised for demonstrating how the African peasant could move away from subsistence agriculture. As the project would take some years and be of value to both Central and East Africa, it fitted appropriately into the CD & W system.[45] However, the Treasury was, not unnaturally, concerned about the proceeds of any assets that might be disposed of by the Tanganyika Corporation,[46] while the Acting Governor was sure that the unofficial members of the Legislature would reject any proposal to shorten the ten-year railway guarantee.[47] To overcome both of these obstacles, the Colonial Office proposed that both assets and liabilities should be transferred by legislation from the OFC to HMG, which would then execute an agency agreement whereby both were transferred to the new Corporation, subject to certain conditions and limitations.[48] The proceeds of the disposal of assets at any time would thus be at the discretion of the Secretary of State, while the railway guarantee would remain until the scheme expired, when it could be dealt with on its merits.[49] The proposal was acceptable to the Treasury at the official level.[50]

However, when it came to draft the purpose of the new Corporation, it was found that the Chairman of the OFC was thinking of permanent settlement, involving the alienation of land.[51] This was outside the purposes laid down in Cmd 8125 and meant that the Secretary of State would have to consult Parliament.[52] The Secretary of State's Agricultural Adviser, Sir Geoffrey Clay, thought that any large settlement project of the kind mentioned should be financed locally, not by HMG.[53] But the official dealing with the matter felt that, whatever the Office view might be, the Chairman's proposals should be carefully considered on their merits and the decision whether to adopt them reserved for the Secretary of State.[54]

Subsequently, it was found that there were legal difficulties involved in the agency agreement idea which made it an unacceptable instrument for effecting the changes in mind.[55] It was, therefore, thought that the general proposal should be put to Treasury Ministers, as the view might be taken in Parliament that the assets were being 'given away' in addition to the rest of the £6 million.[56] The Financial Secretary to the Treasury, Mr Boyd-Carpenter, agreed in principle with the broad proposition that the assets of the OFC should be transferred to a Tanganyika Agricultural Corporation for use for approved purposes, subject to their disposal being in the hands of the Secretary of State, with the concurrence of the Treasury, and the proceeds being paid to the Exchequer.[57] It was realised that the drafting would be a delicate and involved operation, and it was assumed that the matter would be submitted to the Cabinet before any question of public comment arose. The proposal was then put to the Governor of Tanganyika Territory for approval,[58] which was given both by him[59] and by the Executive Council.[60] The Secretary of State, Mr Lyttelton, submitted a memorandum to the Home Affairs Committee, stating his intention to introduce a Bill to amend the ORD Acts, 1948–1951, in order to provide for (a) the winding-up of the OFC and the continuance of its work by a statutory corporation to be set up by the Tanganyika Government, (b) the writing-off of certain advances, approximating £4 million, made to the East African Railways and Harbours Administration for building the Southern Province port and railway, (c) the writing-off of net capital losses and the waiver of interest in certain schemes abandoned by the CDC, involving a sum of approximately £5 million.[61] The memorandum was considered at a meeting of the Home Affairs Committee on 9 March 1954. After the Parliamentary Under-Secretary of State for the Colonies, the Earl of Munster, explained the purpose of the proposed Bill, the Financial Secretary to the Treasury supported, with two reservations, the proposals of the Secretary of State as a necessary salvage operation. He urged that the liability of the Exchequer to support the new Tanganyika Agricultural Corporation should not be extended beyond the balance of £1,550,000 remaining from the £6 million voted in 1951, and that the waiving of advances to the EARHA should not be extended beyond the advances made up to 31 March 1953, so that advances made after that date, some £750,000, should be repaid. The Committee approved in principle the introduction of legislation on the lines proposed, and invited the Secretary of State to submit a draft Bill for that purpose to the Legislation Committee. A draft White Paper and a draft Bill were approved by the Secretary of State on 14 May 1954 after being generally agreed with the Treasury and the Tanganyika Government. The draft Bill was approved by the Legislation Committee on 19 May 1954[62] and, on the same day, the White Paper, *The Future of the Overseas Food Corporation*, was published.[63] The latter included, as an appendix, a memorandum by the OFC which stated (i) Kongwa should be operated until September 1957 with one arable farm run in conjunction with a ranch as a large-scale experiment in cattle and pasture improvement; (ii) at Urambo, the area of cleared land should be consolidated by a controlled form of settlement based primarily on the production of flue-cured tobacco; (iii) the agricultural experiment in Nachingwea, where the eventual objective was co-operative production under the control of co-operatives, should be reconsidered after a further two years.

The new plans were welcomed on all sides in the debate in the Tanganyika Legislature on 26 May 1954. Those who spoke included Mr R. W. R. Miller, a former Member for Agriculture, who sat as an unofficial member; he it was who had suggested the scheme originally to the late Mr F. Samuel of the UAC and he now strongly supported the Bill. The Member for Lands and Mines, Mr A. H. Pike, who was at one time Provincial Commissioner for the Southern Province, said: 'This African tenant-farming scheme in Nachingwea has certainly struck the imagination of the Africans and they feel that, for the first time, they have had brought to them mechanised farming and a way of integrating mechanised farming into their own peasant agriculture which may prove a pattern for the future.'[64] The *Tanganyika Standard* of 28 May of 1954 welcomed the Bill in its editorial, which ended: 'Government can be assured that it has the full support of the people of this Territory in its new enterprise.' The Ordinance, No. 15 of 1954, to establish the Tanganyika Agricultural Corporation received the Governor's Assent on 1 June 1954.[65] In the interests of continuity, it was agreed by the Executive Council that the Chairman, Mr Gillett, and certain of the existing members of the Board should be invited to continue to serve, together with some new members, including an African with agricultural experience and someone with a successful record in business and agriculture.[66] The Overseas Resources Development Bill, 1954, received the Royal Assent on 25 November 1954.[67] The date of transfer was to be 1 April 1955. After consultation with the Secretary of State, the Governor in Council appointed the following to be members of the TAC: Mr S. Gillett, CMG (Chairman); Mr A. Gaitskell, CMG; Chief Humbi Ziots, MBE; Messrs A. M. A. Karimjee, OBE, A. A. Lowrie, D. Parker; and the Member for Agriculture and Natural Resources.[68]

v. A POLICY FOR AFRICAN AGRICULTURE

It is now necessary to return to the basic policy discussions which proceeded from the receipt of the Chairman's letter of 2 September 1953, with which he enclosed a secret memorandum on future policy.[69] Experience as Chairman of the OFC had convinced Mr Gillett that (a) the existing OFC unavoidably operated at a loss, and so commitments should be hived off as soon as practicable: (b) The areas were unsuited to fully mechanised agriculture for the large-scale economic production of food crops, but did lend themselves to crop production by Africans, aided by partial mechanisation and the necessary control and advice; and (c) flue-cured tobacco offered possibilities for the opening-up of the Urambo area on an economic basis. Additionally, he assumed that HMG wished the seven-year experiment to result in a viable enterprise, and therefore, felt that the experiment should consider socio-economic implications as well as agronomic aspects. Rights of tenure for Europeans and Africans alike would, consequently, follow the successful working of the scheme rather than precede it. Equally, private enterprise should operate with the Corporation until it was considered wise to hand over the responsibility to a co-operative body.

The next stage, according to the Chairman, was one of 'consolidation' by means of multiracial settlement with the ultimate object of permanent settlement involving alienation of land. For the introduction of tenants on an increasing scale would, in his view, both use most fully the experimental work already done and husband the remaining resources of the OFC, thus maximising the chances of carrying on the experiment until September 1957, the terminal date, on the basis of the £6 million allocation.

Urambo was thought to be ready for the policy of consolidation. Food crops were to be grown alongside flue-cured tobacco, so there was no danger of mono-culture. While in the long run development would be along the lines of an African tenant scheme, in the meantime viability meant European production and, in order to introduce Africans more quickly, an African visiting-tenant farmers scheme was to be promoted, enabling Africans to retain their tribal lands but to visit the organised scheme annually during the cropping period. To avoid any suggestion of racial differentiation, the Board of the OFC agreed that, while there would have to be different terms for Europeans and Africans because no European would settle and put money into a farm without some security of tenure, the two types should be designated simply Grade A and Grade B farms.[70] Europeans unable to participate were to be offered leases, either on an annuity and redemption basis, repayable over a period of twenty years, or on a tenancy basis for a period of thirty-three years, with an option to purchase after occupancy for five years. These were to be subject to the satisfactory farming of the area and disposal of crops through the Corporation, as was the African visiting-tenant scheme. Africans were to begin with 25–30 acres each, while European farms of 1500 acres were envisaged; these were expected to show net profits of £80–£100 p.a. and around £1850 p.a. respectively, after allowing for food crops. Of the 60,000–65,000 acres of cleared land at Urambo, 50,000 acres was suitable for this settlement programme and this was thought by the Chairman to be sufficient to try out a pilot scheme. A further argument was that Urambo was situated within an immense area of tsetse-infested *miombo* bush in Western Tanganyika: it would, therefore, be cheaper to protect 65,000 acres occupied by tenant farmers than an area of 10,000 acres occupied by the OFC.

Kongwa presented a different problem as dry-land farming was much too hazardous for African tenant farming. So the Chairman proposed that the farmers there should be invited in the spring of 1954 to continue on their own account, which would keep 12,000–20,000 acres under cultivation. The rest of the 70,000 acres should, in the Chairman's opinion, continue to be ranched under European supervision until 1957. Nachingwea, which started after the other two areas, was, in the Chairman's opinion, progressing well on the original lines of agronomic experimentation. It had the best rainfall of the three and a strong African visiting-tenant scheme, but no conclusions could yet be drawn, and so the experimentation was to continue until 1957 before the area could be considered ripe for conversion to a viable area.

The Agricultural Adviser to the Secretary of State, Sir Geoffrey Clay, was dubious both as to whether a settlement scheme covering some 50,000 acres could be called a 'pilot project' and of the apparent desire to abandon the experimentation planned in 1951 for 'development based on limited experimentation and, in the main, short-term results'.[71] Mr Frank Sykes, however, was favourably impressed both with progress at Urambo and Nachingwea and with the Corporation's African farming scheme, which emphasised the need to produce a class of African agricultural capitalists to provide the social incentive to move from subsistence farming.[72] When the proposals were discussed by the Board of the OFC, the Chief Secretary of the Tanganyika Government expressed the agreement of the Governor and himself as they felt that 'it would be wrong either to go on wholly experimentally without an early trial of practical application on realistic lines or, alternatively, to allow the land to revert to bush'.[73] The Board approved, in principle, the Chairman's policy statement, which was also endorsed, subject to clearance with the Tanganyika Government, by a meeting of officials at the Colonial Office which the Chairman attended.[74] It was realised that the new proposals could not properly be construed as within the terms of reference of the White Paper, a view the Treasury was likely to take as the Treasury had enquired before the meeting whether the new proposals were (i) within the terms of Cmd 8125; (ii) likely to cost more than the £6 million earmarked by Parliament to September 1957; and (iii) commonsense.[75]

On 28 May 1954, the day after the Tanganyika Agricultural Corporation Bill passed through all stages in the Legislative Council, the Chairman of the OFC submitted a further memorandum on future policy for discussion in the Colonial Office.[76] At a meeting on 20 November 1953 it was decided that the approval of the Secretary of State should not be sought for the proposed changes until (a) all the parties concerned had considered and approved the changes; and

(b) fuller details were supplied concerning the settlement proposals at Urambo. By the time the details were available, both the Government of Tanganyika Territory and the Board of the OFC had approved, while the original proposals for consolidation in the Urambo area had been modified in the light of further experience. It was realised that, although 12 to 15 acres per family was usually sufficient, more progressive and enterprising tenants could successfully tackle twice that acreage with the same amount of mechanical appliances. So the next 2000 acres were to be divided into holding of 25 acres under arable, with the possible extension to 50 acres. Next, after one year on probation, it was desired to offer tenants year-to-year leases, providing the terms and conditions of the lease were fulfilled. Finally, after discussion with the Government of Tanganyika, it was considered that the African would prefer to receive the whole proceeds from the sale of his crops after deducting the cost of preparing and administering his holding.

As the result of another difficult agricultural year in Kongwa, the Board decided to concentrate its attention on the cattle project, but to continue one arable farm so that the experiment of mechanised agriculture under dry farming conditions could be continued. The cattle project was expected to be self-supporting 'given average years'. At Nachingwea, the experiment was to continue, though financial provision was to be made to 'consolidate' the area, possibly along the lines of Urambo, at a later date.

The Governor of Tanganyika Territory, Sir Edward Twining, confirmed his Government's full support of the policy outlined by the Chairman, adding: 'Indeed, we attach a great importance to his proposals, which may bring about revolutionary changes in African agriculture.'[77] The Agricultural Adviser to the Secretary of State remained sceptical, especially as he felt that the OFC might be embarking on tenant settlement at Urambo before it was able to advise tenants on cropping systems.[78] The Adviser on Co-operatives, Mr B.J. Surridge, agreed, adding that some comparatively high-priced crop would be necessary to make the proposals financially worth while and a co-operative marketing scheme was suggested for the marketing of secondary crops.[79] These points were raised at a meeting at the Colonial Office between officials, Advisers and the Chairman.[80] In answer to the first point, the Chairman said the new proposals represented the application of the experimental data which the Corporation already possessed. He accepted the view on co-operatives, though he felt its immediate application would be unwise because it was necessary both to ensure that tenants paid their debts to the Corporation and to avoid discrimination between farm lease tenants and African tenants. The Secretary of State, Mr Lyttelton, was not altogether happy about the Urambo scheme as: 'Experiments for three years in agriculture are usually not considered long enough in Africa to establish a really firm foundation'. But, with some misgivings and subject to the approval of the Government of Tanganyika for the terms of the leases, he agreed.[81]

Early in January 1955 the Colonial Office sent a draft of a CD & W scheme to the Treasury for advice.[82] After discussing detailed points with the Treasury and the Government of Tanganyika, the Scheme was approved and sent to the Acting Governor of Tanganyika Territory on 15 March 1955.[83] The main provisions were that (a) the net expenditure of the TAC in respect of the CD & W scheme should be met up to 30 September 1957; (b) a sum of the order of £1.3 million was available from the sum of £6 million originally voted; (c) the programme of work in the three areas would be devised from year to year by the TAC and submitted, in a memorandum and in budget form, through the Governor, for the approval of the Secretary of State; (d) provided no new project was undertaken without the authority of the Governor and the Secretary of State, the TAC could vary the approved programme of work as might be found necessary in practice; (e) virement between the items of the approved expenditure estimates were allowed, except for that between the provision for capital expenditure and the provision for recurrent charges, which required prior approval.

While, however, the control from London was no more onerous than before, the need to negotiate through the intermediary of the Government of Tanganyika instead of direct was found irksome by the Chairman, who felt he could not have reorganised the OFC under the new arrangement.[84] He was assured of the Colonial Office's complete confidence in his administration and told that, once the current round of negotiations was completed, he could look forward to five years of comparatively straightforward financial assistance, at least as far as the United Kingdom was concerned. Naturally, owing to their direct interest, the Government of Tanganyika had to be a partner in the matter.[85] Yet, at the end of the year, the Chairman was desperately anxious to know what funds would be available so that he could start planning the next year's programme well ahead, especially if he should be required to reduce the farming staff still further.[86] Not for the first time, immediate and longer-term plans had to be considered together.

VI. THE TANGANYIKA AGRICULTURAL CORPORATION ACT, 1957

In June 1956 the Colonial Office informed the Treasury that the Governor of Tanganyika requested consideration of the future of the TAC after September 1957, i.e. when the period provided for in Cmd 9158 came to an end.[87] It had been recognised in paragraph 4(ii) of Cmd 9158 that plans for the future would have to be made in good time. After discussions with the Chief Secretary of Tanganyika, Mr R. de S. Stapledon, and with the Chairman of the TAC, it was accepted that the work envisaged in Cmd 9158 could not be completed by the end of September 1957. A five-year extension to 1962 was felt to be necessary to complete the work which, in fact, had relevance for the whole of East and Central Africa. Thus, the East Africa Royal Commission 1953-1955 had reported that the process of experimental development was likely to be slow, laborious and expensive, and had shown that the amount of fertile land capable of immediate development was restricted and unevenly distributed.[88] Consequently, the Colonial Office argued that it would be cheaper, and more efficient, to complete the existing experiment than close it down in 1957 and then have to begin again when the problem of land became pressing. It was proposed that the estimated balance of £664,000 from the maximum of £1.7 million made available under section 2 of the ORD Act, 1954, should be used to meet the net expenditure of the 'transferred undertaking' for the following five years. Owing to the wider relevance of the scheme, on the one hand, and the inadequacy of Tanganyika's existing CD & W allocation, on the other, it was not thought that Tanganyika should be expected, or in any case could manage, to absorb the transferred undertaking into her CD & W programme. Accordingly, an amendment to the ORD Act was proposed to allow for the use of a sum of the order of £500,000 over the period 1 October 1957 to 1 October 1962 so that the experimental development might be fully consolidated.

The initial reaction in the Treasury was uncompromising, rather surprisingly so in the circumstances. The argument was that the TAC was essentially a salvage operation after the failure of the Groundnuts Project, undertaken for a period which was now coming to an end and that if there was one extension, there might be yet another.[89] As it benefited Tanganyika, it was considered that it should be paid for, in one way or another, by that Territory, without any supplement to its CD & W allocation. It was recognised that, if no help was given, the

TAC might be closed down and the money already spent would be wasted, but it was felt that this should be accepted without much argument as 'it would be inconsistent with a request to slow down CD & W expenditure to continue this separate subsidy beyond the original period'. However, despite the current economy climate, from which it was said the Colonial Office tended to regard themselves as exempt, it was not thought to be a case for dying in the last ditch, even if a real saving on CD & W could be secured, if the Secretary of State pressed the case strongly.[90] So, while the first answer to the Colonial Office would be to refuse to continue assistance beyond October 1957, if further assistance was necessary it should be on the basis that the Tanganyika Government accepted responsibility for the TAC in return for the releasing of £500,000 as requested. Thus, no question of further direct assistance by HMG would arise.[91] The Financial Secretary to the Treasury readily agreed to this latter suggestion.[92] However, the Colonial Office was told only that the Treasury was not convinced of the rightness of the proposal;[93] in its reply, the Colonial Office pointed out that if the tap was to be turned off at the arbitrary date of October 1957, the areas would soon return to bush and the plan announced in Cmd 8125 and 9158 would then be widely regarded as having failed. The Colonial Office reply continued:

> This is a situation which the Secretary of State could not possibly defend before Parliament, nor our Accounting Officer before the Public Accounts Committee, against a background that what was needed, and indeed has been sought by the Tanganyika Government, was not more money than Parliament had agreed to provide in the first place, but simply more time in which to spend up to that amount of money wisely and in the way most likely to bring the experiments to a satisfactory conclusion.[94]

And, for good measure, it was remarked that a refusal to extend the time limit from 1957 to 1962 'would be all the more inexplicable and indefensible to Parliament in the light of the keen public interest in the Report of the Royal Commission on East Africa and the importance the latter attached to the successful prosecution of the transferred undertaking'.

An examination of the budget forecasts of the TAC for the five years commencing 1 October 1957, to find anything questionable about them,[95] turned out to be fruitless, giving no grounds for asking for a reduction.[96] Lacking both the material and the expertise to criticise in detail the estimates for expenditure over the following five years, it was suggested that the sum should be brought down to £350,000, or, at most, £400,000 by rounding down and presuming that economies could be made.[97] Accordingly, the Colonial Office was offered £300,000 or, at most, £350,000, on the understanding that the Tanganyika Government accepted full responsibility for the Corporation.[98] While the Tanganyika Government was agreeable to the latter proviso, neither that Government nor the Colonial Office was willing to accept the reduced amount as being adequate to complete the programme envisaged.[99] The Colonial Office pointed out that revenue was more difficult to estimate than expenditure and, in any case, forecasting six years ahead was hazardous. As a result, the Treasury agreed to raise the sum to £500,000 in the form of a once-for-all grant.[100] This was acceptable to the Colonial Office, providing it was acceptable to the Tanganyika Government. The essential purpose of the once-for-all grant, after the Tanganyika Government had agreed to accept responsibility, was to avoid amending legislation in the United Kingdom, which was thought likely to be somewhat embarrassing to the Government 'because of the scheme's connection with the ill-fated groundnuts project' and, at the same time, to avoid payments by means of annual CD & W schemes. The latter was to be avoided, first, because it might involve providing the whole of the unspent balance, estimated at £850,000, instead of the £500,000 which was in mind as a limit; secondly, there would be no real control over expenditure and, thirdly, it would be more difficult to resist a request for further assistance.[101] Limitation of the amount to £500,000 by amending legislation might, it was thought, lead to accusations of parsimony. Yet the Treasury Officer of Accounts was not happy with the once-for-all idea because of probable objections by the Public Accounts Committee,[102] and it was decided to revert to annual grants.[103] The Colonial Office was informed accordingly and, in turn, informed the Governor of Tanganyika, who accepted the financial proposals.[104] When the proposal was put to the Economic Policy Committee by the Minister of State for Colonial Affairs, the Earl of Perth,[105] the Committee readily accepted, in principle, the proposed extension of the period of assistance to the TAC, but suggested that further consideration should be given to the possibility of effecting the change by means other than legislation.[106] However, Treasury and Colonial Office officials came reluctantly to conclude that further legislation was unavoidable because (i) for policy reasons, HMG had given an undertaking that, subject to Parliamentary approval, aid to the TAC would be continued until 1962 and, in due course, this undertaking would have to be announced publicly both in London and Dar-es-Salaam; (ii) such an announcement would include a period for which no CD & W funds were yet voted, i.e. 1960–62; and (iii) the Public Accounts Committee could criticise the continuance of annual grants for 1957–60 under the Appropriation Act, as previously the funds were provided by specific legislation.[107] Therefore, it became necessary to draft the TAC Bill, which passed through Parliament after being approved by the Legislation Committee on 28 May 1957.[108] It received the Royal Assent on 31 July 1957. It provided for the payments of grants, not exceeding in aggregate £500,000, for carrying on the transferred undertaking between 2 October 1957 and 30 September 1962.[109]

VII. MOVING TOWARDS A SELF-SUPPORTING AGRICULTURE

In a memorandum which accompanied the TAC's budget estimates for the financial year 1 October 1957 to 30 September 1958 it was stated that the first phase for the long-term experiments with which the TAC was charged would be generally completed by 30 September 1957.[110] The major objective remained one of establishing a system, or systems, of agriculture which enabled the cleared land to be fully utilised for self-supporting agricultural production. At Kongwa, large-scale arable production had been discontinued. With the exception of an African Tenant Scheme and an Experimental Station engaged in research in pasture improvement, the whole of the cleared land was utilised for beef stock-raising. At Urambo, satisfactory results over the preceding two years suggested that the area could be operated successfully by a system of tenant farming depending largely on the production of flue-cured tobacco. It was proposed to complete the capital programme as originally planned, and the estimates to September 1958 provided for that to be done. Adequate allowance was included for the extension of the African Tenant Scheme and the construction of medium-size farms for African tenants able to farm on their own account with a minimum of supervision and assistance. At Nachingwea, farms had remained largely unchanged, while a study of the economics of mechanised, or partially mechanised, agriculture was being conducted. The field-work was expected to be completed by 30 September 1957, and future developments depended on the outcome.

The Colonial Office was pleased with the progress and invited the Treasury to approve the estimates,[111] which it did without question.[112] In the memorandum accompanying the estimates for 1958–59, there was nothing to add to the previous report on Kongwa and Urambo, but at Nachingwea, it was stated, the reorganisation measures, which were planned on the completion of the economic studies in the area, had made considerable progress.[113] The Colonial Office, noting that the main object of the TAC was the establishment of self-supporting agricultural enterprises in the three areas, approved the estimates as they stood and sought the concurrence of the Treasury,[114] which quickly obliged.[115] However, by the time the 1959–60 estimates were submitted, doubts were arising over the Nachingwea area, and it was hoped to reach a decision on future activities after a further year's operations.[116] The Treasury commented that the Corporation had not tapered off its level of expenditure as originally envisaged; and, while the annual deficits were within the forecasts, it raised the question of what was to happen in the future.[117] The Treasury did not expect to subsidise after 1962 and so felt the TAC should be gradually wound up. [In reply to an enquiry concerning lack of insurance on a motor vehicle that had been damaged beyond repair, the Treasury stated that it did 'not allow grant-aided territories to insure except in special cases' – item 52 in EAF 382/205/01, Part B. The poor Colonies had to take risks which others could eliminate by paying a fixed charge – a curious aspect of 'Treasury control'!]

The Colonial Office replied that paragraph 6 of Cmd 9158 stated that, in addition to its task of administering the experimental scheme that it took over from the OFC, the Corporation was to be regarded as a permanent organisation through which the Tanganyika Government could pursue some of its own agricultural development plans.[118] Indeed, it had already been given a number of such responsibilities – for example, the management and administration of two CD & W projects, the running of a tobacco farm, and the development of a ranching scheme. The East Africa Royal Commission, the United Nations Visiting Mission of 1957 and the IBRD Survey Team had all recognised the useful role that the Corporation was playing, and neither the Colonial Office nor the Tanganyika Government accepted the view that the Corporation should be wound up by 1962, or some later date. Its future was to be considered with the Governor in the light of the expected report of the IBRD Survey Team. Meanwhile, the Treasury, still feeling it was for consideration whether the Corporation's activities under the TAC Act, 1957, should be wound up, approved necessary financial provision only for the period to 31 March 1960.[119] As the Corporation's financial year was geared to the crop year, planning had to proceed as from October for the whole year and could not be cut half-way, while the Governor had been assured already, with Treasury agreement, that as from 1 October expenditure could continue on the basis of the 1958–59 estimates. In these circumstances, the Treasury relented and approved the estimates for the whole year, on the understanding that economies could be called for if the review so indicated.[120]

The Governor raised the matter of the future of the Corporation in November 1959, in relation to the disposal of its assets, including the accumulated funds, indicating that, if the assets and funds were not vested in the Corporation on 30 September 1962, it would be necessary to liquidate the Corporation after the following cropping season.[121] The Secretary of State agreed, asking for forecasts of probable expenditure and receipts for the years 1960–61 and 1961–62 and a statement of the Corporation's role after 1962.[122] Preliminary details were provided by cable,[123] but matters were left until the new Chairman of the TAC, Mr R. E. T. Hobbs (previously Agricultural Adviser to the Uganda Development Corporation), was available for discussion. The latter confirmed that there had been a change of policy in respect of Nachingwea, because it was not found possible to hand it over by stages to tenant farmers, and so the Corporation had had to continue to farm the area itself, thus maintaining gross expenditure and, as an offset, gross revenue.[124] The Chairman felt that the decision whether to continue operations or not should be deferred until September 1960, when it would be possible to assess the value of the new strain of soya bean seed. If it was then decided to close down, it would not be sensible to do so before September 1961, on the basis of an organised run-down. The Colonial Office accepted this view. The Treasury wanted to know in September 1960 whether, whatever happened at Nachingwea, 'the transferred undertaking will be viable by September 30, 1962'.[125]

However, the Government of Tanganyika took up the matter. On 5 January 1961 the Council of Ministers considered a Memorandum by the Minister for Agriculture and Co-operative Development, Mr Bryceson, on the future of the Corporation.[126] The need for an early decision was noted in view of the approaching end of the period for which HMG was providing finance and of the recommendation of the IBRD Mission that the TAC should be established on a permanent basis. It was recognised that of the three projects only a part of one, namely the ranch at Kongwa, could be regarded as a self-supporting commercial proposition. The remainder were settlement schemes, which were likely to require subsidisation until they became fully viable self-contained co-operatives. Of the various schemes, only the production farm at Nachingwea had realised a substantial profit, which it did for the first time in the 1959–60 season. It was recommended that the TAC be reorganised so that it could undertake (*a*) on an entirely self-contained and self-supporting basis, commercial schemes which were profitable, and (*b*) on an agency basis, Government schemes desirable from a long-run, indirect or experimental point of view. Ministers were asked to agree, in principle, that the TAC be established on a permanent basis and that negotiations to that end should be put in hand accordingly. The Council of Ministers agreed, subject to the necessity to inform the Secretary of State.[127] The proposals were acceptable to the Colonial Office, which recognised it would be necessary to amend the ORD Act, 1954, as far as the TAC was concerned, and to settle the terms for the transfer of assets and of funds, although it seemed to the Colonial Office that there was 'very little in this transfer which will call for negotiation'.[128] The Tanganyika Government sought, at the pre-Independence discussions at the end of June 1961, (i) the balance of the £500,000 remaining at 30 September 1962; (ii) relief from the liability to former members of the staff of the OFC, then numbering 29, amounting to £29,000; (iii) a grant of £200,000 towards the establishment of adequate reserves; and (iv) the vesting of the remaining assets of the transferred undertaking in the Tanganyika Government.[129] Naturally, the Treasury was not amused and felt the Paper augured badly for the talks.[130] The United Kingdom delegation 'took note' of the proposal at the meeting of the Finance Working Party held on 29 June 1961. The final arrangements agreed at the June discussions were confirmed in a Despatch in November 1961.[131] The Secretary of State, Mr R. Maudling, welcomed the proposal that the TAC be established on a permanent basis as an instrument for agricultural development in Tanganyika and agreed to (i), amounting to £109,000, and (iv) above, and also to phase the repayment of £50,000 outstanding over the ten years to 30 September 1971.

Tanganyika became an independent country within the Commonwealth on 9 December 1961. The TAC had already been taken over by the Government of Tanganyika. The takeover was announced on 9 May 1961 by the Minister of Agriculture, Mr Paul Bomani, at a public meeting at Kongwa.[132] In the course of his speech, he stated that, because of low and erratic rainfall in Kongwa, the TAC had decided tenant farmers should gradually change from arable to livestock farming. The settlement scheme was to be expanded and water supplies were to be improved still further. At Kongwa, ranching was complementary to the tenant scheme: 'From the ranch, cows are hired to the farmers. The ranch provides improved bulls for servicing the cows. It is also a ready market for the tenant farmers for their surplus steers. Without profit from the ranch, there would be no money to pay for the expensive water supplies and dips to enable cattle to be kept in the area.' He stressed the need for and the benefits deriving from the TAC, remarking that, by adopting the tenets of good husbandry, cattle which after two to four years reached 300 lbs would double their weight on a tenant farm. Quality would be improved and 'the better the quality, the better the price'.

The Chairman, Mr R. E. T. Hobbs, voluntarily resigned the chairmanship on the independence of Tanganyika and Chief H. M. Lugusha, CBE, who had been a member of the Legislative Council and an Assistant Minister before independence, became Chairman, with Mr Hobbs as managing director with a seat on the Board. With his previous experience in Uganda, Mr Hobbs felt that Tanganyika should move in the direction of a Development Corporation, with the TAC as its agricultural arm, and other sections concerned with industry and mining, and thus be in a better position to spread risk and raise capital. The TAC and TDC were amalgamated in December 1964 to form a National Development Corporation.[133]

The situation at the time of independence was that the TAC was a statutory Corporation established under the Laws of Tanganyika. It undertook agricultural development projects for the Government as its managing agents. The projects were (a) self-supporting enterprises, run on a commercial basis, and (b) those of a development nature with planned settlement of local farmers, on a tenancy and co-operative basis. The commercial schemes operated by the Corporation were:

(1) Kongwa ranch: a cattle-ranching project, started in 1950, which covered 100,000 acres of cleared land at Kongwa. The stock, amounting to about 12,000 head of cattle, was the product of selective breeding from indigenous Zebu to Boran stock. There were 3000 head of breeding cows. Apart from providing a source of improved foundation stock for further ranch projects and for sale to progressive farmers, chilled meat was supplied from the ranch abattoir and chilling plant to butchers and for canning.

(2) Mkata ranch: formerly a Government project, it was handed over to the TAC as managing agents. It extended over 210,000 acres and held some 8000 head of cattle with a breeding herd of around 2000 cows.

(3) Ruvu ranch: established in 1956 by the TAC on behalf of the Government. The object was to purchase male cattle from the

overstocked areas and sell them as good-quality beef cattle. Some 3000 steers were sold each year.

(4) Nachingwea production farms: 11,000 acres were cropped annually under a system of large-scale mechanical farming. The main crops produced were soya beans, groundnuts, and maize, together with 2000 acres of permanent cashew.

(5) Lupatingatinga tobacco farm: this was taken over in September 1957 by the TAC as managing agents for the Government. The farm was run on commercial lines to prove the suitability of the area for the production of flue-cured tobacco with a view to the introduction of a settlement scheme. Potential tenants spent a year at a training school, where they were paid for the tobacco they grew, and then went to a small farm with the possibility of moving to a medium-sized or even a large farm. Several African farmers on TAC farms enjoyed incomes of well over £1000. For the year 1961, the average profit per tenant farmer was approximately £100 in cash, in addition to the food crops obtained. In a country where the *per capita* income was around £20 per annum, including cash and subsistence crops, this was, as the press release stated, 'definitely an encouraging beginning'.[134] The objective became one of concentrating activities in order to produce annual incomes of £100–£200 p.a. per tenant.

With the object of assisting farmers to progress from subsistence-level cultivation to become efficient, self-reliant yeoman farmers, the TAC operated the following scheme:

(1) Urambo tenant farms: large and medium-sized farms designed for the annual production of 60 and 20 acres, respectively, of flue-cured tobacco, together with ancillary farming enterprises such as cattle and maize. The Corporation provided the full range of buildings required and the farms were leased to tenants having the necessary skill and working capital. It was largely due to the methods evolved by these farmers that the potential of the area was realised.

(2) Urambo farming settlement scheme: farms ranged from 20 to 40 acres each of cleared land and were designed for a maximum production of four acres of flue-cured tobacco per year. Each homestead, built by the tenant, included tobacco barns, store and well. The aim was to enable the small farmer to grow and to carry through all the processing of the tobacco crop with his own resources.

(3) Kongwa farming settlement scheme: started in 1954 with 19 tenants, it had by 1961 a total of 145 farmers with 12 acres of land apiece and an average of 12 head of cattle. The aim was to teach farming under dry-land conditions and proper cattle management. All foundation stock hired to the farmers came from the Kongwa ranch. The objective was to allow each of the farmers to build up a herd of 20 head of cattle and to sell all surplus stock in order to earn additional cash on top of their arable acreage.

(4) Nachingwea settlement scheme: although the first such scheme, it never enjoyed the popularity of subsequent schemes. During the 1960–61 season there were only 23 tenants farming a total of 341 acres. Experience was expected and farmers were being resettled there from other areas.

(5) Lupatingatinga settlement: started in 1960 with four tenants and extended in the 1961–62 season to take 30 new tenants.

(6) Mbarali irrigation scheme: A CD & W scheme, which was started in 1957 with the TAC as managing agents for the Government. Approximately 5000 acres of fertile alluvial soil in the lower Rufiji plain were available for irrigation. The planned programme was to settle 100 farmers by the 1963–64 season on five-acre plots with a rotation including groundnuts, maize and beans.

SOURCES

1. File 42553/1A East Africa, Tanganyika, 1951, item 3, letter of 18 Apr 1951 from Sir Leslie Plummer to the Rt Hon. John Strachey, MP, telling of the contents of a letter received from Mr George Raby, General Manager of the OFC.

2. Ibid., item 6, copy of the letter sent by Mr Strachey to the Minister of State, Mr J. Dugdale, on 4 May 1951.

3. Ibid., item 8, letter of 15 May 1951 from the Minister of State for Colonial Affairs, Mr J. Dugdale, to the Rt Hon. John Strachey, MP.

4. File 42553/50 East Africa, Tanganyika, 1951, item 1, report dated 24 Apr 1951 on a visit by Mr G. F. Clay, Agricultural Adviser to the Secretary of State, to the three areas of the Groundnut Scheme in Tanganyika between 19 Feb and 2 Mar 1951.

5. File 42553/40 East Africa, Tanganyika, 1951, item 2, letter of 14 Feb 1951 from the Chairman to the Permanent Secretary, Ministry of Food.

6. Ibid., item 22, meeting at the Colonial Office on 4 May 1951.

7. Ibid., item 11, programme for 1951–52 submitted on 31 Mar 1951 by the Chief Scientific Officer to the Chief General Manager.

8. File 42553/38/8, East Africa, Tanganyika, 1951, item 5, letter of 8 June 1951.

9. File EAF 53/56/01, 1 August 1951 – 9 March 1954, item 9, letter of 12 November 1951. Much of the report was outlined in the *Tanganyika Standard*, 8 Dec 1951.

10. File 42553/51 East Africa, Tanganyika, 1951, minute of 25 June 1951 by the Secretary of State.

11. File EAF 53/02, Part A (10 Oct 1951 – 5 Feb 1953), item 10, a Review dated 4 Jan 1952 of the Overseas Food Corporation's Activities in relation to Cmd 8125.

12. Ibid., item 12, Note on talks at the Colonial Office on 22 Jan 1951.

13. Ibid., item 13, Note of 25 Jan 1951 by the Agricultural Adviser. See also his letter of 6 Feb – item 21 in ibid. Mr S. J. Southgate minuted on 25 Jan 1951 that 'What we want to know is what the costs are likely to be and how can the losses be kept down.' Unfortunately, the OFC lost its Costings Officer at this time.

14. Ibid., item 17, Note of a Meeting with Ministers at the Colonial Office on 29 Jan 1951.

15. Ibid., item 22, Confidential letter of 24 Feb 1952 from the Secretary of State, Mr Lyttelton, to the Governor, Tanganyika Territory, Sir Edward Twining.

16. Ibid., item 28, Confidential letter GH.1023/II/68 of 29 Apr 1952 from the Governor, Tanganyika Territory, to the Secretary of State.

17. Ibid., item 30, Secret letter of 16 May 1952 from the Chairman.

18. Ibid., item 35E.

19. Ibid., item 40, 'Future of the OFC: Conclusions of a meeting held in the Secretary of State's room in the House of Commons on 5 July 1952'. Besides the Secretary of State, the Governor and the Chairman, there were Mr H. Fraser, MP, and six officials of the Colonial Office.

20. Ibid., item 38, 'Proposed Revision of the Long-Term Plan' – Note of a meeting held at the Colonial Office on 18 July 1952.

21. Ibid., item 37A, one official minuted on 10 July 1952 that they were not 'in a position to question his proposals unless HMG is prepared to put up more money which I don't think they are. It does not seem to me, therefore, that there will be very much to talk about on Monday morning.'

22. Ibid., item 42, letter of 22 July 1952 from the Chairman.

23. Ibid., item 47A, Statement issued by the Board of the OFC on 15 Aug 1952.

24. Ibid., minute of 14 Oct 1952.

25. Ibid., item 70, letter of 20 Oct 1952 to the Chairman.

26. Ibid., item 75, letter of 7 Nov 1952 from the Chairman.

27. Ibid., items 89, 94 and 95.

28. Ibid., items 81 and 90, letter of 27 Jan 1953 to the Chairman, enclosing a copy of the Secretary of State's statement in the House of Commons.

29. Ibid., item 51, Confidential telegram No. 504 of 14 Aug 1952 from the Governor to the Secretary of State; Confidential telegram No. 426 of 23 Aug 1952 from the Secretary of State to the Governor – item 58 in ibid.; Confidential telegram No. 558 of 6 Sep 1952 from the Governor to the Secretary of State – item 61 in ibid.; Confidential telegram No. 459 of 10 Sep 1952 from the Secretary of State to the Governor – item 62 in ibid.

30. File EAF 53/02 Part B (30 Jan – 9 Dec 1953), item 102, Confidential Despatch No. 126 of 14 Feb 1953 from the Governor, Tanganyika Territory, to the Secretary of State.

31. Ibid., item 133, Memorandum for the guidance of the Tanganyika Government on the probable attitude of HMG.

32. Ibid., item 115, Confidential letter of 5 May 1953.

33. Ibid., minute of 13 Apr 1953.

34. Ibid., item 118, Memorandum of 5 June 1953 on the Tanganyika Working Party's Report on the Future of the OFC.

35. Ibid., item 119, Confidential letter of 9 June 1953 from the Acting Governor, Tanganyika Territory.

36. Ibid., item 127.

37. File EAF 53/36/03, item 6, letter of 28 Apr 1953 from the Chairman.

38. File EAF 53/02, Part B, minute of 17 June 1953.

39. Ibid., item 123, letter of 1 July 1953 from the Chairman.

40. Idem.

41. Ibid., item 127, Note of a meeting with the Royal Commission at the Colonial Office on 8 July 1953.

42. Ibid., item 125, memorandum of 6 July 1953 on 'The Future of the OFC'. The maximum requirement was put at about £300,000. The idea was not mentioned to the Treasury – see minute of 7 July 1953, in ibid.

43. Ibid., item 127.

44. Ibid., item 30, minutes of a meeting held at the Treasury on 16 July to discuss the Treasury Memorandum of 5 June 1953 on the Tanganyika Working Party's Report on the future of the OFC.

45. Ibid., item 134, letter of 19 Aug 1953 from the Chairman.

46. Ibid., item 135, Confidential letter of 22 Aug 1953 to the Chairman of OFC.

47. Ibid., item 136, Confidential letter No. 50196/143 of 24 Aug 1953 from the Acting Governor, Tanganyika Territory.

48. Ibid., item 137, letter of 8 Sep 1953.

49. Ibid., item 139, letter of 15 Sep 1953 to the Chairman of OFC.

50. Ibid., minute of 17 Sep 1953.

51. File EAF 52/03, 1954–1956, item 1, letter of 2 Sep 1953 from the Chairman.

52. File EAF 55/02, Part B, item 141, Confidential and Personal Telegram of 25 Sep 1953 from the Secretary of State to the Chairman. Answered by telegram of 28 Sep 1953 from Chairman, item 142.

53. Ibid., minute of 18 Sep 1953.

54. Ibid., minute of 25 Sep 1953.

55. Ibid., item 150, letter of 27 Oct 1953.

56. Ibid., item 156, letter of 9 Dec 1953. The Secretary of State agreed in principle on 30 Dec 1953 – minute in file EAF 52/01, Part A, 1954–56.

57. Treasury file IF 488/02, Part B (beginning 11 Oct 1953), minute of 8 Jan 1954 by the Financial Secretary.

58. File EAF 52/01, Part A, 1954–56, item 4, Confidential Despatch No. 36 of 15 Jan 1954 from the Minister of State to the Governor, Tanganyika Territory.

59. Ibid., item 11, Confidential telegram No. 73 of 11 Feb 1954 from Governor's Deputy to the Secretary of State.

60. Ibid., item 22A, Confidential letter No. 50196/II/166 of 26 Feb 1954 from Chief Secretary.

61. Ibid., item 23, H.A. (54) 26, 5 Mar 1954.

62. File EAF 52/01, Part B 1954–56, item 103. LC 11(54) item 1.

63. *The Future of the Overseas Food Corporation*, Cmd 9158, 19 May 1954.

64. Ibid., item 130, extract of *Hansard*.

65. Ibid., item 113. The Tanganyika Ordinance was published in July 1954 as Cmd 9198, *The Future of the Overseas Food Corporation (Tanganyika Ordinance)*.

66. Ibid., items 135 and 136, Telegrams Nos 518 and 522 of 19 and 20 Oct 1954 from the Governor's Deputy, Tanganyika Territory, to the Secretary of State.

67. 2 and 3 Eliz. 2, Ch. 71.

68. Treasury file IF 36/24/04, Part A, item 64, Confidential telegram No. 185 of 14 Mar 1955 from Governor's Deputy, Tanganyika, to the Secretary of State.

69. File EAF 52/03 (1954–1956), item 1, Memorandum Ch/14 of 1 Sep 1953, which gave the Chairman's personal views; they had not been discussed with the Board of the OFC or the Government of Tanganyika.

70. Ibid., item 6.

71. Ibid., item 2, minute of 18 Sep 1953 by Sir Geoffrey Clay.

72. Ibid., item 5, Agreed Note of a meeting with the Royal Commission held at the Colonial Office on 8 July 1953.

73. Ibid., item 6, minute No. 967, Sixteenth Meeting of the Board Members of the OFC held at Dar-es-Salaam, 21 and 22 Oct 1953.

74. Ibid., item 7, Note of a meeting held at the Colonial Office on 20 Nov 1953.

75. Ibid., minute of 20 Nov 1953.

76. Ibid., item 17, Memorandum CH/24 of 25 May 1954 enclosed with letter of 28 May 1954 from Chairman.

77. Ibid., item 20, letter No. GH.1023/2 of 31 May 1954 from the Governor, Tanganyika Territory.

78. Ibid., item 21, minute of 3 June 1954.

79. Ibid., item 22, minute of 8 June 1954.

80. Ibid., item 33, Note of a meeting held at the Colonial Office on 14 June 1954.

81. Ibid., minute of 15 July 1954 by the Secretary of State.

82. File EAF 382/454/01 (1954–1956), item 2, letter and enclosure of 8 Jan 1955.

83. Ibid., items 12 and 9, Savingram No. 369 of 15 Mar 1955 from the Secretary of State to the OAG, Tanganyika, enclosing Memorandum of approved CD & W scheme D.2435 with an initial grant of £176,500 for the half-year 1 Apr to 30 Sep 1955, respectively.

84. File 382/205/01 (1954–1956), item 49, personal letter of 19 Oct 1956, from the Chairman.

85. Ibid., item 50, personal letter of 25 Oct 1956 to the Chairman.

86. File 382/7/02 (1957–1959), item 1, confidential letter T4/4 of 28 Dec 1956 from the Chairman. This was repeated by cable and letter before it was answered – items 3 and 4 in ibid.

87. Treasury file IF 36/24/04, Part B, pp. 78–81, immediate letter of 5 June 1956.

88. Cmd 9475, June 1955, paras 35–7.

89. Treasury file IF 36/24/01, Part B, minute of 6 June 1956.

90. Ibid., minute of 8 June 1956.

91. Ibid., minute of 11 June 1956 by Sir Alexander Johnston.

92. Ibid., minute of 11 June 1956 by the Financial Secretary to the Treasury.

93. Ibid., p. 105, letter of 22 June 1956.

94. Ibid., pp. 106–10, letter of 13 July 1956.

95. Ibid., p. 112, minute of 17 July 1956.

96. Ibid., p. 113, note of 18 July 1956.

97. Ibid., p. 114, minute of 19 July 1956.

98. Ibid., p. 115, letter of 20 July 1956.

99. Ibid., pp. 117–21, letter of 20 Dec 1956.

100. Ibid., pp. 127–8, letter of 14 Jan 1957.

101. Ibid., pp. 140–2, minute of 13 Mar 1957.

102. Ibid., pp. 135 and 138–9, minutes of 26 Feb and 4 Mar 1957.

103. Ibid., p. 148, minutes of 1 and 2 Apr.

104. Ibid., p. 155, Confidential telegram No. 210, from the Governor of Tanganyika to the Secretary of State.

105. EA(57) 41.

106. EA 9(57) item 1, 1 May 1957.

107. Treasury file IF 36/24/01, Part B, p. 164, Note of a meeting held on 7 May 1957.

108. LC 11(57) item 1, 28 May 1957.

109. Tanganyika Agricultural Corporation Act, 1957 (5 and 6 Eliz. 2, Ch. 54).

110. File EAF 382/205/01, Part A (1957–1959), item 4, enclosed with savingram no. AN/1/41/025/15 of 1 Aug 1957 from the Governor, Tanganyika, to the Secretary of State.

111. Ibid., item 12, letter of 4 Oct 1957.

112. Ibid., items 16 and 18, formal notification of 16 Oct 1957 of the issue of £25,000 to the Vote for Colonial Services; and letter of 18 Oct 1957.

113. Ibid., item 28, enclosed with savingram no. AN/1/41/027/22 of 31 July 1958 from the Governor's Deputy, Tanganyika, to the Secretary of State.

114. Ibid., item 32, letter of 2 Oct 1958.

115. Ibid., item 36, letter of 23 Oct 1958.

116. File EAF 382/205/01, Part B, item 51, letter of 10 Sep 1959.

117. Ibid., item 52, letter of 14 Sep 1959. The original forecast was given in paragraph 7 of the letter of 20 Dec 1956, item 41 in EAF 382/7/02.

118. Ibid., item 54, letter of 27 Oct 1959.

119. Ibid., item 55, letter of 3 Nov 1959.

120. Ibid., item 59, letter of 20 Nov 1959, in reply to letter of 11 Nov 1959, ibid., item 58.

121. File EAF 382/7/02 (1957–1959), item 67, Savingram no. ANC 1/41/021/141(1002) of 10 Nov 1959 from the Governor, Tanganyika, to the Secretary of State.

122. Ibid., item 68, priority telegram no. 626 of 24 Nov 1959 from the Secretary of State to the Governor.

123. Ibid., item 69, priority savingram no. ANC 1/41/021/155 (1097) of 9 Dec 1959 from the Governor, Tanganyika, to the Secretary of State.

124. Treasury file IF 36/24/04, pp. 100–2, letter of 12 Jan 1960.

125. Ibid., p. 112, letter of 2 Feb 1960.

126. File EAF 382/7/02 (1960–1962), item 12, Memorandum ANC 1/41/021 of 3 Jan 1961.

127. Ibid., item 13, minutes of the Meeting of the Council of Ministers on 5 Jan 1961, item 14.

128. Ibid., item 20, letter of 12 June 1961.

129. Ibid., item 21, Tanganyika Government Paper, F 13.

130. Ibid., item 22, letter of 22 June 1961.

131. Ibid., item 37, Despatch No. 1668 of 24 Nov 1961 from the Secretary of State to the Governor of Tanganyika.

132. Ibid., item 24, Press Release of 8 May 1961 issued by Tanganyika Information Services (ref. CH/56/61: AG/5/2).

133. CRO file 2 EAE/18/22/3, item 1, letter of 3 Dec 1964 from the British High Commission, Dar-es-Salaam.

134. CRO file ECA 35/22/1, item 41, Press Release of 4 June 1962 issued by the Tanganyika Information Services.

5 The Colonial Development Corporation: Policy and Functions, 1952–1961

1. MANAGEMENT AND FINANCIAL STRUCTURE, 1952–1955

From the spring of 1952, division grew between the Colonial Office and the Chairman of the CDC, Lord Reith, who had already developed into something of a juggernaut with two basic ideas to press. (According to the *Concise Oxford Dictionary* a juggernaut is a 'notion to which persons blindly sacrifice themselves *or others*' [italics added].) The first idea – for the second, see p. 98 below – was that all the shortcomings of the CDC stemmed from three years of mismanagement by the first Chairman. This was stated in the Annual Report for 1950, which the new Chairman called 'a most unconventional and frank document'.[1] These critical comments were made by a Board which, though reconstituted early in 1951, still included the Deputy Chairman and the five members, Mr R. E. Brook, Sir Charles Darwin, Mr H. M. Gibson, Mr H. N. Hume and Lord Milverton, who had signed the 1950 Report and the previous reports. These were the six Directors, along with Mr A. J. Mitchell, who became a Director in November 1949, whose allegations against Lord Trefgarne were the subject of an independent enquiry by Mr Gerald R. Upjohn, KC, who in due course found the allegations largely failed.[2] Meanwhile, Ministers had naturally not committed themselves to the view that the new Chairman adopted and, as one official minuted on an answer the Chairman proposed should be sent concerning certain new complaints, 'it is not a full answer to complaints about things which have happened since Lord Reith took over'.[3] In fact, neither does mismanagement loom large among the reasons for abandoning schemes up to the summer of 1953 nor were all the abandoned schemes inherited from the period of office of the first Chairman. The list was as follows:[4]

TABLE 5.1   Schemes abandoned by the CDC, 1951–1953

Projects	Date started	Date abandoned	Reason for abandonment
Andros Agricultural Development	1950	March 1953	Failure of crops and difficulties with Mexican produce in US market
Atlantic Fisheries	1949	September 1951	Fishing and factory: vessel too expensive to run, and collapse of market price of shark-liver oil
British Honduras Stock Farms	1950	March 1952	Commercially impracticable owing to heavy development expenditure
British Somaliland Camel and Sheep Abattoir	1951	March 1952	No demand for camel hides and local sheep not acceptable in UK meat market
Castle Bruse Estate, Dominica	1949	April 1952	Estate too remote
Fruit Packing Station, Dominica	1949	October 1953	Too large to be operated economically with quantity of fruit offered
East Africa Ramie	1951	September 1953	Poor crops
Gambia Poultry and River Farms	1940	May 1951	Disease of poultry and failure of crops
Gambia Rice Farm	1949	April 1952	Uneconomic – capital cost of development too high
Kitario Gold Mine	1950	July 1951	Prospecting results poor
Nigerian Fibre Industries	1950	September 1953	Local products could not compete with imported jute sacks and cotton yarn
Nyasaland Fisheries	1948	May 1951	Inefficient management and slump in price of Vitamin A oil
Seychelles Fisheries	1950	July 1952	Catches of fish were not large enough to make the project commercially attractive
South Atlantic Sealing	1948	September 1952	Not enough seals and poor price for oil
West African Fisheries	1951	May 1953	Numerous difficulties, including poor fishing and drop in demand for fish

Of the 15 projects listed, inefficient management is specified as a reason for abandonment in only one (Nyasaland Fisheries), where it is coupled with a fall in price. Lack of adequate preliminary investigation is a more usual reason and it is as true for projects started in 1951 as for those started under the first Chairman. As the official just quoted commented again nearly two years later, 'now that Lord Reith has been in the saddle for three years and the CDC while under his control has probably spent over £20 million including sums spent on schemes "inherited" from Lord Trefgarne, it will be increasingly difficult to claim that capital write-offs are merely intended to dispose of the inheritance.'[5] Thus, the first of the Chairman's basic ideas was not accepted at the time outside the confines of the CDC nor, on later examination, can it be accepted as explaining much of the difficulties which befell the CDC.

Lack of adequate preliminary investigations and the need for pilot schemes were respectively stressed as a reason for and a lesson of the experiences. If the preliminary investigations included market surveys and cost analyses, which do not appear to have been undertaken, at least not satisfactorily, for many of the abandoned projects, the lack was a serious cause of loss. But, as regards pilot projects, the practical answer is less straightforward. It was seen that the CDC was instituted at a time when there was felt to be a great need for the early expansion of Colonial supplies and, while the Corporation was primarily intended to develop Colonial resources, it was also expected to be of advantage to the United Kingdom in providing non-dollar imports. At the time, a series of small pilot projects, which in agriculture and animal husbandry require a few years to show results, would not have been well received. Nor would such projects have necessarily focused attention on the main economic limitations of the time on the successful handling of large-scale projects, namely the scarcity of good management and skilled, including professional, services. Sufficient size of project was both a necessity for the CDC's operations, as otherwise overheads would have been even higher than they were, and a drawback in view of the shortages of the necessary labour. A pilot project which tested on a small scale the suitability of soils and climate for a crop would not be an infallible guide when it came to the economic application of the results.

Rather than harp on 'mismanagement', it would have been better to have examined the intrinsic strengths and weaknesses of the Corporation concept in the field of Colonial development. There was little thought given to this as a whole, as distinct from the usual method of *ad hoc* attention according to the problem in hand. However, the

Economic Adviser, Dr F. Benham, to the Commissioner-General for South East Asia, Mr M. Macdonald, did make such an attempt as part of the preparations for the visit of the Secretary of State to Malaya in 1951.[6] The memorandum was divided into three parts. In the first, it was noted with approval that the Corporation recognised, in principle, its particular role in these words:

> The Corporation's potential influence in the Colonies is apt to be exaggerated. In relation to population and to the new investment needed to achieve any considerable improvement in living standards, £100 million is a small sum; the effects of its deployment will not be very obvious. This was always realised; nobody thought that £100 million could do all that was required. Corporation investments should be so laid out as to attract other capital, and to stimulate capital accumulation within the Colonies. They cannot be lifted out of the speculative sphere; the Corporation was formed to undertake work which others were not prepared to do and so pave the way for further development.[7]

Yet it is doubtful whether the principle was always observed, for, later on, it was reported that: 'arrangements for part of the cost to be carried by CD & W, or other special funds, would make possible schemes in areas where anything like commercial development is at present impossible.'[8] The proposal was that the Corporation should embark on schemes which were expected to show losses, provided the losses were shared with D & W funds. Capital was already tied up in schemes which were not expected to make an adequate profit and which had been undertaken because the Corporation had been 'pressed' or 'urged' to do so by the Colonial Government. These included the Belize Hotel, the Dominica Grouped Undertaking, the Falkland Islands Freezer, the Jamaica Cooling Store, the Turks and Caicos Salt Industry, the Marudu Rice Farm, Nyasaland Fisheries Ltd, the Vipya Tung Estates, the Tanganyika Coalfields Investigation and Tanganyika Roadways Ltd.

Owing to losses on such undertakings, the Corporation sought abnormally high profits elsewhere in order to break even. According to the memorandum a scheme for assisting West Coast fishermen had to be abandoned when a return of 20 per cent net was found to be unlikely. Indeed, private interests took up various schemes which the Corporation found insufficiently attractive. Another criticism was that projects had to carry unduly large head office overheads.[9]

This led to the second part of the memorandum, because the high overheads were in large part due to the size of the head office staff which totalled 340 with a salaries bill of £250,000, according to the Annual Report for 1950. This, in turn, was a reflection of the functional rather than geographical organisation of the CDC: 'The result is that the people on the spot have no one person to whom they can look as a final authority. Any one of twenty or more persons at the head office could issue instructions and demands for information about any given scheme.' But as crops, marketing arrangements and labour problems varied from one place to another, it was suggested that a small head office consultancy staff would suffice to assess information from the field. Management should, it was submitted, either be handed over to an established firm which specialised in the appropriate activity, or, failing that, 'local people with knowledge and experience relevant to the project should be invited to take shares and become Directors of the company.' Once it was set up, the local representative of the CDC should become a Director of the company, which would only refer major issues of general policy to head office. 'In each region there should be one first-class man – one is enough – as the local representative of the Corporation.'[10]

This was the policy that the Secretary of State, Mr Oliver Lyttelton, adopted. He told the House of Commons in July 1952 that he had talked with the Chairman 'about our plans for achieving our common aim, which is to build up a system of separate companies under the regional controllers and above all to try to impart a more functional organisation to the Corporation'.[11] In an aide-memoire on a conversation with the Secretary of State,[12] the Chairman began:

> Secretary of State said that he could not help thinking every now and again of the almost impossible task that the Corporation had; the vast diffusion and diversity. He was very pleased that we were working so much towards private enterprise partnership, and, of course, to regional devolution, and he was certainly not going to suggest anything that would be inconsistent with that, or that would interfere with the redding-up [i.e. setting in order, tidying up] process. He wondered, however, whether it might not be possible, and desirable, to have some wholly-owned functional subsidiaries, with two or three Corporation directors and two or three functional experts – e.g. one concern for mining, one for tropical agriculture.

They might be capitalised at £500,000, with £100,000 paid up. They might be charged with investigations which, if projects resulted, could lead to varying partnership arrangements. The Chairman said that the Corporation was joining with private enterprise at the investigatory stage so that decisions of the Corporation on projects would be on the basis of expert, private advice. The Corporation was planning for separate companies for its various schemes with, if the office went to the Corporation, the regional controller as chairman.

The Chairman was pinning his faith on his regional controllers and giving the Corporation a regional form. The first Chairman inaugurated a system whereby head office consisted of the Board, Executive Council (Chairman, Deputy Chairman, two Joint Controllers and Director of Finance), nine Divisional Managers and six Departmental Heads. There were plans for five Regional Corporations overseas, each under the chairmanship of a member of the London Board. In time, CDC (Engineering) Limited was formed to carry out public works contracts. This was the position when Lord Reith became Chairman, except that the Regional Controllers had failed to materialise. There were, however, what were known as Colony Representatives in each of the larger territories though Project Managers were responsible directly to London. The new Chairman closed down CDC (Engineering) Limited, passing its functions over to a new Works Division within the main Corporation. The Colony Representatives were discontinued and five Regional Controllers were appointed with higher status and authority over the Project Managers. The devolution of responsibility to the Regional Controllers, who had their own staffs, made it possible to dispense with the Divisional Managers. In time, the Chairman was relieved of his full-time functions as Chief Executive, and the Deputy Chairman, Mr R. E. Brook, left and was replaced by a part-time Deputy Chairman with no executive functions. The post of General Manager was created to take over the executive functions of the Chairman and Deputy Chairman. In the Annual Report for 1953, the organisation consisted of a Chairman, Deputy Chairman and Board of six others, all of whom were part-time. There was a General Manager, four Head Office Controllers (Administration, Finance, Operation A and Operation B – Operation A included agriculture, animal products, fisheries, forestry; Operation B included factories, hotels, minerals), Head of Personnel and a Chief Accountant. There were five Regional Controllers, to whom projects went for preliminary consideration and who returned likely ones to London, where the Controllers decided whether they should go to the Board. There was an advisory committee of scientists to assist with the technical appraisal of schemes and difficulties that arose in their operations. The number of staff in the United Kingdom was 183 in 1953 compared with 248 in 1952, while the number of staff in the regional offices was 106 compared with 114 in 1952. Total administration costs were £392,249 compared with £457,642 in 1952. In line with the change of organisation, there was a change in the operational procedure. Whereas in Lord Trefgarne's time the Corporation was undertaking direct management of projects, new projects involving the Corporation in operational as well as financial responsibility were not adopted unless there was a partner with 'know-how' or a managing agent available to run them. The Annual Report for 1953 stated: 'Results of private enterprise participation and management are still uneven.' But that is to anticipate.

In the third part of Dr Benham's memorandum, two issues were commented upon. There was, first, the lending by the CDC of funds on debenture, as in the case of the £4 million loan to the Central Electricity Board of the Federation of Malaya. It was a way of raising money on the part of public utilities overseas which the Capital Issues Committee was unable to sanction on the London capital market, and so was a new source of public utility finance, which the CDC was never intended to provide. Secondly, the memorandum commented on the suggestion that the Corporation should enter into partnership with local Governments in joint undertakings. Yet, if the Corporation was to keep clear of investments which would not yield an adequate profit even when successful, which was the principle stated in the Annual Report for 1950 as quoted earlier, then it should avoid precisely the projects likely to be put forward by local Governments, who had no reason to participate in a venture which was attractive to private enterprise, i.e., a profitable one. Nor would the delays and lack of enterprise of local Governments be likely to provide the CDC with the partnership it was seeking.

Inevitably, an examination of the Chairman's first notion – early mismanagement – has touched upon the second notion, which was that the statutory basis and administrative procedures concerning the Corporation required drastic overhaul. It is true, as shown earlier, that, following the failure in The Gambia, the Treasury requested a change in the Concordat so that it might be allowed to assure itself of the likely commercial soundness of a project. But the Chairman, not without the sympathetic understanding of the Secretary of State at first, began[13] a campaign to change the conditions under which the CDC operated. This, had it been completely successful, would have changed the whole conception of the CDC as it had been promoted in 1948.

In the Annual Report for 1951 it was stated that

The Corporation is constituted to operate commercially, but its financial circumstances and conditions are at variance with commercial practice and purpose; the crucial distinction lies in the fact that the capital structure includes no ordinary shares, but only debentures; the crucial result is inelasticity; moreover any loss – the normal result in the first phase of development – means failure to fulfil the obligations to pay interest and principal.[14]

It was concluded that: 'The result must be to deflect Corporation from its primary purpose of opening up new fields of development until times – and roles – change, unless the case which Corporation has presented to Government on these fundamental financial difficulties leads to some measure of relief.'[15] HMG was unable to accept this thesis. The issue was fully treated in a Note on Financial Structure, a copy of which was sent to the Chairman.[16] This was used by the Parliamentary Under-Secretary, the Earl of Munster, in replying to the Debate in the House of Lords on 28 May 1952.[17] HMG took the view that the Corporation's claim that it was at a disadvantage compared with private enterprise was ill-founded. Firstly, there was no requirement on the Corporation to make each and every scheme pay, for it was required to pay interest on its operations *as a whole*. Secondly, no commercial concern could expect to attract £100 million unless it had the prospect of earning something much higher than a gilt-edged rate of return. Thirdly, the Corporation appeared to assume that the purpose of having a portion of equity capital was to be able to lose it with equanimity, but that was not the Government's understanding. Turning to the recent increase in the rate of interest, it was not thought that the CDC was worse affected than others and, if the possibility had not been allowed for in the past, it should be in the future rather than any expectation of being sheltered from it. In the Annual Report for 1951, it was said that the loan to the Malayan Central Electricity Board at 4 per cent would, with the increase in the rate charged to the CDC, yield only 0.2 per cent profit. As regards repayment, HMG felt that, provided it managed its affairs in a businesslike way, the CDC should, in time, be able to liquidate its capital obligations, especially as it was a permanent organisation and one which could spread its operations over so much capital. However, these matters were not the crux of the problem, which was rather the combined result of the inevitable difficulties of its task coupled with past mistakes and failings. A sound footing was wanted whatever was done about the capital structure. HMG was prepared to: (i) waive interest on abandoned schemes and (ii) provide advances for ten years at 3¾ per cent, in addition to the usual forty-year capital. But it could not agree to the Corporation's proposal that there should be an allocation of £20 million out of the £100 million capital for investigations and marginal cases and that, meanwhile, some part of the existing CDC resources should be allocated for this purpose with guaranteed replenishment. For HMG felt that the CDC should proceed, as any commercial concern would, by investigating only where there appeared to be a good prospect of an economically worthwhile return. Other investigations should be left to Governments, though borderline cases might be jointly financed by the CDC and the local Government on an *ad hoc* basis.

Following the Debate, the Chairman, by letter[18] and in discussion,[19] contested both the content and the tone of the Government's views. As an official minuted the day after the Debate, the Chairman had a mistaken view of the Corporation as a Fairy Godmother.[20] In case some Colonial Governments shared that view, it was decided to state HMG's views 'quite categorically, without inviting further debate', in a Circular Despatch, which would accompany a copy of the speech of the Parliamentary Under-Secretary in the Debate. The Despatch drew attention to the points already mentioned in connection with the Note on Financial Structure.[21] The Secretary of State restated the Government's policy on the main issues in the debate on Colonial Affairs on 17 July 1953.[22] He felt that 'the original conception of the CDC was not fully thought out, and that many of the canons which govern commercial enterprises were ignored'[23] and stated that, save in exceptional circumstances, sanction would not be given for a project to proceed unless one of four criteria were satisfied.

> They are: First, is the Colonial Government in whose territory the project lies willing to participate in it if it has the money to do so? Secondly, where there is local knowledge and where there are local experts, have they been mobilised, so to speak, and are they to be on the board of the operating company in that territory? Thirdly, where there is local capital, has it been offered a participation and has it accepted? Fourthly, has the Corporation tried to associate with itself any company in the United Kingdom or elsewhere carrying on the same kind of business?[24]

The Secretary of State prefaced these remarks with the statement that the Chairman and Board of the CDC had assured him that 'before I arrived on the scene, they were already proceeding on these lines and thinking in these directions'.[25] The Chairman reminded the next

Secretary of State, Mr Alan Lennox-Boyd, of this acknowledgement[26] after the latter had told the House of Commons on 3 December 1954 that the line had been laid down by his predecessor, and adhered to by himself, 'that there ought to be, as far as possible, an association by the Colonial Governments themselves or by private enterprise in the CDC projects'.[27]

When, on 22 July 1952, the House of Lords considered the *Report on the Colonial Territories for 1951–52* (Cmd 8553), Lord Ogmore referred to what he considered to be 'a complete difference of approach between the Government and the Opposition in the matter of the Colonial Development Corporation'. He saw the difference thus: 'The Government regard it merely as they would a private enterprise corporation which has not had the success it might have had. We regard it as an entirely new application in Colonial development, and we do not believe that the setbacks it has suffered should make us put it into cold storage, as the Government appear to feel'.[28] The Parliamentary Under-Secretary, Lord Munster, was content to refer to his own speech and that of the Secretary of State so recently given.[29] However, in his reply to the debate on the Annual Report for 1952, the Parliamentary Under-Secretary argued that the CDC had been thought of by the late Government 'as an alternative instrument to private enterprise in developing exactly that field of development which had previously been the exclusive preserve of private enterprise'. He asked whether the speakers from the Opposition benches supported the theory 'that good schemes should always be for the field of private enterprise and that bad schemes should always be for the field of the CDC', adding: 'That certainly is not what the Corporation was founded to do.'[30] As in its Report for 1950, the Corporation again in its Report for 1952 accepted the principle of profitability but sought permission to avoid it in certain cases. Thus, it stated: 'Application of a commercial criterion to the Corporation's general funds is salutary: efficient managements may lose heart if they see their hard-won profits swamped by losses on "welfare" projects'; but went on to suggest that 'it should be able to finance projects that are of great value but unlikely to be profitable; that such investments should be separately recorded in the accounts; and their results judged on other than a profit basis.'[31] While the Parliamentary Under-Secretary accepted the relevance of genuine pilot schemes intended to test whether a scheme would be an economic proposition, he held that 'a general experiment into the agricultural or industrial potential of any area without any particular scheme in mind is obviously not a pilot scheme. Such expenditure may be very necessary, but it does not seem to fall within the scope of the

Corporation.'[32] But the CDC persisted, pressing the idea that the Colonial Office and the CDC should act simultaneously to encourage the planning of peasant farming schemes in which CD & W finance might be used jointly,[33] and having to be disillusioned, gently but firmly, because it was primarily for Colonial Governments to consider whether they wanted to use them and, in any case, could do so only on the basis of individual schemes.[34]

Pressure for 'integrating' the CDC and the CD & W arrangements came not only from the CDC but also from Parliament, where much was said on this point in the debates on the CD & W Bill of 1955. When the Parliamentary draftsman found it rather easier when consolidating the ORD Acts to include the CD & W Acts rather than exclude them,[35] it was felt that this would be misunderstood as an intention to 'integrate' the two activities, and so add confusion. For, while both the CDC and the CD & W arrangements were intended to develop Colonial resources, the two organisations were basically different in character in that the CDC was required to balance revenue and expenditure 'taking one year with another' while no such obligation could arise over CD & W monies, which were grants and loans for specific purposes made direct by HMG to Colonial Governments or other Administering Authorities. Consequently, the Secretary of State had rather different functions and responsibilities in regard to each of them, and the methods of financing the two activities were entirely different: advances to the CDC were made from the Consolidated Fund whereas CD & W money was provided by annual votes of Parliament.[36] For reasons of policy, therefore, there was a firm preference that the ORD Acts should be consolidated on their own.[37]

II. AGRICULTURAL SCHEMES IN THE BECHUANALAND PROTECTORATE, 1950–1959

It is well to turn away for a while from these matters of general policy to examine the working relationship of the CDC with the Colonial Office and other Government Departments over a group of agricultural schemes in the Bechuanaland Protectorate. On 16 August 1950 the then Chairman applied for capital sanction in the sum of £910,000 for the creation of an Abattoir and Cold Store at Lobatsi, Bechuanaland. Some days earlier the Minister of State, Mr J. Dugdale, decided that, in view of the large amount of money, namely some 20 per cent of the total sanction of £26 million, already committed by the CDC in the High Commission Territories, a standstill in the approval of further schemes for that area should be imposed until the end of the year.[38] The Chairman said the Board had passed the scheme before the Minister's decision was known and so applied for sanction. He was supported by the Commonwealth Relations Office and the scheme was sanctioned in September 1950.[39] When Lord de la Warr wrote to the Secretary of State, Mr J. Griffiths, to question whether it was realised that the CDC was committing itself to a very large programme of agriculture in arid country with a most erratic and unrecorded rainfall and without soil analysis,[40] the CDC, which was asked to advise on a reply, insisted that the supposition that the Corporation was committing itself to a very large programme of agriculture in Bechuanaland without first securing analyses and indications of the cropping potential of the area was unfounded.[41] The Secretary of State wrote accordingly, suggesting that Lord de la Warr should, if he still had doubts after his further visit to Rhodesia, arrange to discuss with the Chairman who was responsible for the schemes.[42] The Secretary of State for Commonwealth Relations, Mr Patrick Gordon Walker, later Lord Gordon-Walker, felt it necessary, in September 1951 to repeat, in writing, the anxiety he had expressed in talk that the ranching project in the North of the Bechuanaland Protectorate should be a success, for

apart from all other considerations, it would be most damaging to us politically in the Union and Southern Rhodesia if, close to their borders, the Corporation met with a serious failure, due to attempts to develop too fast in a wild and little known area. Criticism would, I think, be particularly strong if this failure was in ranching. In the past, there have been several bad ranching failures in Southern Rhodesia. We should also come under fire if either the scheme was managed by someone without ranching experience in the Rhodesias or in Bechuanaland, or, alternatively, if the appointed Manager with such experience was overridden and then there was a failure.[43]

Clearly, there were doubts in the CRO about the way the project was shaping, but no inkling of them was given to the Colonial Office following requests from October 1951 to May 1952[44] and despite a rather difficult passage at Question Time in the House of Commons on 13 March 1952. Yet, in the Annual Report for 1951, it was reported that 'Development work in 1951 made a bad start, manager and several staff had to be replaced; much money and effort wasted; later abnormal rains impeded all work.'[45]

On 21 October 1952 the CDC asked for a further capital sanction of

£252,000 for the Lobatsi Abattoir and Molopo Holding Ranch as the £910,000 sanctioned on 21 September 1950 was nearly exhausted.[46] The reason given was the unexpected increases in prices and costs as well as the need for further working capital for the abattoir to bridge the gap between payments for cattle and receipts from sales. Discussions between the Colonial Office, the Treasury and the CRO raised a number of points – in particular, marketing prospects and the basis for calculating the working capital requirements – and the CDC was asked to discuss these matters.[47] The Corporation countered with a request for a note on the points requiring discussion, which was sent, and written answers were invited if the CDC preferred. In the reply, the accuracy of the information in the original application was given as a reason for not providing fuller explanation with the application for a supplementary allocation, despite the extent to which the original cost and price figures had turned out to be wrong. One official after 'again reading through the voluminous correspondence and the "not-so-clear" reports of progress by the CDC'[48] was highly sceptical, asking whether it really was 'the normal incidence of commercial operation', as stated by the CDC, 'to fail to appreciate that stock prices might rise following on bulk-buying, that in Africa rains fail and crops do not survive the drought, that supplies of equipment may be delayed nowadays, that housing is required for European staff and water required by stock. To me as an ex-Director of an African Veterinary Department these were the normal risks one had to take and try to anticipate.'[49] He went on to say that he realised the difficulties the CDC was up against 'in their endeavour to aid in the development of areas, or industries, which are so much of a gamble that neither Government nor private concern has felt it safe to enter into during the many years Africa has been crying out for development of a kind requiring heavy financial outlay'. Nevertheless, he wondered whether the CDC's experts were themselves 'aware of the risks they run when they so confidently challenge nature'.[50] It was, he said, a recurring question: 'Only yesterday, I dealt with the Falkland Islands file: here again we find bad planning and estimating, managers dismissed, the site of the factory unsuitable, the refrigeration plant of the wrong type and the type of mutton of a lower quality than originally expected.' On the information available, and more was desirable, he felt that whether the whole scheme paid its way or not 'depended entirely on the efficiency of management – which of course is not our business – for so much of the financial side is no more or less than a gamble'.[51]

The main purpose of the scheme and of the main Bechuanaland Ranch was to supply meat to the Central African areas. It was generally agreed that there was a great shortage of beef in the region, and the usefulness of the whole proposition was not in dispute once satisfactory agreements were made for the sale of the meat. It was doubted whether the project would do more than break even but, providing it did so, it was regarded as a valuable project from the point of view of African development.[52] Capital sanction was consequently agreed. Two months later, the Colonial Office heard for the first time that the Government of Northern Rhodesia regarded the abattoir as 'a very grave economic imposition', 'disadvantageous' and 'wasteful', mainly because Northern Rhodesia was obliged to make up the losses that would inevitably be incurred in South Africa owing to price control and transport costs.[53] At the same time, the South African livestock trade was offended by the appointment of a firm to handle hides and skins without inviting competitive bids,[54] though less weight was naturally attached to this trade criticism than to that of the Northern Rhodesian Government. However, the Colonial Office felt unable to take any action on either because commercial judgement – the prerogative of the CDC – was in question. The Quarterly Reports of March and September 1953 reported delays in opening, due to faulty construction, which did not inspire confidence that the reorganisation and new appointments over the previous three years had led to better performance 'in the field'.[55] It was a dismal story that unfolded, although the Chairman blamed his predecessor's appointee.[56] A supplementary capital sanction of £66,000 was requested because of the constructional deficiencies.[57] This application brought the total capital sanction for the project to £1,032,000. In a list of projects that the CDC submitted for capital write-off, the estimated final loss on the abattoir was estimated to be £60,000 because of over-capitalisation.[58] In addition, the Colonial Office and the CRO were perturbed when the CDC appealed for help, because it had somehow accepted under contract 'an unlimited obligation' to supply the Congo with meat. The CDC realised that such an obligation would cut across the division of trade established prior to the CDC's arrival in Bechuanaland and, for that reason, would be resented by South Africa.[59] The matter had considerable political importance, not only in relation to South Africa, but also because of the implicit understanding with the Protectorate Government over the operation of the abattoir.[60] It was thought that, in future, the terms of any contract between the CDC and outside bodies should be scrutinised in advance to see whether there were undesirable political, or financial, commitments ultimately pledging the good faith of HMG.[61] Meantime, the Colonial Office could not intervene directly, although it was felt that 'bungling of the Congo contract is the culmination of a pretty dark record of muddling in Bechuanaland'.[62]

Reference to the Annual Reports show that 1955 was the first full year of operation with a net profit (of £97,943), although 'teething troubles' were persisting with insulation, water supply and waste disposal.[63] The last of these continued into 1956 and, while sales increased, net profit fell to £60,798,[64] which turned into a loss of £187 on nearly the same volume of sales in 1957.[65] 1958 was 'another vexing year'; discussion proceeded with the Bechuanaland Government concerning the terms on which the abattoir business should be transferred to a local company.[66] In 1959 it was reported that participation by the Protectorate Government and the cattle industry had been agreed; the abattoir assets of £600,000 were transferred to the local company of which the CDC became managing agent. The CDC received 300,000 of £1 shares and £300,000 of 6 per cent first mortgage debentures, and arranged to sell half the equity to the Government and to trustees for the cattle industry.[67]

Despite considerable doubts at several points, the Colonial Office felt unable to intervene further in the scheme because of the CDC's right of commercial judgement once the initial case for the scheme was agreed. The Secretary of State's Adviser on Animal Health minuted in December, 1952: 'When one contemplates this doleful history, there would seem to be a good reason for wanting more information about the schemes which still survive but need more financial support.'[68] But, as in this case, by the time supplementary capital was required so much has been invested that there was virtually no choice but to provide the extra. In the scheme under discussion, there were two weaknesses. First, the technical expertise of the Colonial Office could not be brought to bear on the initial planning and the considerable doubts dispelled, because of the unwillingness of the CDC to provide really adequate initial information. Secondly, as the Adviser on Animal Health rightly stated, the efficiency of management was crucial and was at several points found wanting, both at the London and at the local ends.

III. THE WORKING RELATIONSHIP OF THE CDC WITH GOVERNMENT DEPARTMENTS, 1951–1955

In an attempt to achieve more flexibility in their relationship, the Minister of State, Mr Dugdale, and the Chairman decided early in

1951 to discontinue the regular monthly meetings and to replace them by meetings at quarterly intervals, at which any matter of major policy could be discussed.[69] It was agreed that the CDC would supply any information requested and that *ad hoc* meetings could be called at the official level as necessary. One immediate result was that the next quarterly report on schemes under active investigation was not given the general consideration in the Colonial Office it otherwise would have had.[70] There were only 31 items, compared with 50 in the previous report, and the next report listed just 30. So the rush on projects seemed to be tailing off, which was understandable, though one official raised the question whether basic development had, in fact, gone far enough in many Colonies to offer the kind of enterprise the CDC sought, which had to be profitable yet not compete with private enterprise.[71] Over the succeeding years it was to be often argued that the original conception of the Act was wrong, and that the 'gap' in the field of commercial investment which the CDC was supposed to fill did not exist. It was, therefore, urged by those holding this view that the Corporation should be given something to do which would enable it to earn a good return, to the taxpayer's ultimate advantage; if there were no useful function for the Corporation to perform in the field assigned to it, then the logical course was for it to be wound up. The funds which the Corporation would have devoted to lending, without other active involvement, could then be available to be administered otherwise, so that they did not have to carry the costs of the CDC's overheads and of the CDC's losses on speculative enterprises. However, the Corporation had some useful projects in the commercial field, both financial and direct investment, even if they were not as many, or as easy, as the optimists who created the CDC had expected. It is principally with the continuing adaptation of the Corporation in the light of the changing estimates of the gap that this study of the role of the CDC in Colonial development is concerned.

Meanwhile, it is well to consider the relations of the Corporation with Whitehall. For, despite the early hopes of an easier relationship, first with the coming of the new Chairman and then with a new Secretary of State, there was in fact a clear deterioration. As one official remarked, 'Incidentally, it is a measure of our difficulties that we have to open a file designed for the consideration of means of attaining a reasonable working relationship in correspondence with the Corporation.'[72] The Colonial Office asked the Treasury to help it improve relations with the Corporation by not insisting on the withdrawal of a marketability clause from a loan agreement, and the Treasury agreed, being 'very mindful of the desirability of avoiding unpleasantness with the Corporation on minor issues at the present time; there are some major matters on the CDC front and this is no time for impairing your relations with the Corporation where that can be avoided.'[73] On 27 September 1954 the first meeting of a Working Party to discuss the relations of Government Departments with the CDC met at the Colonial Office, under the chairmanship of Mr E. Melville, with two representatives each from the Colonial Office, the Treasury and the CDC.[74] The Working Party was called because both the Secretary of State and the Chairman of the CDC thought it was an appropriate time to review the general state of relations between the Government and the Corporation, with particular reference to what the Chairman called 'the conditions precedent to capital sanction', in order to identify and, if possible, suggest ways of smoothing out difficulties that had arisen. The Act was taken as it stood, though, if irreconcilable difficulties were encountered, consideration was to be given to its amendment. Specific projects were to be considered only to illustrate general problems. A written report was to be submitted to the Secretary of State at the end of the discussions. It was agreed to discuss (a) trading losses, (b) loan transactions, (c) amount of capital sanction – contingencies, and (d) official handling of applications for capital sanction. After nine meetings and several drafts, the report was circulated in its final form of 10 October 1955.[75] But it was already out of date, having been overtaken by events. It was a lost opportunity. More than a year later, the Secretary of State emphasised to the Chairman that he was still worried by the failure to establish good working relations between the Colonial Office and the Corporation.[76]

iv. 'FINANCE HOUSE' ACTIVITIES

The immediate cause of the shelving of the Report of 10 October 1955 arose in this way. A CDC loan for African housing in Nyasaland was agreed in principle by the Treasury on 6 May 1955. The loan would have enabled nearly 3000 African houses to be built, about half of them for African Government employees, and there was no doubt that this would have made a substantial contribution towards easing the acute housing problem which existed in the territory. The loan proposal in its final form was received from the CDC on 28 July and forwarded to the Treasury for final approval on 30 July. In their reply, the Treasury enquired whether the housing of Government employees under the Nyasaland scheme could be considered as falling within the functions of the CDC as laid down in Section 1(1) of the ORD Act, i.e.

whether housing for Government employees could be considered a project 'for developing resources of Colonial territories with a view to the expansion of production therein of foodstuffs and raw materials, or for other agricultural, industrial or trade development therein'. The Treasury expressed the view that to permit the CDC to lend money for African housing at all involved a considerable stretching of its functions as laid down in the Act, and to extend permission to include the financing of houses for Government employees was a further and difficult stretching. The Governor said it was not possible to substitute other types of houses than those to be built for Government employees. However, the Legal Adviser to the Secretary of State gave his opinion that the Nyasaland scheme as a whole, and not just the part concerning housing for Government employees, was outside the spirit, the letter and the intention of the Act.[77] It was not the first CDC venture in housing – the first was the sanction in 1949 to buy and expand the Federal and Colonial Building Society in order to overcome the shortage of housing of the professional and middle classes in Singapore. No questions of principle were raised in the consideration of the scheme. The then Secretary of State, Mr Creech Jones, in conveying sanction to the then Chairman wrote that 'this scheme should be a most beneficial one in relieving the present housing shortage of Malaya'.[78] The urgency of housing in relation to economic development was thus accepted by Ministers, and it had been assumed that, in so far as the CDC was promoting economic development, even indirectly, it could be said to be carrying out its duties under the Act. The CDC, equally, had no doubt that it was acting within its legal powers and disputed the legal opinion given to the Secretary of State. The Law Officers of the Crown agreed with the Secretary of State's Legal Adviser, and their Opinion of 25 November 1955 ruled out the housing schemes currently under consideration and negotiations were suspended.[79] Apart from validating legislation to legalise existing schemes, it was necessary to consider how the Corporation should be empowered to proceed in the future and the Chairman was asked for any views he might have on that.[80] Meanwhile, Colonies were told that the CDC had been requested to suspend negotiations on all outstanding proposals for housing schemes.[81]

Sharp protests were received from Colonial officials and the CDC's representatives at the suspension. The most heartfelt came from Nigeria. The Chief Secretary of the Federation was 'deeply disturbed' to hear of the suspension and explained

so many times in my service in Lagos have I had to recapitulate the sorry tale of the failure of successive Governments to grapple with the slum problem in Lagos, and a feeling almost of desperation comes over me when I have to do it yet again so shortly after having to do it in the Council of Ministers a week or so ago. Nearly thirty years ago, there was a plague in Lagos. A special statutory body was set up to ensure that physical conditions conducive to plague were not perpetuated. This statutory body was hampered by lack of funds. Then came the war years, bringing great economic growth to the country and a tremendous pressure on accommodation in Lagos. The slums got worse. The local authorities were unable and unwilling to give effect to the laws designed to prevent people from creating slum conditions. Thus, the country's Capital got into the disgraceful state which is the subject of such unfavourable comment by almost every visitor we have from overseas.

We have tried mightily to get the cumbrous legal machinery working. We had a Slum Clearance Scheme. The politicians said we should not give effect to it unless we provided alternative accommodation for the people to be dispossessed, regardless of the fact that the majority of them were in illegal occupation of the slum tenements in which they lived. We then set up a Mortgage Scheme to enable people dispossessed under a Slum Clearance Scheme to borrow money in order to build houses of suitable quality upon their developed land when it had been returned to them. Last week, the Minister responsible came to the Council almost in a panic because it had dawned on him, for the first time, that the essential element of the Slum Clearance Scheme, namely the acquisition of land, the development of it and the re-sale of it (with priority to original owners), was supposed to be self-supporting, and he professed to see in this a dark scheme for getting rid of the indigenous owners and handing the land over to aliens. It took some forceful argument to persuade the rest of the Council that, unless something like this Scheme was done, the Capital of the country could hardly rely on the continuing mercies of Providence to keep it from some frightful outbreak of pestilence and, even if we were spared that, the commercial capital of the country would soon cease to function because traffic could not flow through its choked arteries. Lagos cannot continue to exist as an effective capital of the country, as an efficient port and as a live commercial centre unless its housing problems are tackled vigorously and successfully.

I hope that neither I nor any other member of the Council of Ministers will have to go to the Council and tell them that the Statutory Corporation set up by the United Kingdom for 'Colonial

Development', upon which such high hopes were founded and which has so seriously disappointed all those hopes, is now deemed to be permanently unable, under the law, to do what it has been successfully doing in Singapore and the Federation of Malaya for the last seven years, namely, to operate a Building Society, and that in going to this Corporation and getting from it an expert to report to us on the local possibilities of a Building Society, we had gone to quite the wrong person and, in fact, gone to someone who had no legal power to do what he was doing. This is the sort of argument that no one could sell successfully to the Nigerian Council of Ministers. Unless we can get out of this legal difficulty in some way, then I think that nothing is more certain than that all the fears you expressed so many months ago will be realised in full measure, pressed down and brimming over, and we shall have to go to the next Constitutional Conference and say that the Federal Government has been unable to do anything to improve housing in Lagos.

We had hoped that with the help of the Colonial Development Corporation we would not only set up a Building Society which would enable Lagosians generally to build good quality houses in newly developed areas, but also we would be able to make use of the expert staff brought into the country for the Building Society's purposes to give us much needed help in settling re-building problems arising out of slum clearance. If the CDC project fails, therefore, we are suffering a double loss. The old story which availed the Lagos Executive Development Board for so many years, 'shortage of men and materials', is now to be replaced by a new story – 'We are sorry, the law does not allow us to do it'. We shall be very grateful if you will look into this for us and assure us that something is going to be done right soon to enable us to go ahead with a project which has been so long maturing here with the CDC.[82]

He was assured that the Colonial Office '*fully* share your concern', and that Lagos was not the only casualty. Meanwhile, he was advised to look elsewhere for money and management for his Building Society as it would take months to prepare and pass the necessary validating legislation, whose terms could not, at that time, be foreseen.[83]

When new legislation came to be discussed it was realised that a number of schemes other than housing, as, for example, hotels, certain electricity supply schemes, Castries Reconstruction Agency and the Bantu press, might also be invalid. So it was proposed to validate all CDC schemes. It was found difficult, however, to validate all past doings and to provide a greater measure of flexibility as well as to place a limit on the Corporation's powers to engage in social or administrative activities or in commercial activities whose connection with the economic development of Colonial territories was remote.[84] Even when this was accomplished, officials resigned themselves to the inevitability of continued conflict with the CDC, which it was felt would contrive to judge the merits of a project primarily from the point of view of the bearing it might have on its balance sheet – 'The bearing that it might have on genuine Colonial development is likely to take second place.'[85] The Secretary of State, Mr Lennox-Boyd, initialled his agreement with this view, and later wrote to the Chairman that 'even if the Bill does not do everything the Corporation would like, it does go a very long way indeed, and gives the Corporation a very wide field in which to exercise all its talents.'[86]

The ORD Act, 1956,[87] received the Royal Assent on 2 August 1956, and a copy was sent to Colonies under cover of a Confidential Circular, which emphasised that the Act (i) did not alter the general organisation or mode of operation of the CDC; (ii) did not imply a new emphasis in the Corporation's functions; (iii) prevented the Corporation from exercising powers in the field of social and administrative services where it had never been intended that it should function; and (iv) provided that the CDC might engage in transport or telecommunications even when these were not wholly located within Colonial territories, provided the Secretary of State approved in those cases where they functioned partly outside the Colonies.[88]

The Circular was not shown to the Corporation in draft because it was felt, rightly as it turned out, that the Corporation would not wish to be associated with what was said about 'finance house' activities.[89] It was stated that

> Her Majesty's Government have hitherto accepted the Corporation's view that a reasonable proportion of 'finance house' business is necessary if the Corporation is to 'break even' taking one year with another. But there has been considerable criticism in Parliament and elsewhere that an undue proportion of the Corporation's resources was being used for this type of activity, and I recently gave an assurance that the Corporation, in consultation with the Government, will do all it can to see that this does not become a top-heavy aspect of its activities. This matter will therefore be considered further with the Corporation.[90]

The criticism referred to included adverse comment by the Public

Accounts Committee on the high proportion of safe investments in secured loans (see *Third Report, Series 1953–54*). The percentage was then 16 as compared with 42 when the PAC considered the matter again in 1956–57.

After being reminded of 'the somewhat doubtful propriety, or wisdom, of the Corporation's representatives commenting to Colonial Governments on the contents of confidential messages which have been copied to the Corporation for their information'[91] the CDC official replied that no such action would be taken, although the Corporation reserved the right to make its own attitude clear to a Colonial Government 'if it is raised in connection with any particular scheme'.[92] The precise meaning of the warning was not clear, but it was realised in the Colonial Office that an impossible situation would result if Colonial Governments were incited against HMG whenever the CDC was refused capital sanction.[93]

The Secretary of State assured the House of Commons that 'a proper balance' would be preserved between finance house and other business and, in order to carry out that pledge, the Colonial Office sought factual material from the CDC.[94] However, the latter questioned the assumption, arguing it was not too much 'finance house' business but too little of directly-run risks, preferably in agriculture, that was the trouble and blaming three inhibitions on the Corporation for that.[95] These were (i) the long-term rate of interest charged by the Treasury, then $5\frac{1}{4}$ per cent; (ii) the legal ruling that Treasury advances were not available to finance losses; and (iii) the burden of the Special Losses Account.[96] This ignored the assurance of the Secretary of State and misconceived what critics and Colonial Office officials had in mind, namely that the CDC should itself take more initiative in seeking out and planning projects for direct Colonial development and in getting them under way 'instead of sitting in Hill Street dealing with a queue of applicants for loans to enterprises in the planning and execution of which the CDC play little or no part'.[97] The position was extremely difficult because practically all applications were of the 'finance house' type and, to avoid a running quarrel, it was necessary to reach a general understanding on the problem and the limits within which transactions of the type might be sanctioned.[98] The position was discussed with the Treasury, which had, in the course of discussions in 1953, tentatively proposed that there should be 'a percentage restriction on finance house business as part of the whole capital sanction,' but that was deemed an artificial method by Colonial Office officials.[99] However, following a meeting in August 1956[100] with the Colonial Office, the Treasury felt otherwise. After acknowledging their former views, it was felt to be 'arguments of expediency' which pointed the other way.[101] They were twofold. First, a limitation on the CDC's finance house business could strengthen their case for capital write-offs and, indeed, make it impossible to repay their debt with interest to the Exchequer. The Treasury did not wish 'to abandon any part of the CDC's debt, unless it was absolutely unavoidable', which it was not felt to be at that time. Also, unless the CDC's borrowing limit was raised, any limitation proposed could not be large. Secondly, it provided a useful supplement to the London Loan Market, which was short of funds.[102] A further, though subsidiary, consideration was the difficulty of defining what was meant by 'finance house' business. A practical criterion that was considered in the Treasury was whether or not the investment was in a company on whose Board the CDC was represented, which provided a possible way of carrying out the Secretary of State's assurance 'without prejudicing our position in regard to write-off'.[103]

As this reaction shows, the finance house business was not an isolated issue. Indeed, there were four major issues at the time which were interrelated, namely finance house activities, capital write-off, the £100 million limit and the role of the CDC in Colonies on independence.[104] Quite rightly, it was felt that solutions to these four problems should not be deferred whilst a general review of the CDC was undertaken.[105] The issues will be examined in turn.

The new Treasury outlook, as expressed in the letter of 15 October, was discussed between Treasury and Colonial Office officials. It was decided to invite the CDC to participate in further talks on the basis of the Colonial Office definitions of finance house activities so that, at least, the facts would be established with the CDC before a paper was submitted to the Secretary of State.[106] The problem of definition was difficult, and the Colonial Office suggested that finance house activities should be regarded as 'those cases in which the Corporation is not directly concerned in, and assumes little or no responsibility for, the inception, planning or execution of a project, or in which the principal, if not the only, activity of the Corporation in relation to the project is to make a loan against a satisfactory guarantee or security'.[107] On the basis of that definition, some 45 per cent, i.e. £35.8 million, of the CDC's total commitments were so employed. The CDC was invited to comment on the definition and to supply information. However, the Colonial Office–CDC meeting of 14 November 1956 was inconclusive and the problems remained: how to define such activities, what was a proper balance and what action was required. The CDC preferred a narrower definition, namely loans to Governments and Government-guaranteed loans, thus excluding debentures, as these included a risk of loss; and so the total was brought down to £34.5 million. As the Corporation expected to make a net annual profit of £1 million over the next few years, after taking account of interest payments to the Treasury, the latter's doubts were not justified on the score of making the CDC liable to default if finance house business was effectively restricted.[108]

This issue and also that of increasing the Corporation's ceiling were both very closely tied up with the problem of finding loan finance for Colonial Governments. While this last was being discussed between the Colonial Office and the Treasury further attention to the finance house issue was postponed.[109] It was not until August 1957 that the Colonial Office wrote to the Treasury[110] for their approval of a draft letter to the CDC. Meantime, it had not been found possible to agree on a satisfactory definition of finance house activities for the purpose in mind; so it was proposed instead to exclude as not normally appropriate for future financing by the CDC (a) straight loans to governments, (b) loans guaranteed by governments, and (c) straight loans to statutory bodies. While the Treasury preferred the earlier formula, this was accepted.[111] The CDC was prepared to accept these conclusions as part of Government policy but was unwilling, in addition, to agree normally to limit its lending to businesses to the sum invested in equities or its right to appoint a director, because this was regarded as a matter of commercial judgement.[112] The reply was regarded as 'a bit tough' in view of the fact that no absolute rule was proposed.[113] However, the Office brief prepared for the officials who were to appear before the Public Accounts Committee on 20 February 1958, where the main item on the agenda was to be the question of finance house activities of the CDC, largely argued the case for the Corporation, principally because the Office was working up a new approach to the question of loan finance for Colonial Governments.[114]

v. LOAN FINANCE FOR COLONIAL GOVERNMENTS AND SUBORDINATE COLONIAL AUTHORITIES

The principal factors in the situation were (a) first and foremost, the serious situation with regard to Colonial Governments' borrowing programmes in London, and (b) the position of subordinate Colonial borrowers.[115] An regards (a), when the 1955 CD & W Act was being drawn up in 1954, the Office estimate of the amount of new money that would need to be provided under the Act was £115 million, making a total of £155 million with the carry-over of £40 million from the previous Act. In fact, the amount of new money provided under the Act was only £80 million, making a total provision for the five-year period up to 1960 of £120 million with the £40 million carry-over. The main justification for the reduction in the amount of new money to be provided under the Act was the Treasury estimate that Colonial Governments would be able to raise on the London Market an average of £20–25 million a year. The forecast was doubted in the Office and the Secretary of State, Mr Alan Lennox-Boyd, sought from the Chancellor of the Exchequer, Mr R. A. Butler, an assurance that, if loan finance of that amount was not forthcoming from the Market, special steps would be taken by HMG to ensure that such finance was available. The Chancellor replied on 17 November 1954 that: 'As regards external borrowing by the Colonies, I am sure that we should wait until the difficulty actually arises before we consider what special measures should be taken; but you have my assurance that, if the occasion arises, we shall do our best to find some suitable way to help.'

TABLE   5.2 Colonial Loans issued and Amount taken by the Crown Agents and Locally, 1955–1957 (£ million)

	Total issued	Amount taken up by Crown Agents or by local reservations
1955	9.448	4.75
1956	11.265	3.50
1957	15.500	3.50

The amounts actually raised are shown in Table 5.2, while the firm programme of borrowing requirements for 1958 totalled £27 million. It was not felt that a sum of that order could all be obtained from the market, basically because investors feared for the security of their long-term, usually 20–25-year, loans owing to the likelihood that these Governments would become independent before the loan matured.[116] Another factor was the sharp decline likely in the extent to which Colonial loans in London would be taken up by other Colonial Governments. In the years 1951–56 no less than £83¼ million was contributed locally or taken up by Colonial Government funds under the management of the Crown Agents and only £32¾ million of the total of £116 million was contributed by United Kingdom investors, i.e. 28 per cent. In future, the Crown Agents would not be able to

contribute so much because Colonial Governments wished increasingly to use their resources locally, and the funds held on behalf of
Ghana and Malaya were no longer available for such use. Nor did the
Secretary of State feel that the CDC should involve itself significantly
further in the provision of loan finance for Colonial Governments. The
only feasible method of meeting the shortfall in loan finance that
Colonial Governments could expect to raise on the London Market
was held to be the provision of loans from the Exchequer.[117] It was
suggested that the Exchequer should be regarded as a lender of last
resort and carry a full sinking fund, so making them dearer, and also
that such loans should be made solely on the recommendation of an
independent body, appointed by the Secretary of State with the
concurrence of the Treasury. A total of £140 million was proposed for
the seven years to March 1965. The general view of the Economic
Policy Committee was that it would be extremely difficult to evade the
moral commitments which had been undertaken in respect of the
current Colonial development programmes.[118] In relation both to
total overseas investment and to the economic and political importance of the issues at stake, the amounts involved were small and, it was
thought, it might still be obtained from the market. The Secretary of
State was invited to circulate his memorandum to the Cabinet,[119]
which considered that the necessary legislation could be postponed
provided that Colonial Governments were assured that HMG would
make good any shortfall in borrowing on the market by one means or
another.[120] Later such assurances were given to the Government of
Uganda and to the Government of British Guiana. However, on 2
December 1957 the Chancellor of the Exchequer, Mr Peter Thorney-
croft, wrote to the Secretary of State, Mr Alan Lennox-Boyd, to say
that, in the light of HMG's current policies, he thought that no more
money should be provided from the United Kingdom for Colonial
development in 1958 than had been provided in 1957 and, consequently, the Cabinet decision of 4 June that Colonial development
programmes should be permitted to proceed as planned, would have
to be revised.[121] By a Secret Unnumbered Circular of 18 September
1958 the Secretary of State informed Colonial Governors that HMG
would announce, at the Commonwealth Conference at Montreal,
their decision to seek Parliamentary approval for a system of
Exchequer loans to Colonial Governments to supplement the resources of the London Market. The intention was to include provision
for the scheme in the CD & W Act, which was expected to come into
force on 1 April 1959.

The second factor in the situation was the ban on direct borrowing in London by subordinate Colonial borrowers. The ban did not stem from the Control of Borrowing Order but was imposed administratively. Its effect was to require that the borrowings of constituent parts of a Federation, statutory corporations, municipalities and other local government bodies should be met through borrowing by the central governments concerned. Exception was made for Nairobi City Council as Nairobi was virtually the economic and financial capital of East Africa as a whole and its requirements would have taken a disproportionately large share of the loan finance that could be raised by Kenya. This ban bore hardly on the Colonies, because statutory corporations had been established to run a wide variety of public utility, including transport and power undertakings, which, in the absence of local sources of finance, had to borrow through their central governments which were, at the same time, finding difficulty in raising external loans for their own requirements.

Consequently, the Office recommendation was that loans by the CDC to Colonial Governments should be banned but 'approved' loans to statutory bodies which could not otherwise find finance should be authorised, the latter condition being intended to limit the use of funds to cases of the greatest need. It was, in addition, considered that the CDC would in this way more effectively contribute to Colonial development than by participating in commercial-type undertakings with business partners. Also, it was felt that the conditions on which the CDC normally insisted before making a loan to a Colonial statutory body imposed a degree of financial discipline that was a valuable aspect of the arrangement. Finally, as regards loans made by the CDC to commercial bodies, it was accepted that conditions should not be laid down which affected the CDC's commercial judgment.[122] So it was concluded that no restrictions should be placed on the lending by the CDC to private enterprise, 'provided that the project is within the CDC's legal competence, is a worthwhile piece of Colonial development and is *prima facie* technically and commercially sound'. A draft Circular was prepared along the lines of the Brief but 'put by' as the finance house issue became part of the general enquiry into the future role of the CDC.[123] One issue was that of raising CDC's borrowing limit.

vi. THE CDC'S BORROWING LIMIT

When the Chairman discussed the CDC's borrowing limit with the Secretary of State on 16 July 1956 he estimated that the Corporation would run out of money by 1958, if not earlier, on the basis of what he regarded as 'commitments'[124] and he subsequently asked for a doubling of borrowing powers to £200 million.[125] After discussions within the Office, the Treasury was consulted and the CDC asked for fuller information, but progress was slow, partly because of simultaneous consideration of the future role of the United Kingdom in the development of independent Commonwealth countries and partly because of discussions of future borrowings by Colonial Governments on the London Market.[126] A draft memorandum was passed to the Minister for Colonial Affairs, Lord Perth, on 7 March 1957, which surveyed the future capital requirements of the CDC. It recommended that, without consulting the CDC, the Office should, subject to the review of the CDC's role in newly-independent Commonwealth countries and providing the separate proposals for Exchequer loans were agreed, put to the Treasury a proposal that the CDC's borrowing powers should be increased by £30 million. This was based on an estimate of £5–6 million a year over the following five years, in addition to the further £16.4 million available from the remainder of the £100 million for existing projects. It was felt that the CDC should not be consulted before the Treasury was approached as it would 'react violently against what they would regard as a very low "offer" of £30 million, and would begin "lobbying"'.[127]

It had been found that the Chairman supplied a brief to all participants in the debate of 20 June 1956 in the House of Lords on the Annual Report of the CDC, but not to the Colonial Office spokesman. The Parliamentary Under-Secretary, Lord Lloyd, was understandably indignant that he, as Minister replying to the Debate, should only have heard of the brief by chance.[128] Furthermore, the Chairman was due to discuss several of the points with the Secretary of State, and so the Parliamentary Under-Secretary of State was unable to reply meantime.[129] The Financial Secretary to the Treasury, Mr H. Brooke, thought that the Chairman had transgressed the rules for, in seeking to enlist the support of other Peers on matters where his views were at variance with that of the responsible Minister, he was 'engaging in political activity' on matters affecting the Board and not showing 'proper discretion'.[130] Meantime, the Chairman published a turnover article on Public Corporations in The Times of 3 July 1956, and the Secretary of State took up both matters with the Chairman who, however, remained unrepentant, holding that the Boards of Public Corporations had a right and a duty to join public issue with the Minister concerned whenever they saw fit to do so.[131] The Secretary of State discussed the matter with the Lord President of the Council, the

Marquis of Salisbury, and the Financial Secretary to the Treasury, Mr E. Powell, with a view to action to render any recurrence unlikely.[132] On 17 July 1957 the Chairman transgressed again when he voted against the Government when the Report of the CDC was debated. The Secretary of State for Commonwealth Relations, the Earl of Home, was anxious that this vote should not be allowed to create a precedent.[133] Eventually, the Chairman sent[134] what the Secretary of State chose to regard as a 'full and adequate apology'.[135] The Prime Minister subsequently circulated, after agreement with Ministers, a revised text of the rules governing political activities of members of Public Boards. The Secretary of State, Mr Lennox-Boyd, sent a copy of the revised rules to the new Chairman of the CDC, Sir Nutcombe Hume.[136] These events exemplify the Secretary of State's view that: 'Our relations with the Corporation – largely because of Reith's attitude and personality – are always difficult and tiresome.'[137]

To return to the CDC's borrowing limit, the Office recommendations were endorsed by Ministers[138] and the Treasury agreed, saying that any greater sum would involve a cut elsewhere.[139] Although the Chairman had meantime asked for an increase of £75 million,[140] the Secretary of State proposed that (a) the Corporation's borrowing powers should be increased by £50 million, so that it might have outstanding at any one time a maximum of £10 million temporary loans and a maximum of £150 million medium and long-term loans; and (b) the amount which the Corporation might borrow from the Exchequer should be increased by only £30 million.[141] So the Corporation would only be able to enter into commitments in excess of £130 million to the extent that it was able, as it claimed it was for specific projects, to raise loans either in the United Kingdom, where the CDC required the consent of the Treasury under the Control of Borrowing Order before borrowing, or elsewhere. The proposal was approved by the Economic Policy Committee[142] and, in due course, included in the ORD Act, 1958, which gave effect to this and other Government proposals set out in paragraphs 31 to 34 of the White Paper on 'The United Kingdom's Role in Commonwealth Development' (Cmnd 237, July 1957).

VII. CDC'S ROLE IN NEWLY-INDEPENDENT COMMONWEALTH COUNTRIES

On 19 April 1956 a Deputy-Under-Secretary of State at the Colonial Office enquired:[143] 'Has any thought been given to the question whether territories now within the statutory ambit of the CDC will remain in it after becoming independent?' He went on to explain that the point had been put in his mind by a letter from the Chairman of the CDC to the Secretary of State, in which he said that the CDC would like to participate in the Volta River Project 'as HMG's agent' and added: 'As the Volta River Project will not start till after Gold Coast independence, one is tempted to reply "*ultra vires*" on territorial grounds.' But that would have been wrong because 'Colonial territory' in section 1(1) of the ORD Act, 1948, was defined in section 19(a) of that Act as a territory to which section 1 of the CD & W Act, 1940, applied at the commencement of the Act of 1948. So territories to which the 1948 Act applied would not cease to be eligible, after they became independent, unless the United Kingdom Act granting independence effected some alteration in the position.[144] Officials considered the position was, if anything, too flexible in that, unless the Act was amended, the CDC would be able to go on financing schemes in what might have become independent countries.[145] This was thought to be contrary to the original intention of Parliament. It was suggested that the CDC should be debarred from embarking on new schemes in territories after they attained independence, but existing schemes could be maintained and the injection of further capital into them, though normally to be avoided, should be permitted where necessary.[146] The Secretary of State thought 'this general principle is quite right'[147] and, with the concurrence of the Treasury and the CRO, wrote accordingly to the Chairman of CDC.[148] The latter told the Permanent Under-Secretary that, unless the Corporation could continue to operate in territories which had graduated from Colonial status to independence, it was 'finished' – already the possibility was influencing first-rate people in taking up appointments with the CDC.[149] This was doubted; it was, in fact, thought that the Chairman had 'some rather grandiose ideas of becoming the major instrument of Commonwealth, as opposed to Colonial, development'.[150] The Office view was that this would change the whole character and purpose of the CDC and noted that, as recently as 13 November 1956, Mr James Griffiths explicitly recognised that the Gold Coast and the Caribbean Federation would, on attaining independence, 'cease to be Colonies and to be entitled to any advantage and benefit derived from the two principal methods of granting such help, through the CD & W Act and the CDC'.[151]

The draft Gold Coast Independence Bill included the following clause: 'Without prejudice to the continuance of any operations commenced by the CDC in any part of Ghana before the appointed day [6 March 1957], as from that day the expression "Colonial territories" in the ORD Acts, 1948 to 1956, shall not include Ghana or any part thereof.' It was feared, rightly as it turned out, that the CDC would attempt to start four substantial new investments just before the appointed day in Ghana and Malaya, and it was recommended that those of long standing should be allowed while recently-conceived schemes should be vetoed. In the second category were the Gold Coast Cement factory, which was first proposed after the new policy had been communicated to the Chairman, and the Port Swettenham extension, a pure finance-house transaction of £3 million. In the first category were the Federal Land Development Authority, first proposed in August 1955, and the Malayan Industrial Development Corporation, which had developed from early proposals.[152] When communicated to the Chairman, the latter argued strenuously against any restrictions.[153] The main argument was that 'Independence will not mean less need for these services [of the CDC]: on the contrary, the gap between demand and supply for both types may well become greater, due to withdrawal of official support, both in men and money, and political security. What then? and who then?'[154] It was, in fact, the potential threat rather than the actual position over Ghana that mattered. But that was, apparently, not realised by those Members of Parliament, including Mr Griffiths and Mr White, who supported Sir Albert Braithwaite in pressing, in the debate of 30 November 1956, for the CDC to be allowed to continue to operate, including starting new schemes, in newly independent territories. The Secretary of State for Commonwealth Relations, Lord Home, felt that the critics of planned Government action had 'a point of some substance' and suggested that 'some transitional provision' should be considered.[155] He recognised that

the pure milk of the doctrine, of course, is that a Colony which becomes independent should take the full responsibilities of that state, including standing on its own feet financially; if it requires capital from abroad for development, it should be able to borrow in the ordinary way in the market. But the creation of investors' confidence in a country like Ghana must take some considerable time. There is, thus, a danger that a country like Ghana, on emerging into independence, may find itself falling between two stools, being neither eligible for further funds from the Colonial Development Corporation, nor for some years in a position to raise a market loan in London or to attract other capital on commercial terms. I think it would be unfortunate politically, and wrong in principle, if we were to leave a country in this position simply to sink or swim as from the day of independence.

So he made a proposal of the continuance of full involvement of the CDC for, say, three years with the possibility of renewal for another three.

Official opinion in the Colonial Office was opposed to this view.[156] First, it was thought to be the result of lobbying by the Chairman, and it would be wrong to submit to such pressure after a contrary decision had been taken on policy grounds. Secondly, the transitional period was thought to have no logic, particularly in the Gold Coast where the CDC had hitherto merely contracted for road construction, involving a commitment of the order of £350,000, largely because it had equipment on hand. Any transitional arrangement inevitably meant expanding the CDC's involvement, which could be substantial if it included participation in the Volta River Project. Thirdly, it would constitute an undesirable precedent for other territories. Fourthly, although the Secretary of State for Commonwealth Relations felt that the same argument would not apply to CD & W assistance, once the CDC was allowed to be involved there 'could be no real reason for not doing the same in respect of CD & W'. Finally, the suggestion would be administratively difficult to operate as the Colonial Office could not supervise CDC projects in independent Commonwealth countries, while joint control with the CRO would give the CDC opportunity to queer the pitch. It was not considered that full responsibility could yet be transferred to the CRO.

The Secretary of State for the Colonies, Mr Lennox-Boyd, agreed in conversation with the Secretary of State for Commonwealth Relations, Lord Home, that it might be necessary to make some concession in the debate on the Ghana Independence Bill, but felt the right course was to use the Commonwealth Development Finance Company.[157] The Secretary of State for Commonwealth Relations was doubtful whether the CDFC was the right answer and wished his own proposal to be considered, first by officials and later by Ministers. It was so considered and it was decided not to proceed with it.[158] The Ghana Independence Bill was moved, as originally planned, on 11 December 1956.[159] Mr Lennox-Boyd promised that the role of the CDC 'in the Gold Coast and elsewhere' would be considered at length at the Committee stage. The intention was misunderstood in some quarters: thus The Economist of 8 December 1956 believed that the CDC would have to abandon existing projects and not be allowed to complete projects in hand. The sub-clause 3(4), which excluded

Ghana from benefiting from new projects, encountered considerable criticism in the House of Commons at the Committee stage on 8 January 1957, and in the Second Reading Debate in the House of Lords on 24 January 1957. Indeed, it was feared that the subsection might not be accepted. Accordingly, the position was discussed in the CRO by Ministers from the CRO and the Colonial Office and officials from both Departments and the Treasury.[160] Subsequently, a Memorandum was submitted jointly by the Secretary of State for Commonwealth Relations, Lord Home, and the Minister of State for Colonial Affairs, Lord Perth, to the Colonial Policy Committee.[161] After rehearsing the position, the Memorandum recognised that there were two issues involved: (a) whether financial help should be given from United Kingdom Government funds to newly-independent countries; and (b) whether, if (a) was conceded, the channel should be the CDC, this being distinct from the question raised in Parliament that it was desirable that the CDC's managerial and technical 'know-how' should be retained in some form for the benefit of the newly-independent territories. It was, in fact, felt that the view that the CDC had some unique competence in the field of overseas development was fallacious, 'though it is difficult to say this outspokenly in Parliament in view of the "mystique" about the CDC which Lord Reith has created', for its main activity had been financing, while its development operations had been in partnership with established businesses. There remained much for the CDC to do in the Colonies after the independence of Ghana and Malaya.[162]

It was felt highly desirable to retain the sub-clause without making any concession but, if a concession were necessary, it was considered that it should be neither of the sub-clause nor of the principle that United Kingdom Exchequer money could not normally be made available for the development of independent Commonwealth countries. Instead, a review should be made of the whole question of the United Kingdom's role in the development of newly-independent Commonwealth countries and, if there was a decision arising that the services of the CDC should be retained, legislation would be introduced to amend the ORD Acts accordingly and Ghana should be brought within any such arrangements. This recommendation was endorsed by the Colonial Policy Committee.[163] The Secretary of State for Commonwealth Relations found it necessary to intervene early in the Debate on the Committee Stage to make this concession.[164] The Cabinet invited the Colonial Policy Committee to consider further the tactics to be adopted in the resumed debate in the Lords.[165] It concluded that there was no alternative but to retain Clause 3 in the

Bill if it was wished to have power to terminate CD & W schemes already in being and to withdraw the CDC's freedom to operate in Ghana.[166] The Lord Chancellor, Viscount, later Earl, Kilmuir, explained the legal position when the debate was resumed on 5 February. Opposition to the Clause was however maintained, and the House divided, first on a notice to omit subsection 4 of the clause and later to omit Clause 3 as a whole. Both motions were rejected, the Committee stage was concluded and the Bill was read a third time and passed.

While the protests of Labour and some Tory critics are easily understood, it is at the same time doubtful whether a decision to carry on with CD & W and the CDC as before would have been the right answer. *The Economist* of 9 February 1957 put the point admirably in this way:

> Nevertheless, the Government's decision was the right one. The CDC, which wants to extend its empire, is not the right instrument for financing independent countries; the need is for a separate (and small) fund which will help to tide over these new countries until they establish their own creditworthiness, not for the mixture as before. The question of development in new Dominions is a general one, which could not appropriately be dealt with by way of an amendment to the independence bill. . . . The only really justifiable criticism is that, if the Commonwealth is to make some special provision for its members, it is a pity that this was not arranged before Ghana's independence, since the bill has cut off aid with an unfriendly abruptness.

This neatly summed up the position. The Government was taken unaware of the need for broad planning. Within their own assumptions and concerns, the Colonial Office was correct and, when the Secretary of State for Commonwealth Relations proposed a transition period, this might have stood some chance of acceptance if the CDC had earlier accepted the six months' notice of the termination in Ghana and, therefore, not allowed the planning of a cement project to proceed.[167] As an official very reasonably minuted, it demonstrated again that the Chairman's 'misdeeds can be made to appear to be the fault of the British Government. In my view, this is one more argument in favour of not letting the CDC operate freely in Commonwealth countries, whose relations with HMG can well be prejudiced by such behaviour.'[168] There was general agreement at the time between the Secretary of State and his chief officials, on the one side, and the

Chairman, his colleagues and General Manager, on the other, that there were 'unfortunate differences of outlook between the two bodies' and that their 'relations left room for improvement'.[169] Had this not been so, the necessary review of the policy of Commonwealth economic development might well have been put in hand earlier. Critics of government policy unknowingly weakened a good case by centring their recommendations on the CDC rather than on the general issues. The Chairman of the CDC had overplayed his hand without heeding that HMG always held the trump card and, in the end, would use it.

At the Colonial Policy Committee,[170] the Foreign Secretary, Mr Selwyn Lloyd, drew attention to the need for a reappraisal of the general problems involved in financing the future development of the African territories, as it was necessary to avoid the imputation of drawing wealth from them without an adequate return, and also to forestall unwelcome offers of assistance made as part of the Soviet economic offensive. As, in the pursuit of the latter aim, grants and loans were being made to countries outside the Commonwealth, it was arguable that Commonwealth countries should continue to receive aid as they became independent. However, the Ghana Independence Bill could not wait for the fundamental review of policy that this submission involved. Even so, it led to the process of review. On 3 December 1956 the Permanent Under-Secretaries of the Colonial Office and the CRO discussed the future relationship of their two Departments and the following month the Colonial Office sent to the CRO a description of the advisory and other services available to Colonial territories.[171] The Colonial Office was, in fact somewhat embarrassed over the uncertain future of the mass of such services that had been built up and, possibly in part for that reason, suggested that it would prove helpful if the existing arrangements were geared to the needs of newly-independent states. The CRO felt that apart, possibly, from dropping 'Colonial' from the names, Ghana and Malaya could use the services they were interested in and reorganisation should await evidence of the use to which the services would be put by emergent territories.[172]

The Secretary of State for Commonwealth Relations invited his Parliamentary Under-Secretary, Mr C. Alport, to consider the need for, and possible form of, a Commonwealth Advisory Service and to make a recommendation.[173] The paper which the Parliamentary Under-Secretary quickly prepared[174] was divided into five parts. First, it listed the several categories of assistance, both technical and capital. Then it indicated political and economic considerations, including

(a) the wish of the Conservative Party to undertake a development in the field of Commonwealth economics comparable with the inauguration of the CDC and CD & W under the earlier Labour administration (though in fact CD & W was not inaugurated by the 1945–51 Labour administration but in 1940 by the war time Coalition Government), as developments in the Commonwealth field had largely consisted of changes in the political and constitutional relationships between the United Kingdom and various Colonies, so weakening the political influence of the United Kingdom; (b) the dangers of Communist political penetration in Africa and elsewhere; (c) even more imminent dangers of economic penetration by Germany and Japan, initially by means of long-term credits; and (d) possible measures to keep emergent countries within the Sterling Area. After stating that any proposals must effectively cope with these considerations, the paper proposed (i) the provision of technical advice and training through the creation of a Commonwealth Technical Service within the CRO by an expansion of the existing Colombo Plan Department; (ii) the establishment of a Commonwealth Atomic Energy body to advise and assist emergent countries; (iii) the creation of a Commonwealth Development Bank to invest in public utilities and offer guarantees to outside capital against risks of political instability and administrative uncertainty; (iv) for normal risk investment, special encouragement was suggested for the CDFC, which was unlikely to become involved in political complications, as would the CDC, and was developing a useful advisory service. Finally, it was suggested that the various proposals should be announced together by HMG as part of 'A technical co-operation plan for the Commonwealth', and, subsequently, other Commonwealth countries should be associated. As the Prime Minister aptly commented, the problem was to get a surplus in the balance of payments: 'You cannot invest a deficit. But you can invest "know-how", etc.'[175]

The Colonial Office, meantime, examined the suggestion that the advisory, technical and personnel services then operated by, or under the aegis of, the Colonial Office should be hived off, along with the administrative departments concerned with their work, and entrusted to a new Overseas Services Office under a junior Minister jointly responsible to the Colonial and Commonwealth Secretaries. It was provisionally concluded that the establishment of anything of that nature would be premature and, instead, Advisers in the Colonial Office should be given a limited status in the CRO.[176] The Parliamentary Under-Secretary of State, Mr C. Alport, did not favour a similar proposal that had been made for a new Department, partly because it perpetuated the link with the Colonial Office and partly because joint responsibility was likely to prove unworkable.

At a time of eager groping for a satisfactory answer to the problem thrown up by Ghana's independence, there was a real danger of uncoordinated efforts. Thus there was, it was thought at the time, the possibility that the Committee on Commonwealth Economic Development would pursue policies in conflict with those of the Economic Policy Committee.[177] For the latter had commissioned the Economic Secretary to the Treasury, Mr N. Birch, to produce studies, *inter alia*, of ways in which the United Kingdom could reduce the scale of its investment in the Commonwealth, while the former had commissioned papers on the assumption that the United Kingdom should increase its investment in the Commonwealth. The conclusions that the CCED had come to were that it was impossible to launch an imaginative plan for Commonwealth development

> at a time when the United Kingdom is scraping the bottom of the barrel to an extent which compels her to look overseas for sources of investment both for herself and for her Commonwealth partners. Even a radical departure in organisation demands more money to match, if it is going to succeed. So our best policy at present is probably to feel our way fairly humbly, in the hope that something bigger will grow – at the right time – out of modest beginnings in such fields as the CDFC and technical co-operation.

In his paper, the Parliamentary Under-Secretary accepted that the CD & W and the CDC alike would not be available in the emergent countries and favoured a reinforcement, via the Bank of England, of the resources of the CDFC.[178] The CCED had by mid-March 1957 provisionally concluded that there was no case for extending the operation of the CDC to emergent countries and the resultant diminution of functions should be accepted. Nor was there thought to be a case for combining the CDC and the CDFC or, as additional funds on a significant scale were not available, for the establishment of a new financing institution.[179] The role indicated for the CDC agreed with that proposed by the Colonial Office in its submission to the CCED.[180] This was reflected in the Report of the CCED, which argued that, unless the Colonial Empire shrunk unexpectedly fast, the CDC would for many years find sufficient scope in the Colonial territories for the sort of assistance which it was established to provide, 'though a greater degree of initiative may be required in promoting development in economically less attractive areas'.[181] In its final

Report on the Provision of Capital, which was circulated to the Cabinet on 29 May 1957 as C(57) 129, the CCED concluded that the policy set out at the time of the Ghana Independence Bill should be followed. It also recommended that (i) the policy should be implemented by means of an amendment to the ORD Acts; and (ii) at the same time, the CDC should be authorised to second staff on the request of the Government of an independent Commonwealth country or to undertake the management of a project on a managing agency basis, without commitment of the Corporation's funds. These recommendations were accepted by the Cabinet.[182] So, unlike the Ghana Independence Act, the Malayan Independence Bill did not include any provision regarding the position of the CDC in the Federation after independence and, until the ORD Acts were amended, the policy was effected by administrative action.[183] Although the legality of this latter course was doubted in the Debate on the Ghana Independence Bill by the Lord Chancellor,[184] the new situation was distinguished from the earlier one by the decision to amend the ORD Acts, and by the acceptance of exclusion by the CDC[185] and by the Chief Minister of Malaya.[186]

It was not possible to make progress with the ORD Bill until the various questions of policy involved were settled. These were announced in the White Paper, *The United Kingdom's Role in Commonwealth Development* (Cmnd 237, July 1957, paras 31–3), after which the Bill was given high priority.[187] Prolonged discussions were, however, found to be necessary with the CRO in particular, and when the Chief Whip asked that the Bill should, if possible, be presented before Christmas,[188] it had not even been drafted.[189] The Bill provided that (a) the borrowing powers of the CDC should be increased from £100 million to £150 million; (b) Exchequer advances to the CDC should be increased from £100 million to £130 million; (c) the CDC should be able to continue, after a Colony became independent, with projects commenced before independence and, if necessary, to provide further capital for them; and (d) the CDC should be able to undertake the management of any project on a managing agency basis, without commitment of the Corporation's funds, in any independent Commonwealth country, subject to the agreement of the Government of the country concerned. Power was included in the Bill, at the request of the CRO, whereby the Secretary of State – in practice the Commonwealth Secretary – could require the Corporation to cease any managing agency activity. The reason for this was that the CRO feared that, should political repercussions result, a distinction was unlikely to be made between the CDC and HMG and so the only solution would be for the Corporation to withdraw.[190] The contentious section 3(4) of the Ghana Independence Act was repealed. The ORD Act, 1958 (6 and 7 Eliz. 2, Ch. 15), received the Royal Assent on 13 March 1958.

In opening the Debate on the Second Reading on 28 January 1958, the Secretary of State, Mr Lennox-Boyd, stated that 'Given the White Paper policy, the Bill has [the CDC's] full support, although it would have preferred it to cover a number of other financial matters. . . . These matters are being studied afresh, but I am not in a position to say more about them at this stage.'[191] As he suspected, the points were raised in the course of the Debate; they included the provision of an equity element in the CDC's capital, because of its need to undertake certain risk investment, and the fixing of a rate of interest at the beginning of a project rather than the charging of the Treasury rate at the time that additional capital was required. The Parliamentary Under-Secretary of State for Commonwealth Relations, Mr Alport, declared, in his speech winding up the Debate, that 'all those matters which are connected with the reconstruction of the CDC's capital structure . . .' were 'a matter of investigation and consideration at present'.[192] At the Committee Stage the Parliamentary Under-Secretary made a revealing statement about attitudes. He said:

> The hon. Member [Mr J. Johnson, Rugby] has accused the party on this side of the Committee of being concerned with ideological matters. The truth is that if we had been concerned supremely with our own particular point of view, we should not be giving, as we are through the Bill, increased opportunities . . . for the CDC to play its part in accordance with certain definite limitations in a wider sphere. Indeed, had we followed the ideological line to which the hon. Member has referred, we should not at present be providing the CDC, as we are under the Bill, with an additional £50 million.[193]

Before issues concerning the capital structure of the CDC are examined, it is convenient to refer to two subsidiary points arising from the present discussion. The first concerns the ORD Act, 1959, and the second the housing activities of the CDC. As regards the first of these, Parliamentary Counsel drafted in February 1958 a Bill to consolidate the ORD Acts, many of whose provisions were by that time spent,[194] and this was welcomed in the Colonial Office as of great practical assistance.[195] A consolidating Bill, as was explained to both the CDC[196] and enquiring Members of Parliament anxious to press for changes,[197] does not and may not add to the law in any way: it merely brings together a series of existing enactments in a more convenient form and repeals any provisions which are spent. The ORD Act, 1959, received the Royal Assent on 23 March 1959 (7 and 8 Eliz. 2, Ch. 23).

Turning to the second matter, namely the housing activities of the CDC, it will be recalled that the ORD Act, 1956, specifically recognised that housing projects were *intra vires*. However, when the Minister of State, Lord Perth, discussed an application for capital sanction in the sum of £1 million for the CDC's Jamaica Housing Scheme, he approved but, at the same time, expressed the view that housing was not development of the type which the CDC was primarily intended to undertake, and suggested that a cautionary note to that effect should be sounded when the CDC was written to.[198] The Treasury asked for further information on the 'sort of people' likely to be accommodated, and suggested that, as a general principle, the CDC should not contribute more than half of the cost of such schemes.[199] The Colonial Office explained the first point and, providing it was interpreted 'with sensible flexibility', accepted the second.[200] The CDC noted the point but wished to avoid acceptance of even a flexible rule, although it was agreed 'that housing projects already constitute a large enough part of the CDC's operations to justify some care in choice and shape of new projects to preserve a proper balance overall – and that some restriction of the CDC support for housing projects may be desirable'.[201] As the proportion of housing sanctions (£9.5 million) to total sanctions (£92.7 million) did not suggest that there was any immediate danger of upsetting the balance, the Colonial Office accepted the CDC's assurances and invited the Treasury to do so too, which it eventually did.[202] That settled the matter[203] until April 1961, when the Treasury observed that the CDC had been investing 'more substantially in housing projects lately', and asked whether it was considered that 'a proper balance' was being maintained.[204] In its reply, the Colonial Office made two points. First, the total capital sanctions approved amounted to £128.3 million, of which £19.3 million, or 15 per cent, was for housing projects or, on the basis of 'live' sanction, which totalled £114.9 million, it was 16.7 per cent. In the light of these figures, it was believed that a reasonable overall balance had been maintained. Secondly, as regards housing, there was often a political interest and, while HMG did not wish as a rule to urge particular projects on the CDC for political reasons, it naturally looked favourably at schemes which the Corporation put forward with such advantage.[205] Thus, the Colonial Office view was that there was a strong case for agreeing to any proposal that the CDC might submit for issuing a straight loan to the Northern Rhodesia Government, or to its African Housing Board, to assist in African housing in the Protectorate.[206] First, there was a genuine need, fully substantiated in a memorandum prepared for the Prime Minister, Mr H. Macmillan, when he visited Lusaka,[207] for money for African housing. Secondly, the territory had not been well provided with CD & W money nor was it likely to get much Exchequer loan finance, and it depended for much of its development finance on borrowing by the Federal Government on the London Market, which was at the time a rather chancy proposition. Therefore, a loan via the CDC on the basis of a sensible scheme was to be welcomed, not least by the Corporation itself, which was under-invested in Northern Rhodesia.

The Treasury was unable to accept that political reasons should outweigh any objections on policy grounds to a particular investment by the CDC, feeling bound to take the view that economic considerations should predominate, 'especially as the pressure on United Kingdom overseas aid resources increases and it becomes progressively more essential to concentrate these resources where the need is greatest'.[208] However, it was agreed that the CDC might lend £1 million for housing schemes in Lusaka and other towns in Northern Rhodesia, where the Colonial Office efforts were greatly appreciated, even although the loan would 'only make a small dent in our needs for African housing'.[209] Other applications of a similar nature, such as £1,970,000 for the Trinidad Mortgage Agency Company[210] and £2 million for the Caribbean Housing Finance Corporation,[211] were sanctioned without difficulty.

SOURCES

1. File 97357/71, Economic General, 1950–1–2, item 12, letter of 21 Dec 1951 from the Chairman to the Minister of State.

2. Cmd 8560, May 1952, Part V. When the Report had been considered, the Parliamentary Under-Secretary, Lord Munster, told the Chairman that, if he needed to refer to it in the forthcoming Debate, he would say it 'puts everything in its true perspective, that naturally we accept the findings but that no action on the report seems necessary. Let bygones be bygones and let the present Chairman and Board and their staff get on with their job.' – Confidential file 97357, Economic General, Part II, 1952, item 45, letter of 27 May 1952.

3. File 97357/71, Economic General, 1950–1–2, items 10a, 11–14, and minute of 31 Dec 1951. The occasion was Lord Reith's answer to complaints which Mr Peter Smithers, MP, had passed on to the Minister of State.

4. File EGD 81/150/01, Part A, item 2, Appendix to Draft Brief for Minister of State.

5. File EGD 89/169/01, minute of 7 Sep 1953. The Secretary of State emphasised the psychological reasons for writing-off capital on abandoned schemes or schemes that were over-capitalised rather picturesquely as 'getting rid of the tin cans tied to the Corporation's tail' – see item 1 in ibid., giving a record of a discussion between the Chancellor and the Secretary of State with officials on 7 Aug 1952.

6. File 97357, Economic General, Part 1, 1950–1–2, item 38.

7. Annual Report for 1950, p. 5, para. 9(2) and (3).

8. Ibid., p. 5, para. 10(3).

9. File 97357/101, Economic General, 1951, item 1. The Chairman expressed his concern at the unduly high overhead expenditure at the monthly meeting with the Colonial Office on 8 May 1951. The Deputy Chairman stated that one reason was the wide scattering of schemes.

10. File 97357, Economic General, Part I, 1950–1–2: minute of 14 Jan 1952 asserted that: 'The difficulties are now practical rather than theoretical, viz., how to get the right man on the right spot at the right time and implement devolution while maintaining adequate central control.'

11. H. of C. Deb., Vol. 503, col. 2376, 17 July 1952.

12. File 97357/88, Economic General, 1952, item 3, Aide-memoire of conversation with Secretary of State, 3 July 1952.

13. File 97357, Economic General, Part I, 1950–1–2, item 31. In his letter of 1 Nov 1951 the Chairman asked Sir Hilton Poynton whether 'the time has come – particularly with the change of Government – for a serious consideration of policy adjustments in one shape or another'.

14. Annual Report and Accounts for 1951, p. 5, para. 5.

15. Ibid., p. 7, para. 8(9).

16. Confidential file 97357, Economic General, Part II, 1952, item 43, letter of 22 May 1952 from the Secretary of State to the Chairman.

17. H. of L. Deb., Vol. 176, cols. 1549–620, 28 May 1952. In a letter to the Parliamentary Under-Secretary Lord Ogmore, who was due to introduce the Debate, said he would raise two main issues: (i) the Corporation was being compelled increasingly, because of its financial obligations, to undertake projects likely to yield a quick financial return; and (ii) consequently, the Corporation was likely to become a finance house instead of undertaking projects of long-run benefit to Colonial Territories. Lord Ogmore felt that the Corporation 'should be used far more than it is, both by the Colonial Office under the CD & W funds and by the Colonial Governments, as an agency for carrying out of schemes not likely to be quickly profitable and for pilot projects' – letter of 23 May 1952, item 44 in Confidential file 97357, Economic General, Part II, 1952.

18. Confidential file 97357, Economic General, Part II, 1952, items 50, 51 and 56, letters of 4 and 10 June and 7 July 1952.

19. Ibid., item 58: aide-memoire of conversation with Secretary of State and others of 3 July 1952. The Secretary of State contested the version of his own views in the aide-memoire, saying that 'You still have not appreciated the argument about equity capital' – letter of 16 July 1952, item 60 in ibid.

20. File 97357, Economic General, Part I, 1950–1–2, minute of 29 May 1952.

21. Ibid., item 48, Circular Despatch 603/52 of 16 June 1952. A copy was sent to the CDC for information. The Chairman said it read 'not as in confirmation, but as in imposition' – letter of 15 July 1952 – item 62 in Confidential file 97357, Economic General, Part II, 1952.

22. H. of C. Deb., Vol. 503, cols. 2370–6, 17 July 1953.

23. Idem, col. 2370.

24. Idem, cols. 2373–4. Subsidiary issues remained to be settled between the Colonial Office, the Treasury and CDC, and were the subject of much discussion within the Treasury and between the Treasury and the other two parties. A letter of 23 July 1952 listed the issues as the timing of interest rate charges as they affected advances; the waiving of interest in the seven-year fructification period; backdating the agreement on medium-term loans; general authority to borrow from banks on short term; approval for a 'top-hat' pension scheme and identification of the schemes in which 'dead capital' interest could be waived. The Colonial Office was anxious to agree with CDC, but there was some resistance from the Home Finance division of the Treasury. For original letter, discussions within the Treasury and meeting between the three parties on 7 Aug 1952 see Treasury file IF 580/01, Part H, pp. 138–86.

25. H. of C. Deb., Vol. 503, col. 2374, 17 July 1953.

26. File EGD 81/01, 1954–1956, item 19, letter of 10 Dec 1954 from the Chairman to the Secretary of State. This appears to have been a sore point with the Chairman – see minute of 21 Dec 1954, in idem.

27. H. of C. Deb., Vol. 535, col. 499, 3 Dec 1954.

28. H. of L. Deb., Vol. 178, col. 133, 22 July 1952.

29. Idem, col. 168.

30. H. of L. Deb., Vol. 183, col. 1234, 30 July 1953. As Lord Ogmore reminded the House of Lords (H. of L. Deb., Vol. 197, cols 1125–6, 20 June 1956), 'Winding up the debate on the Second Reading of the original Bill in another place in 1948, I said (H. of C. Deb., Vol. 443, col. 2115) "The purpose of the Colonial Development Corporation is to do anything necessary for the starting up of any legitimate productive enterprise *which is likely to pay its way in the Colonies*" [italics added]. These words were carefully considered, naturally, and I am quite sure that I am right in saying that they were the basic underlying impulse of the Government of that time headed by my noble friend who is now Lord Attlee.'

31. Annual Report for 1952, p. 6, para. 7(3) and (4). In reply to a question on the paragraph, the Minister of State, Mr H. Hopkinson, stated that it was questionable whether the suggestion in para. 7(4) was compatible with the provisions of the ORD Act, 1948, and also whether schemes of the kind referred to were not better financed from other sources (H. of C. Deb., Vol. 515, col. 143, 20 May 1953).

32. H. of L. Deb., Vol. 183, col. 1235, 30 July 1953.

33. File EGD 81/167/01, 1954–1956, item 19, letter of 18 June 1954, from the General Manager, CDC, to Sir Hilton Poynton. See also item 17 of 10 Oct 1953 in EGD 89/90/01, which is an account of a discussion with Sir Hilton Poynton when the General Manager first raised the matter, receiving much the same reply as in 1954.

34. Ibid., item 20, letter of 25 June 1954, from Sir Hilton Poynton to the General Manager. In a minute of 22 June 1954 it was suggested that the response to CDC's memorandum on agricultural production was disappointing because 'the CDC ideas were half-baked'. The memorandum and discussions thereon, both within the Colonial Office and with CDC, are to be found on file EGD 89/213/01 of 1953. Sir Hilton Poynton referred to the memorandum as one of the Chairman's toy-balloons minute of 6 May 1953.

35. Confidential file EGD 150/01, 1954–1956, item 1, letter of 6 May 1955 to Sir K. Roberts-Wray.

36. Ibid., minute of 15 Aug 1955.

37. Ibid., item 2, letter of 10 Sep 1955 from Sir K. Roberts-Wray.

38. File 97357/84, Economic General, 1950–51, item 2, letter of 11 Aug 1950 (on behalf of the Minister of State) to the Chairman. The Chairman stated the commitment was 16 per cent, not 20 per cent – item 5 in ibid. The population of the three Territories was slightly more than a million, i.e. less than 2 per cent of the total Colonial population. Apart from the Lobatsi abattoir, the schemes were (i) Bechuanaland ranching project covering an area of 16,000 square miles and expected to take 18–21 years to reach completion; (ii) Swaziland ranching project on an estate of 110,000 acres; (iii) Swaziland forestry project at Usutu on 108,411 acres, of which 75,000 acres was suitable for afforestation.

39. Ibid., item 12.

40. File 97357/105, Economic, 1951–52, item 4, letter of 25 May 1951 from Earl de la Warr to the Secretary of State.

41. Ibid., item 7, letter and enclosure of 1 June 1951.

42. Ibid., item 8, letter of 7 June 1951 from the Secretary of State to Earl de la Warr.

43. Ibid., item 13, letter of 27 Sep 1951 from the Secretary of State for Commonwealth Relations to the Chairman.

44. Ibid., items 14 and 33, letters of 4 Oct 1951 and 19 May 1952.

45. Annual Report for 1951, p. 57, para 54(a)(a).

46. File 97357/105, Economic, 1951–2, item 42, letter and enclosure of 21 Oct 1952.

47. Ibid., item 46, letter of 28 Nov 1952 to the General Manager.

48. Ibid., minute of 5 Dec 1952 by the Adviser on Animal Health to the Secretary of State.

49. Ibid., minute of 23 Dec 1952.

50. Idem.

51. Idem. However, he thought that the scheme could be justified if, by destocking the area, it improved the land which might otherwise suffer from soil erosion. As he realised, that was not the point at issue, nor one for the CDC.

52. File EGD 89/99/01, 1953, minute of 3 Mar 1953.

53. Ibid., item 16, confidential letter and enclosure of 23 Apr 1953 from the Secretariat, Lusaka. See also minute of 13 May 1953.

54. Ibid., item 18, letter and enclosure of 7 May 1953.

55. Ibid., minute of 6 Oct 1953.

56. Ibid., item 36, letter and enclosure of 12 Nov 1953 from the Chairman to Sir Hilton Poynton.

57. Ibid., item 51, letter and enclosure of 18 Dec 1953.

58. Ibid., item 53, letter and enclosure of 30 Dec 1953 from the Chairman to Sir Hilton Poynton.

59. Ibid., item E/45, secret letter of 24 Nov 1953.

60. Ibid., item E/45/1, secret letter of 7 Dec 1953.

61. Ibid., minute of 10 Dec 1953.

62. Idem.

63. Annual Report for 1955, p. 48, para. 76.

64. Annual Report for 1956, p. 50, para. 77.

65. Annual Report for 1957, p. 55, para. 81.

66. Annual Report for 1958, p. 60, para. 81.

67. Annual Report for 1959, p. 63–4, para. 81.

68. File 97357/105, Economic General, 1951–52, minute of 23 Dec 1952.

69. File 97357/79, Economic General, 1950–1, item 7, note of 15 Feb 1951 by Economic General Department.

70. File 97357/65, Economic General, 1950–51, minute of 10 Feb 1951 on item 15, the Quarterly Report No. 10, Oct–Dec 1950.

71. Ibid., minute of 23 May 1951.

72. File EGD 89/05, 1953, minute of Apr 1953.

73. Treasury file IF 580/01, Part K, p. 87, letter of 10 May 1954.

74. Confidential file EGD 81/09, 1954–56, item 2, note of first meeting held on 27 Sep 1954.

75. Ibid., item 43, Report of the Joint Working Party of the CDC, Colonial Office and the Treasury.

76. Confidential file EGD 81/69/01, 1954–56, item 4, Confidential note of 23 Nov 1956 of discussion between the Secretary of State and the Chairman on 23 Nov 1956.

77. Secret file EGD 81/228/01, Part A, 1954–56, item 3, minute of 16 Sep 1955 to the Secretary of State.

78. Ibid., item 1, note of 9 Sep 1955 on CDC Housing Activities.

79. Treasury file IF 580/01, Part L, p. 85, Confidential Circular Telegram of 23 Dec 1955 from the Secretary of State.

80. Secret file EGD 81/228/01, Part A, 1954–56, item 49, letter of 25 Jan 1956 from the Secretary of State to the Chairman.

81. Treasury file IF 580/01, Part L, p. 65, Confidential Circular Telegram of 23 Dec 1955. The suspension was terminated as from 3 Aug 1956, the day after the ORD Act, 1956, received the Royal Assent – unnumbered Circular Telegram of 3 Aug 1956, at p. 150 of ibid.

82. Secret file EGD 81/228/01, Part A, 1954–56, item 66, secret and personal letter of 3 Jan 1956 from the Chief Secretary of the Federation of Nigeria, Sir Ralph Grey.

83. Ibid., item 68, letter of 3 Feb 1956 to Sir Ralph Grey. Underlinings in original.

84. Ibid., item 100, memorandum by the Secretary of State to the Economic Policy Committee of the Cabinet EP(56) 55 of 16 June 1956. The EPC approved the

principles of the draft Bill attached to EP(56) 55 on 20 June 1956 – see EP(56) 11th Meeting, item 104 in ibid. But, in answer to the Chairman, the Secretary of State explained that 'the delay is not due to difficulties over content . . . the real reason why I cannot speed up the Bill is pressure on Parliamentary time.' Letter of 1 June 1956 – item 115 in Secret file EGD 81/228/01, Part B, 1954–56.

85. Secret file EGD 81/150/01, Part B, 1954–56, minute of 26 June 1956.

86. Secret file EGD 81/150/01, Part C, 1954–56, item 154, letter of 24 July 1956 from the Secretary of State to the Chairman.

87. 4 and 5 Eliz. 2, Ch. 71. For the Debates, see H. of C., Vol. 557, 25–7 July 1956, and H. of L., Vol. 199, 1 Aug 1956.

88. Secret file EGD 81/150/01, Part C, 1954–56, item 170, Confidential Circular 967/56, 6 Sep 1956.

89. Ibid., items 177 and 176, letter of 26 Sep 1956 in reply to letter of 24 Sep.

90. Ibid., item 170, Confidential Circular 967/56, para. 2(b). The assurances were given on the Committee Stage of the Bill – see Hansard, H. of C., Vol. 557, No. 201, cols 829, 830 and 838 of 27 July 1956. It is quite clear from the course of the debates that failure to give such an assurance might have prejudiced the passage of the Bill, as the Opposition could have prevented passage before the recess. Failure to implement the assurance could therefore be represented as going back on a Parliamentary commitment.

91. Secret file EGD 81/150/01, Part C, 1954–56, item 77, letter of 26 Sep 1956.

92. Ibid., item 178, letter of 5 Oct 1956.

93. Ibid., minute of 10 Oct 1956. The minute later went on to say that: 'At the present time, it seems impossible for CO and CDC to work in harmony, largely due, some would say, to the personality and attitude of the present Chairman, which are reflected in the letters we receive from the executives of the Corporation. In these circumstances, there seems very little point in replying to (178).'

94. Confidential file EGD 81/136/03, 1954–56, item 4, letter of 21 Aug 1956.

95. Ibid., item 6, letter of 6 Sep 1956.

96. Idem. The Account was created as an alternative to the proposal to write off a part of the capital losses. It was an 'outstanding issue' in the sense that the Corporation did not agree with the Government's decision over the write-off of £4 million because the Corporation felt that this would be taken by the public to mean that they were starting with a clean sheet whereas that would not be so, in its opinion, unless £8 million was written off.

97. Ibid., minute of 7 Sep 1956.

98. Ibid., minute of 9 Sep 1956.

99. Treasury file IF 580/01, Part J, p. 126, note of 21 Oct 1953.

100. Confidential file EGD 81/136/03, 1954–56, item 8, 13 Aug 1956.

101. Ibid., item 11, letter of 15 Oct 1956.

102. Treasury file IF 580/01, Part L, pp. 6–7. In a Note of 1 Nov 1954 prepared for the information of the Economic Secretary, Mr R. Maudling, it was stated that: 'The Treasury do not think that, overall, market finance is in short supply, although we are prepared to keep an open mind on the point that it may become so. If, as it has been suggested the remedy for that is to authorise Exchequer loans,

the CDC as it now exists becomes an anomaly, being a favoured organ drawing money from the Consolidated Fund at cheaper-than-market rates, adding its office expenses and salaries and lending to borrowers at higher-than-market rates.'

103. Confidential file EGD 81/136/03, 1954–56, item 11, letter of 15 Oct 1956.

104. Ibid., minute of 17 Oct 1956.

105. Ibid., minute of 17 Oct 1956.

106. Ibid., item 12, letter and enclosure of 24 Oct 1956.

107. Ibid., item 14, letter of 30 Oct 1956.

108. Ibid., minutes of 16 Nov 1956 and Note of Meeting of 14 Nov 1956; minutes of 19 Nov 1956, ibid. In a talk between Sir John Macpherson, Permanent Under-Secretary at the Colonial Office, and the Chairman on 6 Sep 1956, the latter said that 'any office boy could re-lend money at 1 per cent more than the rate at which he borrowed' and it was indulged in merely in order to cover overheads – ibid., item 9.

109. Ibid., minute of 24 Nov 1956.

110. File EGD 81/136/03, 1957–59, item 4, letter of 13 Aug 1957.

111. Ibid., item 8, letter of 10 Sep 1957.

112. Ibid., item 10, letter of 19 Dec 1957.

113. Ibid., minute of 12 Feb 1958 by the Minister of State.

114. Ibid., minute of 10 Feb 1958.

115. Ibid., item 11, Secret Memorandum on CDC 'Finance-House' Activities.

116. EA(57) 49, 17 May 1957: Loan Finance for Colonial Development – Memorandum submitted by the Secretary of State for the Colonies to the Economic Policy Committee.

117. Idem, pp. 5–7.

118. EA(57) 14th Meeting, 29 May 1957.

119. C(57) 130, 30 May 1957.

120. CC44(57), 4 June 1957, p. 4. The Commonwealth Secretary was invited, in consultation with the Chancellor of the Exchequer and the Colonial Secretary, to prepare a draft White Paper on the contribution made by the United Kingdom to Commonwealth development. The White Paper was published in July 1957 as Cmnd 237.

121. File EGD 81/136/03, 1957–59, item 11, Secret Memorandum on CDC 'Finance-House' Activities.

122. Ibid., item 10, as was argued by the General Manager of CDC in his letter of 19 Dec 1957.

123. File EGD 81/136/03, 1957–59, minutes of Oct–Dec 1958 and Feb 1959.

124. Secret file EGD 81/151/04, 1954–56, item 2, minute of 16 July 1956.

125. Ibid., item 3, letter of 20 July 1956 from the Chairman to the Secretary of State.

126. Ibid., minute of 1 Mar 1957 by Sir Hilton Poynton.

127. Ibid., Future Capital Requirements of CDC, para. 15(ii).

128. Secret file EGD 81/241/01, 1954–56, item 3, minute of 26 June 1956 by the Parliamentary Under-Secretary of State to Sir Hilton Poynton.

129. Ibid., item 5, minute of 28 June 1956 by the Parliamentary Under-Secretary of State to the Secretary of State.

130. Ibid., item 14, letter and enclosure of 15 Aug 1956 from the Financial Secretary to the Parliamentary Under-Secretary. The phrases quoted were from the Rules Governing Political Activities of Members of Boards of Nationalised Industries, as stated by Lord Addison in the House of Lords on 21 March 1951.

131. Ibid., item 18, letter and enclosure of 19 Sep 1956 from the Chairman to the Secretary of State.

132. Secret file EGD 81/241/01, 1957–59, item 1, note of a meeting on 14 Feb 1957.

133. Ibid., item 5, minute of 18 July 1957 from the Secretary of State for Commonwealth Relations to the Secretary of State for the Colonies.

134. Ibid., item 30, handwritten letter of 6 Aug 1957 from the Chairman to the Secretary of State.

135. Ibid., item 33, minute of 2 Sep 1957 from the Secretary of State to the Prime Minister, Mr H. Macmillan. The Prime Minister replied 'I suppose this is the best apology that you can expect from old Wuthering Height. H.M.' – item 40 in ibid.

136. Ibid., item 71, letter and enclosure of 8 Apr 1959 from the Secretary of State to the Chairman of CDC. The term of Lord Reith's appointment had ended on 31 Mar 1959, and his Deputy Chairman was appointed Chairman. Lord Reith was unwilling, after the Prime Minister's invitation to Sir N. Hume was made known to him, to talk to Hume, Sir H. Beaver or Mr W. Rendell – Minute by the Secretary of State of 20 Mar 1959 on his talk with Sir N. Hume: item 22 in EGD 81/69/01, 1957–59. Lord Reith's last act at the CDC was to direct that his chair be taken into the garden of 33 Hill Street and burnt.

137. Secret file EGD 81/241/01, 1954–56, item 20, letter of 16 Nov 1956 from the Secretary of State to the Lord President of the Council. The Secretary of State went on to say that he did not want 'to start a major upset' with the Chairman, presumably because he had already been reappointed. See the statement by the Secretary of State to the Chairman on 23 Nov 1956 – item 4 in Confidential file EGD 81/69/01, 1954–56.

138. Secret file EGD 81/151/04, 1957–59, minute of 1 May 1957.

139. Ibid., item 8, letter of 28 June 1957.

140. Ibid., item 7, letter and enclosure of 17 June 1957 from the Chairman to the Minister of State. As a result of discussions by officials with CDC officials one minuted: 'I think our general feeling was that £30 million was too little, and would too severely restrict the CDC's ability to take advantage of opportunities for worthwhile projects and for bringing potentially large existing projects to fruition. Whether this point would, in practice, be met by increasing the borrowing limit to £150 million is perhaps open to doubt, but if £30 million is the most that can be afforded as regards Exchequer advances I think it would be an acceptable palliative'. – Minute of 18 July 1957, in ibid.

141. Ibid., item 11, EA(57) 94 of 19 July 1957: Memorandum by the Secretary of State: The Borrowing Powers of CDC.

142. Ibid., item 16, EA(57) 21st Meeting, 22 July 1957.

143. Secret file EGD 81/012, 1954–56, minute of 19 Apr 1956 by Sir Hilton Poynton.

144. Ibid., minute of 2 May 1956.

145. Ibid., minutes of 2, 3 and 4 May.

146. Ibid., minute of 4 May 1956 by Sir Hilton Poynton.

147. Ibid., minute of 10 May 1956 by the Secretary of State.

148. Ibid., item 7, letter of 30 Aug 1956 from the Secretary of State to the Chairman.

149. Ibid., item 11, minute of 8 Sep 1956 by Sir J. Macpherson.

150. Ibid., item 14, minute of 20 Aug 1956 and note for the Secretary of State's talk with the Chairman. The Chairman had already suggested a change of name because of the sensitivity of some territories to the word 'Colonial', and it was hoped to change the name to 'Overseas Development Corporation' when a suitable legislative opportunity presented itself, because CDC would be operating outside the Colonies once territories in which it had projects changed their status – item 22 in ibid.

151. H. of C. Deb., Vol. 560, col. 768, 13 Nov 1956, quoted in note for the Secretary of State's talk with the Chairman of the CDC; item 29 in ibid.

152. Secret file EGD 81/012, 1954–56, item 30, additional note for the Secretary of State's meeting.

153. Ibid., items 32 and 33, Paper handed to the Secretary of State when he spoke to the Chairman on 27 Nov 1956.

154. Ibid., item 32, para. 4.

155. Ibid., item 54, letter of 6 Dec 1956 from the Secretary of State for Commonwealth Relations to the Secretary of State for the Colonies.

156. Ibid., item 50, minute of 6 Dec 1956.

157. Ibid., minute of 6 Dec 1956 by the Permanent Under-Secretary, CRO, Sir Gilbert Laithwaite. The Secretary of State for the Colonies, according to Sir Hilton Poynton, 'after some misgivings, had finally agreed with the official view that the CDC ought *not* to continue after independence' – see note of 10 Dec 1956 by Sir Alexander Johnston at pp. 236–7 in Treasury file IF 580/01, Part L. The intended formation of the CDFC was announced at the time of the Commonwealth Economic Conference held at Ottawa in Dec 1952. It was incorporated on 24 Mar 1953 as a public company.

158. Ibid., minute of 12 Dec 1956.

159. H. of C. Deb., Vol. 562, cols 231–42, 11 Dec 1956.

160. Confidential file EGD 81/67/01, Part A, items 7 and 8, notes of meetings on 25 Jan 1957.

161. CPC(57) 2, 28 Jan 1957.

162. Idem, para. 7(iv).

163. CPC(57) 2nd Meeting, 29 Jan 1957.

164. H. of L. Deb., Vol. 201, 31 Jan 1957, cols 355–56. Lord Ogmore moved to leave out Clause 3(4).

165. CC 6(57) 7, 1 Feb 1957.

166. CPC(57) 3rd Meeting, 4 Feb 1957.

167. Secret file EGD 81/012, 1954–56, item 47, letter and enclosure of 4 Dec 1956 from the PS of the Chairman of CDC to the PS of the Secretary of State.

168. Ibid., item 49, minute of 5 Dec 1956.

169. Ibid., item 66, note of a meeting between the Secretary of State and Members of the Board of CDC held in the Colonial Office at 6.30 p.m. on 17 Dec 1956.

170. Confidential file EGD 81/67/01, Part A, 1957–59, item 12, CPC(57) 2nd Meeting of 20 Jan 1957.

171. Secret file of the Cabinet Office 10/4/63, Part 2, letter and enclosure of 16 Jan 1957 from the Permanent Under-Secretary of State, Colonial Office, to the Permanent Under-Secretary of State, CRO.

172. Ibid., minute of 21 Jan 1957 from the Permanent Under-Secretary of State to the Secretary of State for Commonwealth Relations.

173. Ibid., minute of 25 Jan 1957 by the Secretary of State for Commonwealth Relations.

174. Ibid. A copy was sent to the Prime Minister on 12 Feb 1957 by the Secretary of State. The paper was entitled 'Commonwealth Development Policy'.

175. Ibid., minute of 12 Feb 1957 from the Prime Minister, Mr Macmillan, to the Secretary of State for Commonwealth Relations, Lord Home.

176. Ibid., letter of 6 Mar 1957 from Sir Hilton Poynton with Proposals for Reorganisation and Adjustment of Whitehall machinery to enable Colonial Office Advisory and Technical Service to be made available to newly independent Commonwealth countries.

177. Ibid., note of 14 Mar 1957 to Sir Norman Brook on Commonwealth Economic Development. The CCED was inter-departmental under the chairmanship of the Minister of State for Colonial Affairs, Lord Perth.

178. Ibid., paper by the Parliamentary Under-Secretary for Commonwealth Relations, Mr C. Alport.

179. Ibid., note of 14 March 1957 to Sir Norman Brook.

180. Confidential file EGD 81/67/01, Part B, 1957–59, item 42, CED(57) 22 of 28 Mar 1957: Note by the Colonial Office: 'Future Role of the CDC in the field of Colonial Development'.

181. Secret file of the Cabinet Office 10/4/63, Part 2, draft Report of CCED, para. 53.

182. CC 44(57) 1, 4 June 1957.

183. Confidential file EGD 81/67/01, Part B, 1957–59, item 55, Federation of Malaya Independence Bill: Brief on the position of the CDC, para. 88–16.

184. H. of L. Deb., Vol. 201, col. 428, 5 Feb 1957.

185. Confidential file EGD 81/67/01, Part B, 1957–59, item 52, note of a meeting held on 20 June 1957.

186. Ibid., item 58, Restricted Telegram No. 455 of 2 July 1957 from the Secretary of State to the High Commissioner for the Federation of Malaya.

187. Confidential file EGD 81/150/01, Part A, 1957–59, minute of 18 Oct 1957.

188. Ibid., item 50, minute of 26 Nov 1957 by the Chief Whip, Mr E. Heath, to the Minister of State for Colonial Affairs.

189. Ibid., minute of 12 Dec 1957.

190. Ibid., minute of 18 Oct 1957.

191. H. of C. Deb., Vol. 581, col. 228, 28 Jan 1958.

192. Idem, col. 273.

193. H. of C. Deb., Vol. 581, col. 1296, 5 Feb 1958.

194. Secret file EGD 81/150/02, 1957–59, item 2, letter of 13 Feb 1958.

195. Ibid., item 3, letter of 18 Feb 1958.

196. Ibid., item 29, letter of 12 Nov 1958.

197. Ibid., item 42, letter of 23 Jan 1959 from the Secretary of State to Mr D. Tilney, MP.

198. File EGD 81/228/01, 1957–59, item 2, minute of 7 August 1957.

199. Ibid., item 4, letter of 15 Aug 1957.

200. Ibid., item 7, letter of 26 Aug 1957.

201. Ibid., item 10, letter of 19 Dec 1957.

202. Ibid., item 17, letter of 5 Aug 1958.

203. File EGD 81/228/01, 1960–62: a minute of 29 Dec 1960 suggested that the Treasury view was then fairly favourable to housing projects 'because the CDC's money is well secured and an economic return may be expected'.

204. Ibid., item 2, letter of 17 Apr 1961.

205. Ibid., item 4, letter of 25 May 1961.

206. Confidential file EGD 81/3/05, 1960–62, minute of 25 May 1960.

207. Ibid., item 3, letter and enclosure of 11 Mar 1960, from Ministry of Finance, Lusaka.

208. Ibid., item 22, letter of 14 June 1961.

209. Ibid., item 16, letter of 12 Apr 1961. It was, in effect, a finance house loan to the Government of Northern Rhodesia.

210. File EGD 81/38/05, 1960–62, item 15, sanctioned on 17 May 1961.

211. Confidential file WID 20/224/2, item 6, sanctioned 31 Oct 1963. The scheme was one for providing low-cost housing in Jamaica.

6 The Colonial Development Corporation: Assessment and Reorganisation, 1957–1965

1. THE CDC'S CAPITAL STRUCTURE, 1957–1959

The appropriateness or, rather, inappropriateness of the capital structure of the CDC was a perennial issue. All three of the authorities concerned – the Treasury, the Colonial Office and, of course, the CDC, particularly under the chairmanship of Lord Reith – acknowledged, if sometimes only to themselves, that changes were inevitable. They differed on the kind of changes and the timing of those changes. Early internal Treasury views may be gleaned from the following examples. The first occurred after the receipt of the Secretary of State's letter of 25 February 1952, which dealt with two questions: (a) the amount of information to be supplied by the CDC in its applications for approval of any schemes, and (b) what was to be done about the CDC's 'bad debts'. On the second question, it was 'admitted that the Corporation has had a difficult, perhaps even an impossible, task assigned to it, of supplying risk capital to territories and ventures where private risk capital is not available, and of breaking even in its overall accounts. The original conception may have been at fault. But there is no evidence that a radical revision of the Corporation's Charter is necessary at this stage.'[1] The Chancellor, Mr R. A. Butler, duly postponed action 'to a rather later date'.[2]

The second example came some two years later, in May 1954, though the time for a radical decision was still not thought to have arrived:

We have perhaps all been rather too inclined to expect to get too quick results from the CDC 'experiment' – an 'experiment in

financing' it certainly is. It has now been going on for seven years. Of
these, the locusts certainly ate five but they have been eating
progressively less in the last two years. I could not agree with the
Corporation on its present showing that it will be able to accomplish
its aim but I think we have to let this instrument of finance run on
very much as it is doing for, I hazard, two years more.[3]

It was, however, not until December 1957 that a definite view was
taken, and this provides the third example of the Treasury's thinking.
At a meeting of the Minister of State for Colonial Affairs, Lord Perth,
and senior officials of the Treasury and the Colonial Office, the
Financial Secretary to the Treasury, Mr Enoch Powell, who was in the
chair, argued that there was, in fact, no middle band between the two
fields of Colonial development, namely the profitable, which would be
undertaken by private enterprise, and the non-profitable, which
would be a matter for Governments. This being so, he felt that it would
be well to vote outright all monies for Colonial development and to
accept that the conception of an intermediate field of activity had
broken down. The natural conclusion of this line of thought was that
steps should be taken forthwith to liquidate the CDC.[4] In a letter of 21
November 1957 to the Minister of State, the Financial Secretary to the
Treasury recognised that before there could be a move to Votes instead
of 'the subterfuge of unrepayable or interest-free loans' there was a
need on the part of Conservatives of 'a *katharsis* of all the humbug we
have talked and allowed to be talked since the War'. However, it was
decided to set up an inter-departmental Working Party to consider the
whole question of future policy in regard to Colonial development. In
a note of a year later – and this is the fourth and final example of the
Treasury's views – it was admitted that there was no prospect of the
Corporation breaking even, over a period of time, and 'that we must
expect heavy deficits to mount up in the 1960s. The position is indeed
deteriorating every day. . . .'[5] Four courses of action were examined.
The first, which was favoured by the Treasury, was to confine the
Corporation to the management of existing enterprises and to provide
no further new capital. The second, which the Minister of State for
Colonial Affairs advocated, was to reconstitute the Corporation on the
basis of equity capital. The third involved the admission that the CDC
could not operate in the marginal field unless interest was provided for
its commercial enterprises at the rate of around 2 to $2\frac{1}{2}$ per cent. The
fourth course was to accept the need, in time, to bail the CDC out of its
financial difficulties by special action but, in the meantime, to take no
action. It was realised that none of these courses was free from
objection.

Until 1957, in fact, the possibility of a radical reorganisation of the CDC's capital structure had not been seriously considered. The interest waiver, granted in 1953–54, and the offer of a partial capital write-off of early losses stemmed not from a conviction that such a reorganisation was called for, but, rather, from the 'new deal' atmosphere that followed Lord Reith's appointment as chairman. Subsequently, the attitude of the Treasury and of the Colonial Office towards suggestions seeking either equity capital or a complete write-off of the Special Losses Account was that, unless and until the Corporation was unable to meet its obligations under the break-even section of the 1948 Act, there was no problem to consider. The Corporation had, however, meantime been assured that, if it became unable to repay capital to the Exchequer, further advance would be made to enable it to do so. That explains why, when the Secretary of State and the Chairman discussed in November 1956[6] matters of mutual concern, they did not talk about the eleven, mainly financial, points which the Chairman had said were 'outstanding between CDC and CO'.[7] There was no immediate problem. The eleven points were (1) Special Losses Account; (2) revival of the CDC application for cancellation of capital lost in abandoned projects; (3) identification of abandoned projects and method of calculating interest waived in accordance with the ORD Act, 1954; (4) interest waiver on reborrowings to meet capital repayments on abandoned projects not covered by eventual agreement on either (1) or (2); (5) revision of capital sanction for abandoned projects and other projects where original intention had been substantially changed; (6) recalculation of long-term annuities involving withdrawal of initial interest-free period; (7) alleged CDC obligation to charge capital portion of long-term annuities as an expense in annual profit and loss account; (8) basis for fixing interest rates on CO advances; (9) basis for fixing interest rates on postponed drawings by Kenya Government and Southern Rhodesia Government against housing loans, if ruling rates were higher when the ban was lifted than the rates effective when advances were suspended at CO's request; (10) the CDC application to raise ceiling above £100 million; (11) change of Corporation's name.

It was only when the future capital requirements of the Corporation came to be considered in 1957, and the Corporation began to produce tentative estimate of future revenue and expenditure, that the capital structure became a matter of serious consideration. Even then, there was no firm evidence of any imminent inability on the part of the Corporation to meet its obligation under the 'break-even' rule. So the case for a revision rested on more general grounds. These included, first, the argument that the Treasury advances at fixed rates of interest were unsuitable for financing commercial-type development of a marginal character, as no buffer was provided against early losses, nor any resources available for investigations or pilot schemes and, therefore, the Corporation needed some equity capital. Secondly, it was argued that the CDC could be embarrassed by increases in interest rates, as the capital that was sanctioned was advanced as it was needed, with the result that later instalments might carry a somewhat higher interest rate than earlier instalments. Thirdly, the CDC wished to have the whole £8 million that it estimated had been lost in early schemes, on which interest was payable, written off or, at least, the instalments of the capital repayment deferred until such time as the Corporation could reasonably be expected to pay them.

In a memorandum on the capital structure of the CDC,[8] the Colonial Office emphasised that the magnitude of the CDC's task in meeting its interest and capital repayment obligations was partly concealed in the 'fructification period', which meant that no interest was payable on long-term loans for the first seven years. The interest deferred during this grace period was charged on a compound basis and included in the annuities, which began with the eighth year and covered interest and repayment of capital by means of 33 equated annuities. The fructification period was a way in which the Treasury paid the annual deficits of the CDC or, as in 1955 and 1956, enabled the Corporation to show a surplus which would, under ordinary commercial practice, have been a deficit. The memorandum concluded that 'the continued working of the fructification period can only lead to progressively greater distortions as the years go by. It is, in fact, virtually impossible to judge under the present structure what the true financial position of the CDC is at any particular time. Moreover, it is inappropriate in the case of straight loans, which now account for £35 million.'[9] According to the estimates in the memorandum, interest deferred through the fructification period would rise from £9.3 million in 1958 to £31 million by 1967 on the basis of the £100 million ceiling.

Quite apart from the possibility that the CDC might over the next ten years be unable to meet its commitments on the existing basis, it was urged that the existing financial structure, coupled with high interest rates and the need to service dead capital, inhibited the Corporation from undertaking the tasks it was intended to perform, viz. direct development in the 'gap' between private enterprise and government activity. Instead of relieving the CDC of some of its burdens, it was recommended that there should be a major re-organisation of the capital structure by dividing the capital into

(a) loan capital and (b) equity capital. The former would be used for lending for a fixed period by the CDC as a finance house, and bear interest from the date of advance, while the latter would be advanced to the CDC in the form of non-interest-bearing bonds, which would be repayable by the CDC only when it was in the same financial position as an ordinary company would be before declaring a dividend. The money was to be used for equity investments, expenditure on investigations and some direct investment projects. The fructification period was to have no place in this new structure.

The memorandum was submitted to the Treasury and discussed at the meeting of 9 December 1957, when it was decided to set up an Inter-departmental Working Party to consider the whole question of the future policy in relation to United Kingdom Government finance for Colonial development. A special sub-committee of the Working Party was set up to consider the future of the CDC and, at its first meeting on 16 April 1958, the Treasury representatives proposed that, in the first place, consideration should be given to the role which the CDC was to play in Colonial development.[10] The Colonial Office accordingly prepared a memorandum in which it contended that there were, after several failures, still a number of substantial continuing projects of the 'gap' type, including Usutu Forests, Fort George Hotel, Kulai Oil Palm Estate, Swaziland Irrigation Scheme, Mostyn Estates, Borneo Abaca, Vipya Tung and Kasungu Tobacco, which could turn out to be both useful and profitable.[11] Thus, it was claimed that the 'gap' existed, though it was not as originally conceived, that is in areas where private enterprise would not venture in any circumstances. Instead, it was thought of as comprising a much wider and more diverse category of commercial-type projects which private enterprise, and occasionally statutory bodies, were unable, or reluctant, to tackle on their own because either capital was lacking or the total amount of capital required for the project was more than they were prepared to invest, e.g. the investment of German capital in Tanganyika through the proposed development consortium, and the W. R. Grace & Co. project in Trinidad where the CDC's participation was regarded as essential by US shareholders. There was also a gap caused by political apprehensions regarding emergent territories so that either only the CDC was prepared to go in or private enterprise would only go in with the CDC. The tendency was for 'mixed enterprise' projects to increase, though old style 'gap' projects still turned up occasionally, as with Mostyn Estates, where the CDC was growing oil palms, a crop which takes 13 years to mature. Under existing policy, finance house activities were being reduced.

At the subsequent meeting of the Working Party, it was agreed that (a) it was unrealistic for the Corporation both to be expected to operate in the 'gap' and also to break even, taking one year with another; (b) there was a fundamental difference between the CDC and the CDFC in that the CDC normally expected to be involved in the management of any enterprise in which it invested but the CDFC did not and, therefore, there was no simple duplication in so far as both were concerned with 'mixed enterprises'; (c) that the CDC should not be restricted to 'mixed enterprises' as 'gap' projects would occasionally arise, and it would also sometimes be useful for the CDC to make a loan to a statutory body; (d) that mixed enterprises would normally be profitable within a reasonable period of time, though realistic forecasts of the Corporation's probable future financial position could not be made by the Colonial Office on the basis of existing information; and (e) that the Corporation should be invited to provide forecasts of revenue and expenditure over the next few years for the consideration of the Working Party.

The tables produced by the CDC showed that a surplus was expected on the annual profit and loss account until 1966 and, by that time, there would be a credit balance on the profit and loss account which would, from a commercial accounting point of view, keep them going for a few more years, though if interest were to be paid on half the new borrowings immediately, the CDC would go into the red in 1964.[12] In other words, while there was not an immediate problem, the trend was clearly unfavourable and would be worsened by a reduction in the fructification period. The only internal possibility of an improvement was the receipt of substantial capital gains from some of the existing investments. The Treasury, in its memorandum, argued that it was not right to provide the CDC with what turned out to be grant money for its commercial ventures, which, as a group, were not of sufficiently high priority.[13] So it wished to provide (i) no further grant money for the CDC's direct investment ventures; and (ii) any further funds for basic development by way of fixed-interest loans to Governments and statutory bodies on a direct Exchequer basis. The CDC should, it was contended, concentrate on managing existing ventures whose disposal, or retention, should in due course be considered. Actually, the Colonial Office envisaged the mixed enterprises that it regarded as the CDC's main concern as profitable ventures, although they were not expected to be alone able to keep the CDC solvent.[14] It was agreed that, if the Corporation did not exist, it would not then be created. However, the Colonial Office did not agree that it should, therefore, be terminated as it doubted whether public and political opinion could be persuaded that the CDC was basically a nonsense and should be abolished. As the memorandum said: 'Better Banquo than Banquo's ghost', as the CDC had become a symbol of post-war policy.[15] The Colonial Office repeated its view that there was no alternative to a radical reorganisation of the CDC's capital structure in the manner previously proposed. Nor was it considered feasible to appoint a new Chairman until the main policy was settled. Also, there was pressure from both sides in the House of Lords for capital reconstruction.[16]

At a meeting between the Financial Secretary, Mr J. Simon, and the Minister of State, Lord Perth, with officials, on 20 November 1958 the Treasury's 'four courses' paper was discussed, and it was agreed that the two Departments should work out a programme for special action when the need arose.[17] But, at a further meeting, the Financial Secretary said he had come to the view that there was no remunerative field for the CDC to operate in and the policy should be to liquidate the risk side of the business but to keep the public utility loan side going.[18] This view was not accepted by the Minister of State, and, after further discussion, it was agreed that an enquiry should be undertaken to decide whether there was a role for the CDC.[19] The Chancellor, Mr D. Heathcoat Amory, asked the Financial Secretary to proceed, and it was agreed between the Treasury and the Colonial Office that the terms of reference should be as follows: 'To examine the functions of the CDC within its existing statutory framework; to consider whether any change in its financial structure is required; and to make recommendations.'[20]

Lord Sinclair of Cleeve agreed to act as Chairman of the enquiry, and Sir Archibald Forbes and Sir Harold Howitt agreed to serve as the other members. (Lord Sinclair of Cleeve, KCB, KBE, 66, was President of the Imperial Tobacco Company and a former President of the Federation of British Industries. Sir Archibald Forbes, CBE, 56, was chairman of the Central Mining and Investment Corporation and another former President of the FBI. Sir Harold Howitt, CBE, DSO, MC, 72, a chartered accountant, was chairman of Messrs Ashwell and Nesbit.) After reporting the Secretary of State's announcement of the enquiry to the House of Commons on the previous day, *The Times* of 9 April 1959 went on to say that

The appointment of this committee is evidently a belated response to the complaints repeatedly made by Lord Reith, chairman of the CDC until last week, about the unsuitable character of the Corporation's capital. The Corporation's annual report a year ago said that the Board had 'repeatedly submitted and urged that financing of oversea risk-bearing projects solely by repayable loan capital is woefully unsound' and that this feature of the capital structure was 'in effect and in fact a financial nonsense'. The Government had recognised at least the possibility that there might be some truth in all these strictures.

11. THE SINCLAIR REPORT, 1959

The *Report of the Committee of Enquiry into the Financial Structure of the Colonial Development Corporation* was submitted to the Secretary of State by the Committee's chairman, Lord Sinclair of Cleeve, on 22 July 1959[21] and was published two months later as Cmnd 786. The Committee interpreted its main purpose as being to determine whether the existing financial structure was suited to the fulfilment of the obligations made on the Corporation and, if not, how it should be changed. No opinion was expressed on the relative value of the various activities undertaken by the CDC in the light of experience over eleven years. It simply took the CDC's own forecast of net profits and losses over the whole field on the basis of existing projects. This showed that, as things were going, there would undoubtedly be losses.

It was pointed out that between 1948 and October 1960 the CDC's area of operations would have contracted by 26 per cent from 1.9 million square miles to 1.4 million square miles, with a population reduction from 86 million to 41 million, owing to the independence of Ghana, Malaya and Nigeria in that period. Over the same period, large amounts of money had been, and would continue to be, applied to Colonial economic development from sources other than the CDC. The figures quoted are shown in Table 6.1.

TABLE 6.1 Funds available for Colonial Development,
1946–1958

	($£$ million)
CDC expenditure, 1948–58	64
CD & W expenditure, 1946–58	155
London Market Loans, 1946–57	187
IBRD Loans, 1946–57	$13\frac{1}{2}$
Local Government Resources, 1946–57	600
External Private Enterprise, 1946–57 (estimate)	900
Total from sources other than the CDC	$1,855\frac{1}{2}$

Looking ahead, the CD & W (Amendment) Act, 1959, provided for the next five years, excluding the Malta dockyard and Nigeria, £25 million a year in CD & W grants and a total of £100 million in Exchequer loans, while independent Commonwealth countries were eligible to receive Commonwealth Assistance loans. So, in the period 1946–1957/58, the CDC's expenditure of £64 million represented just over 3 per cent of total expenditure on development and less than 5 per cent of the total external funds flowing into the Colonies. The Committee went on to note that there were still considerable underdeveloped territories in the Colonies, so that the £40–50 million available to the CDC for further borrowings was not large in relation to the need that existed. However, while the Colonial Office agreed that the need was large, it was felt that the requirement was for basic development, such as in communications, irrigation and education, which it was not the function of the CDC, whose contribution to Colonial development had in any case been marginal, to provide.[22] With the limitations on straight loans, the contribution was expected to be even less relevant in future to the needs of the Colonies.

The rest of Part I of the Report was concerned (a) to trace all changes in direction from direct projects, with many costly failures, to Government-guaranteed loans and, from 1956 onwards, the partnership arrangements with private enterprise or Governments; (b) to show the CDC's financial obligations under the Act; and (c) to deal with the so-called Special Losses, arising from wholly abandoned projects on which interest payments had been waived. A total of £6.1 million of long-term finance and £0.5 million of medium-term finance was involved, and that total of £6.6 million was the amount that the Committee proposed should be converted into 'C' Stock. The Report wrongly stated the amount to be £7.1 million. These losses should be distinguished from the CDC's own Special Losses Account referred to earlier, which included items on which interest payments had not been waived, such as over-capitalisation.

Part II of the Report was concerned with discussion and recommendations. The Committee asked the CDC to submit estimates, relating to existing commitments only, of profit and loss accounts and cash receipts and payments for the years 1959–78, so that it might assess the working of the existing financial structure. The tentative nature of the estimates[23] was emphasised, and rightly so, as no allowance was made for bad debts or abandoned projects. The estimated profit and loss account[24] showed what the Committee described as the 'hopelessness of the outlook' in 1978, with total indebtedness to the Exchequer of £62 million as outstanding borrowing and £19 million as unpaid fructification interest, with a rising deficit on both profit and loss and on capital accounts. It was concluded that the CDC could not both carry out the purposes described in Sections 1 and 2 of the ORD Act, 1959, and meet the financial obligations laid down in Sections 14, 15 and 16 of the Act: either the purposes or the obligations, or both, had to be varied. It was proposed that three kinds of stock would be created, as follows: (i) Borrowing by the CDC for the purpose of finance house business should be in the form of 'A' Stock, on which interest would be payable from the date of issue and the capital repaid according to the redemption arrangements between the CDC and its borrowers; (ii) Borrowings for any other purpose, such as direct projects and equity participation, should be in the form of 'B' Stock, on which a maximum of 5 per cent interest, non-cumulative, would be payable, though the payment of interest and redemption of capital would depend on the results; and (iii) The Special Losses and unpaid 'fructification' interest at 1 January 1959 would be covered by 'C' Stock, on which no interest would be payable and redemption would only operate as and when the whole of the 'B' Stock had been repaid. As at 31 January 1959 the totals of the three kinds of stock would be respectively £17.9 million, £36.3 million and £15.5 million, giving a total of £69.7 million. The nub of these proposals was the conversion of £36.3 million of the Corporation's indebtedness on existing projects into equity-type 'B' Stock. As finance house business was restricted and special losses were fixed, the only significant change could come in the equity-type 'B' Stock.

From the Colonial Office point of view, the main objection was that it would no longer be necessary for the Corporation to establish the likely ability of a project to service and, eventually, to repay its capital. In order to limit the rate of drawing of equity capital, the Colonial Office and the Treasury considered the possibility of maintaining a fairly constant ratio between 'A' Stock and 'B' Stock issues, but that involved relaxing the restrictions on finance house business, for which it was felt the CDC was not set up, and for which the borrower paid unnecessarily high rates because of the CDC's overheads and profit margins. The Treasury was opposed to the 'B' Stock conception because it amounted to an annual, unpredictable, uncontrollable but concealed subsidy. Notwithstanding the Committee's endorsement of the claim of the CDC that it was 'sui generis',[25] the Treasury maintained that it would create an impossible precedent for the nationalised industries. It was felt essential that any subsidy should be overt, rather than concealed, and be handled in a manner likely to minimise repercussions elsewhere. The least objectionable course was to supply above-the-line finance, i.e. voted annually, after a project had been examined and the terms settled *ad hoc*.[26] In the view of the Colonial Office such a course of action would mean the end of the CDC as an independent, quasi-commercial organisation. The Treasury was told that it would be less unacceptable if the subsidy were provided by an annual vote in arrears to cover the actual deficit of the previous year. The Treasury reacted to the suggestion in the same terms as it had to the 'B' Stock conception itself.[27]

III. DEPARTMENTAL DISCUSSIONS, 1959

The Colonial Office felt that the Report showed that the theory that there was available to the CDC a 'gap' type of project, which would pay its way though the rate of profit was below normal commercial rates, should be finally abandoned. In fact, it seemed to the Office in 1959 rather as the former Secretary of State, Mr Oliver Lyttelton, now Lord Chandos, had believed in 1951, that is that experience had shown that no single Board could expect to be competent to deal adequately with the variety of activities in which the Corporation was engaged. The consequent weight of overhead expenditure did not reflect the quality of the service rendered. Two other problems had proved intractable over the years. In the first place, there was no Whitehall control over the direction of investment by the CDC. It was considered that there had been relative over-investment in the Central African and Far Eastern areas, apart from the Western Pacific area and Nyasaland which were thought to need investment most, and under-investment in West Africa and the smaller territories, including Mauritius, the Solomon Islands and the Seychelles. However, the Corporation was free to make its commercial judgements and the Colonial Office could not intervene. In the second place, it was felt that no political goodwill for the United Kingdom had come from the CDC's activities and, indeed, as in the West Indies, they had sometimes been the cause of friction and bad feeling.

It was thought that in the cases of those Colonies aspiring to early independence and of those less politically advanced the need was not for a few hundred acres of plantations, often unprofitable, such as Kasungu Tobacco in Nyasaland, Tanganyika Wattle, Vipya Tung in Nyasaland, or for frequently unprofitable mining enterprises, such as British Guiana Goldfields,[28] Mbeya Exploration in Tanganyika or Macalder Nyanza Copper in Kenya. The need was seen to be rather for agricultural development on the pattern of the Swynnerton Plan – the five-year 'Plan to intensify the development of African Agriculture in Kenya' which was started in April 1954: it was financed by CD & W grant of £5.7 million, subsequently increased to £7.95 million. Such development should be combined with finance for basic social and economic development and, in the view of the Colonial Office, the financial resources employed by the CDC would be better used in helping to meet the basic development needs. Colonial Governments would, it was believed, favour the use of the funds as grants or loans of the CD & W-type for CD & W purposes. If the CDC were liquidated, it was estimated that, in addition to the undrawn sum of £66 million, possibly another £30 million would accrue over the years from existing investments. With the disappearance of finance house business, owing to the availability of Exchequer loans and the increasing doubts within the Office that public money should be invested in limited and usually speculative schemes, the belief grew that, on merits alone, the right course would be to close down the CDC.[29] However, such a course was regarded as politically impossible and, in any case, the CDC was seen to have a function in the mixed enterprise field, where the capital requirements were sometimes too large for a private enterprise alone or the political climate was not sufficiently attractive, or both.[30] The Secretary of State, Mr Iain Macleod, accepted the logic of the official view but the practicality of the advice of the Minister of State, feeling that the CDC was likely to be continued, partly because of the mystique which surrounded it and partly because it had a real, though limited, job to perform on the lines suggested by the Minister, who was accordingly asked to put up detailed proposals.[31] Lord Sinclair felt that any further enquiry to assess projects and organisation would be both time-consuming and unsettling, and the important thing was to get the capital structure right.[32] This view was thought to be illogical, and was regretted in the Office.[33] However, the Minister, at an Office meeting, stated that the problem should be approached on the basis that the CDC was 'sui generis', and that possible lines of action should not be excluded because of supposed repercussions on the nationalised industries. It was decided that further study should be given to the problem on the basis that some direct projects would have to be allowed, and that a financial reorganisation broadly on the lines of the Sinclair Report would be needed.[34]

A paper was prepared and a copy sent to the Financial Secretary to the Treasury, Sir Edward Boyle.[35] The paper proposed that, in future, the CDC should act purely and simply as a lending institution; that its current projects should be tidied up, by means of the writing-off of capital, to the extent necessary to make them viable. Also, as the CDC would, in any case, have existing equity investments, it would be politically impossible to exclude a restricted amount of equity-type investments, totalling around £7.5 million, of 'B'-type finance and the conditions for doing so were suggested in a second paper. It was proposed that HMG should be free to take account not only of the commercial attractions of a project, but also of its own assessment of the political and economic requirements of the territory concerned. The problem of defining direct projects was mentioned, but the only kind of such projects alluded to were wholly-owned subsidiaries.

Over the years, the CDC occasioned several marathons of discussions being run both within and between Departments and itself, beginning with that over the so-called Concordat. The receipt by the Financial Secretary to the Treasury of the letter of 23 December 1959 started a marathon which outran all previous ones, filling, by the time the Secretary of State for the Colonies announced on 27 April 1961 the agreed changes in the financial liabilities of the CDC, half a dozen Treasury files and as many Colonial Office files. In the end, the Chancellor of the Exchequer and the Secretary of State had been unable to agree on the amount of indebtedness to the Exchequer for past borrowings which should be written off. The Colonial Office took the view that the Corporation needed to be relieved of about £18 million, but the Treasury was unwilling to waive more than £7–9 million. The Prime Minister, Mr H. Macmillan, considered that the issue was essentially one for an individual judgement, which he would have given himself had he not been leaving for the West Indies. He asked the Lord Chancellor, Viscount Kilmuir, to arbitrate on his behalf.[36] The difference was resolved in favour of the Colonial Office.[37] This was formally confirmed on behalf of the Cabinet as a whole by the Home Secretary, Mr R. A. Butler, who was in charge of the Government, and the Chancellor and the Secretary of State were notified accordingly.

iv. MINISTERIAL DISCUSSIONS AND DECISIONS, 1960

On 27 January 1960, the Chancellor of the Exchequer, Mr D. Heathcoat Amory, replied to the letter from the Minister of State of 23 December 1959.[38] He declared his firm opposition to lending the CDC any more money for projects of an equity type, adding, for good measure, that he believed there was a very strong case for winding up the organisation. He recognised that the political objections to the latter course, although he did not think they were overriding, He believed they needed careful examination and suggested that should be made by an *ad hoc* meeting of Ministers under the chairmanship of the Home Secretary. The Secretary of State, Mr Iain Macleod, was reminded of the proposal in a letter of 18 February 1960 from the Chancellor and straightway invited the Secretary of State for Commonwealth Relations, the Earl of Home, to take part, and the Home Secretary, Mr R. A. Butler, to take the chair.[39] However, the latter felt there was the need for an agreed analysis of the position before the three senior Ministers met, and suggested that the Financial Secretary, the Minister of State for Colonial Affairs and the Minister of State for Commonwealth Relations should meet for that purpose. Both the Chancellor and the Secretary of State for the Colonies felt a decision should be taken soon at a high-level Ministerial meeting on the question whether the CDC should be allowed to continue to expand within the financial limits allowed by the current Act, or whether it should be required slowly to wind up and, meanwhile, to confine itself to such of its existing enterprises as it could not sell.[40] Accordingly, a meeting was held on 17 March 1960, to consider the future of the CDC, with the Home Secretary, in the chair, and the Chancellor of the Exchequer, the Secretaries of State for the Colonies and for Commonwealth Relations, the Paymaster-General, Lord Mills, and the Chancellor of the Duchy of Lancaster, Dr Charles Hill.[41] In his Note for the meeting, the Secretary of State commented on the two courses open, namely (i) winding-up and (ii) carrying on. In respect of the first, it was acknowledged that Colonial Governments would welcome the transfer to their development projects of the unspent allocation of the CDC's capital and of repayments due to the Corporation.[42] It was also acknowledged that 'There is a mystic belief in the CDC, or something like it, which is likely to lead to a great outcry if winding-up is proposed,' and that there would be residual staffing and project problems with the result that the run-down could neither be quick nor without its own problems. Yet if the CDC was to carry on, a reconstruction of its capital was necessary, as was a new set of working rules, which should include a general ban on 'solo' projects and on engaging in an equity investment if a Colonial Government was the only partner. In any case, it was thought that equity investment should be limited to one-third of the balance of the money available for investment, i.e. to some £5–6 million. The remainder of the uncommitted £18 million should, it was suggested, be lent to statutory corporations, or other public bodies, or businesses to which the Colonial Office favoured lending on grounds of public policy. Even more important, it was contended, was the need to have a Chairman and Board who observed the spirit as well as the letter of any rules. The choice of a new Chairman depended on the decision on the future of the Corporation.

The Chancellor, in his Memorandum, held there was an overwhelming case for winding up the Corporation and diverting the funds so released 'for true development, administered by HMG'. He wished, therefore, to consider how that might be presented to Parliament and the public, so as to minimise political difficulty, for Colonial Governments would strongly support such a proposal and the Sinclair Report had shown how great a failure the Corporation had been. In a comment[43] on the Memorandum, the Secretary of State, while expressing sympathy with some of the Chancellor's arguments for winding-up, felt that such a course was not politically feasible as it would mean defeat in the Lords and considerable difficulty in the Commons. Furthermore, the CDC's results for 1959 were about to be published and would show a marked improvement over those of 1958. On the directly-operated sector of their business, which would be expected to be the least remunerative, the CDC had given figures 'purporting to show profits on capital invested rising from 1.3 per cent to 3.6 per cent in 1958 and an estimated 5.9 per cent in 1959'. Consequently, any announcement of a closure would be especially inopportune at that time, in his opinion.

At the meeting on 17 March 1960, the Chancellor accepted the view that winding-up was not politically practicable, and he proposed instead that the CDC should cease its equity investment activities, manage existing projects with a view to realising the assets as opportunity offered, and make direct loans to Colonial Governments and statutory bodies. After discussion, it was agreed that the CDC should continue in a truncated form, and that its precise functions and financial structure should be examined by officials of the Departments concerned, who would report to the three junior Ministers who, in turn, could refer the matter again to the group of senior Ministers. The final decision was reserved for the Cabinet. The Secretary of State was invited to inform the Chairman-designate, Lord Howick, that whatever the detailed arrangements ultimately agreed, no increase in the scale of the CDC's future activities could be considered.

The Working Party report[44] was considered by the three junior Ministers on 1 June 1960. On the basis of the Ministerial decisions of 17 March, it was stated in the report that the aim of policy was to make the best use of resources within the existing financial ceiling, while from a presentational point of view it was desirable, on the one hand, to keep as close as practicable to the recommendations of the Sinclair Report and, on the other, to expose losses, both actual and expected. (The Treasury's valiant attempts to avoid concealed subsidy sometimes led to curious results. It was rightly claimed by the Treasury that the interest postponed in the fructification period should itself bear interest, otherwise HMG would be out of pocket. The CDC proposed to challenge in the Courts the right to charge compound interest and the Treasury proposed prior reference to the Law Officers, which the Legal Adviser of the Colonial Office regarded as most inappropriate. Colonial Office officials felt that they should try to get simple interest agreed, but when the Treasury suggested increasing the rate of simple interest to give the same effect as compound interest the proposal was regarded as a 'nefarious idea' (*sic*). The history of the matter is to be found in EGD 81/128/03, 1957–1959, which is referred to in a minute of 23 August 1960 by Mr W. G. Boss in Secret file EGD 81/161/07, Part B, 1960–1962. It was explained once more in the letter of 16 September 1960, from Mr A. W. Taylor to Mr A. N. Galsworthy – item 75A in idem.)

The Report comprised one section, which was agreed between Departments, and another which was still a matter of controversy. The Sinclair Committee was regarded, in the Treasury particularly, as having dealt with the situation it had found as if it were a question of reconstructing an insolvent company, and recommended accordingly.[45] But the Treasury, with qualified concurrence of the Colonial Office and the Commonwealth Relations Office, felt that the problem went deeper, and could not be solved simply by a technical reconstruction of the Corporation's financial arrangements, though this might well form part of the solution. It was felt that much of the investment that the CDC had undertaken in the Colonies and High Commission Territories had been justifiable neither on commercial grounds nor by the test of social priorities, and it was necessary to avoid further losses, consistent with the Ministerial decision to continue the Corporation. This led to the recommendation that further equity investment be restricted, though Departments differed on how this was to be effected. The differences between the Departments concerned three issues: (i) whether the Corporation should be allowed to make new equity investments, or only to complete existing investments; (ii) whether steps should be taken to facilitate private borrowing by the Corporation, up to the statutory maximum of £20 million, by allowing such borrowing to rank ahead of the £30–40 million of Exchequer money that the Corporation already had locked up in equity investment; and (iii) whether the Corporation should be relieved of the obligation to repay Exchequer loans already used for equity-type investments, and any further sums that might be so used, through the issue of irredeemable loans.

The Colonial and the Commonwealth Relations Offices took the view that, if the Corporation was to continue, it should be given scope to increase its equity-type investment, to raise money from private investors and to make its balance sheet look respectable. The Treasury view,[46] in essence, was that (a) more equity-type investment would mean more losses, (b) the proposed arrangements for private borrowing would water down the security for the money advanced by the Exchequer and increase the prospective capital losses by anything up to another £20 million, and (c) waiver of capital repayment by the device of issuing irredeemable stock was wrong in principle, as the Corporation already received Exchequer loans on better terms than almost any other public concern and, if it made losses, the fact ought not to be concealed from Parliament. The chairman of the Working Party made the point that they had been considerably hampered by the lack of detailed information in the Colonial Office on the activities of the CDC.[47] He endorsed the view that, for tactical reasons, the more restricted scheme, i.e. the Treasury's, should be put to the Corporation.[48]

At the meeting of 1 June 1960[49] the junior Ministers reached agreement on two of the disputed points in the report of the Working Party. It was agreed that the CDC's total equity investment should not exceed £40 million, which allowed for some £3 million to be invested in existing projects if they could not be profitable or made realisable otherwise. As investments were realised, further equity-type investments would be permissible within the £40 million limit. It was also agreed that the CDC should be given a full explanation of the procedure to be followed for repayment of capital. The meeting asked the Financial Secretary to arrange for officials to prepare a brief for use in discussions with the CDC, and agreed to resume consideration of the outstanding points in the report of the Working Party. However, the Minister of State for Colonial Affairs did not feel that the CDC could be expected to accept two of the Treasury proposals, namely, first, the repayment of borrowings for equity-type investment by means of equal annual instalments of capital and interest over an appropriate period and, secondly, the ranking of borrowing from non-Exchequer sources below that from the Exchequer.[50] The Treasury did not feel justified in agreeing to any significant modification in the first because, if, as was generally expected, the Corporation made further losses, these should be revealed and accounted for, not concealed by giving the Corporation virtually a free hand in its accounting. If it were unable to fulfil this requirement, then the right answer was felt to be to provide for write-off of appropriate sums after review, rather than conceal the fact through accounting procedure, as happened with the fructification period. However, on the second issue, the ranking of Exchequer and non-Exchequer borrowing, a compromise was possible. When the Cabinet considered the Secretary of State's memorandum on the CDC,[51] the Chancellor expressed his willingness to accept the compromise proposed by the Secretary of State that the Treasury should decide *ad hoc* on the appropriate ranking or, alternatively, that private borrowing by the Corporation should rank after Exchequer advances for straightforward lending but before Exchequer advances when the private funds were used for equity-type investment. The Cabinet invited the Secretary of State to consider this further with the Chancellor. There was general agreement that the CDC should be allowed some freedom to undertake equity-type business.

v. THE REPAYMENT ISSUE, 1960–1961

The Cabinet expressed no view on the repayment issue. But, although the Colonial Office still firmly believed that 'the only arrangement which made sense' was 'the one we have advocated all along, i.e. that the CDC should be relieved of any fixed obligation to repay Exchequer Advances,' it was not included in the draft Note for discussion with the CDC as it was unacceptable to the Chancellor.[52] Instead, the Treasury's proposal was adopted and then counterbalanced by a suggestion that repayment might be on a sinking-fund basis. The new proposal struck the Treasury as both tactically bad in negotiating with the CDC, and objectionable in itself, for 'the principle is that Exchequer advances should be repaid, and to repay them only partially would be hardly less improper than not to repay them at all'.[53]

To anyone coming to this question afresh, it might well seem that the whole argument concerned procedures and technicalities. It needs to be considered, however, as the Treasury considered it, that is against an unsatisfactory background. For, after being permitted to write off large losses, the Corporation had built up fresh losses of over £10 million, and also got into a position in which a further £10 million was highly likely to be lost over the next few years. At the same time, owing to the permitted accounting arrangements, hardly anyone outside

Whitehall appreciated the position. A perusal of the Debate in the House of Commons on 7 July 1950 shows that one member was aware of this: see Mr Norman Pannell (Liverpool, Kirkdale) at Column 802. The point was not made in the Debate in the House of Lords on 20 July 1960 (Vol. 225, cols 516–75). Given that background, the Treasury view was that the Colonial Office proposal that Exchequer advances be made to the CDC for equity-type projects without obligation to repay 'would be a circumlocution for giving the money away',[54] and the sinking-fund alternative was suspected to mean 'that the Treasury can, if it wants, maintain in principle that the money is repayable, subject to an understanding that the question will then be put into cold storage for forty years or more'. The Chancellor of the Exchequer asked for the proposal to be omitted from the Note intended for the CDC.[55]

The Chairman of the CDC, Sir Nutcombe Hume, at a meeting with the Secretary of State, the Financial Secretary to the Treasury, and officials said he did not consider it proper for the Corporation, after twelve years' experience, to accept an obligation to repay advances for equity-type investment when it was thought unlikely they would be able to do so. Unless something less onerous was offered, he thought that the CDC might prefer to carry on under the existing arrangements.[56] This view was repeated a week later by the General Manager, who also indicated that the figures in the Sinclair Report were largely hypothetical.[57] In fact, whether because of lack of information or for some other reason, there was from the first a rather curious lack of scrutiny in Whitehall of the nature of the forecasts on which the whole Sinclair thesis depended. The first time this appears to have been stated was in December 1960 when Mr Taylor of the Treasury remarked that the financial picture presented to the Sinclair Committee had, on the CDC's admission, been a pessimistic one, and the Corporation's representatives had since expressed some optimism about future prospects. The Colonial Office agreed that the financial outlook was brighter and said the CDC would produce the figures showing their financial position by 9 December.[58] Much of the strength of the CDC in the whole debate was due to the better realisation of the nature of the forecasts than either the Treasury or the Colonial Office appear to have possessed. The point is one of some significance, and it will arise again later.

The Treasury, while it was prepared to discuss on detail, was wholly unwilling to accept the Colonial Office proposals about repayment obligations in regard to 'equity' capital,[59] and the Secretary of State felt obliged to write to the Chancellor of the Exchequer, Mr Selwyn

Lloyd, to suggest that the latter should either accept the Colonial Office proposal or the matter should be taken back to the Cabinet.[60] It was recognised that, in the light of the political aura that the Corporation had built up for itself, policy would need to be publicly explained on other grounds. Hitherto, it had been possible to say that the CDC could not expect to receive funds on better terms than any other statutory body, but this argument was becoming weaker as certain exceptions were in the offing, although the revised basis for Exchequer advances to the Post Office, namely renewable maturity loans, was not thought to be appropriate to the CDC, owing to the very wide difference between the two bodies in the use of public money. One possible answer, as an alternative to accepting the Secretary of State's 'ability-to-pay' criterion, was to accept the Chairman's offer of 18 July to pay interest after a grace period, while jibbing at the obligation to make repayments of capital where the money was in equity-type investments.[61] But it was felt that, while a 'pay-if-you-can' arrangement should be restricted, maturity loans would be no better if 'when the maturity day dawns, we find that the assets of the companies financed by the Corporation have wasted away and there is no money available to repay our loans'.[62] The Treasury was anxious both to limit possible losses by placing a ceiling on equity-type investment, and to see that, as further losses occurred, they would be brought before Parliament. The Colonial Office 'pay-as-you-can' terms made it impossible to demonstrate losses because the accounts, by hypothesis, always balanced.

The Treasury had for some time felt that the Colonial Office should put a proposal concerning reorganisation to the CDC rather than itself debate with the Treasury what was acceptable to the CDC, and refuse to put anything which it did not regard as acceptable as it stood. On 18 October 1960 the Permanent Secretary to the Treasury, Sir Frank Lee, held a meeting[63] with the Colonial Office and the CDC in which he offered (a) to substitute a system of redeemable maturity loans, with provision for a sinking fund, for the existing annuity payments; and (b) to consider the need, in particular cases, to pledge assets in order to raise private funds, even though this involved deferring the Government's claim on the Corporation's assets. The Chairman of the CDC, Sir Nutcombe Hume, thought that the Corporation might be able to meet its obligations without any appreciable change in the existing arrangements, and the CDC was invited to give further consideration to the possibility that the outlook was such that it could be demonstrated to Parliament that the Corporation stood a good chance of meeting its obligations in such circumstances.[64] But the

CDC proposed instead (i) continuing the existing system of advances 'without any appreciable change'; (ii) writing-off, or sterilising, the Losses and Liabilities Account and (iii) pledging existing assets as collateral for private loans.[65] The Colonial Office privately thought the attitude of the CDC in the face of Treasury concessions was foolish, unless the real purpose was to avoid having even an administrative ceiling placed on the proportion of its capital invested in equity-type investments – a point not mentioned by the Chairman.[66] It was thought that the CDC's new proposals involved such a radical alteration to those of the Government that it would be more practicable to meet the CDC's points by appropriate amendments to HMG's existing offer.[67] After agreeing the reply with the Colonial Office, the Permanent Secretary to the Treasury said that the CDC's proposal for 'a once and for all write-off, or at least sterilisation, of the Losses and Liabilities Account' could not be put to Ministers in full. Detailed discussions were suggested between officials.[68] Meanwhile, the Chairman-designate, Lord Howick, pressed the need for three conditions if the CDC were to have a fair chance to succeed.[69] They were that (i) whilst he accepted that Parliament should not be asked to provide the CDC with further Exchequer funds, the CDC should be enabled to undertake new projects with money released by repayments of capital, whether through the maturing of loans or through the selling of equity-type projects; (ii) the burden of the CDC's obligations, in respect of interest and capital repayment obligations, should not be so heavy that the CDC had no hope of making a profit; and (iii) there should not be an inflexible arbitrary ceiling on equity-type investments within the general financial ceilings. The official comment was that the Colonial Office should for the time being 'concentrate on defeating the Treasury' on the second point, i.e. the obligations to be placed on the CDC in relation to the payments of interest and capital on monies invested in equity-type projects, for 'If we can win our point on this, we can perhaps then leave Lord Howick in subsequent discussions with the Treasury, and ourselves to make his case for flexibility as between loans and equity-type investment.'[70] But, in essence, the Treasury wanted the CDC to admit, and show, such losses as were made, not to guarantee against loss. This came out clearly when, for example, the CDC asked for treatment interest-wise such as was received by the National Research Development Corporation (NRDC) which was said to have an interest waiver clause in its governing statute.[71] However, in fact, the power to waive interest was allowed to lapse in 1958 after a ten-year run, because it was considered inconsistent simultaneously to allow it to

borrow more money and to display a lack of confidence by providing
for it not to pay interest on the money. Meantime, interest had been
held 'in abeyance', rather than waived, and stood at the end of June
1959 at £382,000. In their latest Annual Report the NRDC stated:
'The provisions of the Development of Inventions Act, 1948, require us
to try and balance our revenue account taking one year with another
"in so far as can be done consistently with the fulfilment of their
purposes", i.e. the purposes of the Corporation's functions. It is not yet
apparent when this balance will be achieved, but the requirement is
one of our constant preoccupations.' So the difference was that the
NRDC was in the red and admitted it, while the CDC was in the red
and sought to conceal it. Incidentally, one argument the CDC used
against showing its losses was that eminent businessmen would not be
willing to be associated with a Corporation that was consistently in the
red.

Discussion between officials of the Colonial Office, the Treasury and
the CDC reverted to losses, and what should be done about them.[72]
The CDC view was, broadly, that the nature of their operations was
such that they could not yield a reasonable commercial profit, and that
they should, therefore, be granted a relaxation of the strict rigour of
Treasury advances. This view ignored the statutory obligation to make
ends meet. Also, the CDC was unwilling to accept the logic of its own
attitude, namely to make losses public in some appropriate way. It
wanted, instead, concessions which would enable it to appear to
balance its books, invest its 'profits' and give the impression that it was
a going concern in the ordinary commercial sense. This was an
internally contradictory attitude.[73]

The Treasury view was that the CDC had already lost a lot of public
money and, as far as possible, should be prevented from losing more. It
was generally recognised that there was little prospect of recouping
any of the past losses, or of putting the CDC on a paying basis, though
it was hoped to reduce the drain.[74] Colonial Office Ministers and
officials appeared not to think on the same lines as the Treasury. After
nominating a Chairman-designate, they appear to have been concerned to fit the CDC to the Chairman, and no doubt, once the
appointment had been made, this was unavoidable, for the CDC had
become a vested interest which Whitehall, in the end, had to live with.
By February, 1961, the impression had strengthened in the Treasury
that what was at issue was not so much the finding of a solution to a
difficult technical problem as the settlement of the political question of
how much should be paid, in terms of money and sacrifice of financial
regularity, to the CDC as the price of its goodwill. Unlike other

statutory bodies, the one consideration which stood in the way of the rejection of the proposal was the knowledge that the CDC was ready to stimulate troublesome debates in Parliament, and to be awkward in other ways.[75] The CDC's position is well shown by the nature of an insertion that the General Manager requested should be included in the Note of the meeting of 21 November 1960.[76] It read: 'Mr Rendell said that the CDC could not depart from its view, confirmed by the Sinclair Committee, that, in principle, it is unsound to finance solely with fixed interest capital a concern undertaking highly risky projects. However, CDC now being soundly established, it clearly is in a much better position to meet fixed obligations than it was in the early days, provided they were not too onerous.' That curious qualification led directly back to the question of 'capacity to pay'. And so the marathon proceeded.

At the end of a second meeting between the officials of the Colonial Office, the Treasury and the CDC, 23 November 1960, it was agreed that the CDC would soon put forward a paper with their proposals for the write-off, or sterilisation, of capital sums and, meanwhile, the Colonial Office and the Treasury would discuss how a waiver of interest could best be achieved.[77] The CDC requested relief to be conceded on a total of some £20 million, comprising about half in terms of 'lost' capital and the other half in 'accrued' fructification interest.[78] The justification was conspicuously absent and was asked for by the Colonial Office. When it was received,[79] the Minister of State felt that it was unlikely to justify either a final writing-off of losses or an extension of the CDC's borrowing powers by £10 million, and that CDC's desire to raise private capital could be assisted otherwise.[80] On close examination in the Treasury, it emerged that the key figures, which were in Schedule I of the justification, were 'related to what the position would be if the Corporation were *not* benefiting from the fructification arrangement'.[81] The Colonial Office was, therefore, told that a write-off, or freeze, of £20 million could not be authorised without even a show of evidence that the Corporation would not be able to meet its liabilities until at least the 1970s, i.e. for as far ahead as anyone could reasonably plan.[82] The figures submitted by the CDC could only be made to look more gloomy by revising the views hitherto taken by the CDC about the future trend of prices for rubber and other tropical products – an action the Treasury deprecated.[83] It emerged that the root of the CDC's difficulty was that, by the use of the fructification arrangement, they had put themselves into a position to declare such substantial surpluses over the following few years that no change in their methods of financing future investments would be likely for a long time to bring about any fundamental change in the picture. Extensive renegotiation of those past contracts with the Exchequer which had been unduly favourable to the CDC would have been necessary and, even so, the extent to which a write-off could be justified was limited.[84] The Treasury view was that capital irretrievably lost should be written off, but the accrued liability for interest would not at the same time be cancelled as such cancellation would release funds for use by the Corporation without Colonial Office, Treasury or Parliamentary control.[85] It was realised that a fructification period had been allowed in circumstances, namely finance house activities, where it was not justified, and the Corporation had taken advantage of it to invest in risky projects instead of making provision for the future liability.[86] This, in fact, was the initial error in the operation of the CDC, just as the presumption of the 'gap' was the initial error in the conception of the CDC. A grace period was not required for the fructification of a finance house, i.e. loan, transaction and should not have been extended. However, as the difference was not realised and the concession was extended, the funds arising should have been accumulated by the CDC instead of being used in ventures which created further losses. This point never received the attention it deserved in accounting for the alleged need for altering the initial capital structure of the Corporation.

The Chancellor, Mr Selwyn Lloyd, agreed that the Financial Secretary, Sir Edward Boyle, might negotiate with the Minister of State for Colonial Affairs, Lord Perth, on the basis that (i) there should be a capital write-off amounting to £7.2 million, (ii) one-half of any surplus in excess of (say) £1 million should be applied to repayment of the £7.2 million lost capital, and (iii) fructification arrangements should continue only in the case of equity-type investment.[87] The 'package' was offered to the Minister of State,[88] who felt it would mean that the CDC would be worse off in the short run and not improved in the long run, even though the second and third points made useful concessions.[89] He did not think, in the circumstances of the Sinclair Report and Parliamentary pressure, that 'we can properly allow the CDC to drift on towards bankruptcy, even if it will take a number of years before they are actually insolvent'.

Yet the CDC's prospective difficulties arose essentially from its use of the fructification arrangement, which generated surpluses at first and led to the risk of deficits in the 1970s. The Treasury, therefore, suggested that the terms of some of the Corporation's existing borrowing from the Exchequer should be renegotiated on an actuarially equivalent basis, so that the Corporation's contractual payments fell as evenly as was practicable over the decade of the 1960s.[90] It was also proposed that a Government statement should be made to the effect that, if, in 1970, it appeared that the Corporation could not meet its obligations, appropriate action should be taken to write them off or rephase them. However, the latter proposal was not thought to be either meaningful, as Ministers could not tie their successors, or helpful, as it merely postponed a solution.[91] It seems that the Colonial Office never doubted the reality of the alleged repayment problem, because it was apparently never clearly appreciated that the forecasts on which the Sinclair Committee judged were necessarily based on assumptions and that some, at least, of these were highly debatable.[92] The following is one indication of the margin of error in the Corporation's estimates. The CDC forecast to the Sinclair Committee in the summer of 1959 that the net profit for the year would be £600,000, yet it proved to be £1,334,286, only a few months later.[93] As the Colonial Office apparently never doubted that the forecasts made by the CDC for the Sinclair Committee would inevitably come to pass, it wanted accumulated fructification interest amounting to £10 million to be converted into non-interest-bearing stock, which would be repaid to the extent of half of any 'profits' in excess of £500,000.[94] Rather curiously, the Colonial Office took the view that the test of any new proposals should not simply be whether they provided a sufficient solution to the problem, but also whether the Treasury would be incurring additional cost to the benefit of the CDC.[95] The Treasury held that their proposals resolved the problem of phasing in the 1960s, but did not purport to look beyond 1970.

Officials thus failed to agree, and the Secretary of State for the Colonies, Mr Iain Macleod, sought of the Chancellor, mainly for political reasons, a financial reorganisation of the CDC which would give it 'at least a fighting chance of carrying on their work without accumulating an unpayable load of debt and, at the same time, enable people to see clearly how the Corporation is, in fact, doing year by year.'[96] The main difference between the Treasury and the Colonial Office was over the treatment of the accrued fructification interest amounting, as already stated, to £10 million. The importance of the point was realised by the Colonial Office only when the CDC rejected Sir Frank Lee's offer of 18 October 1960 on capital repayments. As the Secretary of State was informed in the brief prepared for his meeting with the Chancellor,

At the time when Sir Frank Lee's proposal was made, we were all under the impression, which had been created by Sir Nutcombe Hume, that the CDC's main problem was its obligation to repay the capital of the 'B' Stock equity-type project. Subsequently, the CDC officials explained to us that this was not a real problem for them, because they already have authority to reborrow from the Exchequer to the extent that they are unable at any time to meet their capital liabilities, i.e. they were able to postpone capital liabilities indefinitely by a process of re-financing. They pointed out that the core of their problem was that of meeting interest obligations in the long term. Because of this, the CDC were not prepared to accept Sir Frank Lee's proposals, and said they would prefer to carry on as before, so long as steps were taken to write off, or sterilise, the Trefgarne losses and the accumulated fructification interest to date.[97] [Reith losses of over £2 million were added subsequently.]

The Treasury view was, first, that no case had been shown for any waiver in respect of the £10 million, on which the Corporation could demonstrably meet its liabilities for as far ahead as could reasonably be foreseen; and secondly, that to waive liabilities which could be met was equivalent to a concealed subsidy, and such procedure was open to strong criticism on grounds of financial regularity.[98] Failing agreement, the Chancellor was advised that existing arrangements, though imperfect, would be better than putting fresh money into the CDC, although the Secretary of State might regard that outcome as politically indefensible. This latter was found to be so for, at the meeting with the Chancellor, he emphasised the need to satisfy both Parliament and the CDC which, he said, had changed its ways.[99] The Secretary of State revived the proposals of 19 January 1961, when the Minister of State had suggested writing off capital lost on abandoned schemes, 'sterilising' accrued fructification interest, and restricting the seven-year fructification arrangements to equity-type investments. (The word 'sterilising' was a misnomer, as, in fact, the Corporation was defaulting on the interest payment on part of its capital.) The Secretary of State regarded the last restriction, which would prevent an inappropriate use of the arrangement, as requiring compensation for the CDC, as otherwise the Exchequer would 'benefit'. The net cost to the Treasury was estimated to be £18 million, although the Secretary of State claimed it would be 'Nil'.[100] The Chancellor asked the Financial Secretary to see whether he could get agreement with the Minister of State for Colonial Affairs 'on the figures'.[101] But while the figures were agreed at the official level,[102] the junior Ministers felt it necessary to discuss whether loan money would eventually be repaid, which brought them back to the argument over whether policies should be based in 1961 on the assumption that the Corporation would be insolvent in the 1970s.[103] The Minister of State was unwilling to modify the proposal to 'freeze' £20 million of the Corporation's liabilities to the Exchequer, subject to repayment of the capital from profits according to a formula. As compromise was not possible and the issue was not really a suitable one for the Cabinet to decide, the Secretary to the Cabinet sought the Prime Minister's agreement to the issue being referred for decision by a senior Minister, possibly the Lord Chancellor, on his behalf. The Chancellor agreed, and the matter was arranged accordingly.

In both the Secretary of State's Memorandum[104] and in the Minister of State's covering letter to the Lord Chancellor,[105] attention was focused on 'the hopeless long-term trend to which the Sinclair Report drew attention and which cannot be disputed'.[106] During the whole long marathon, the Colonial Office appears to have learnt nothing and forgotten nothing. It was the point to which the Financial Secretary to the Treasury directed the Lord Chancellor's particular attention in his Note and his covering letter.[107] It was fully covered in the Lord Chancellor's summary of the Treasury objections in his report to the Home Secretary,[108] but he too had been, if such might ever be said of a Lord Chancellor, bamboozled by the forecasts supplied to the Sinclair Committee, and the Treasury had completely failed to de-bamboozle him, just as it had in the case of the Colonial Office. That apart, the summing-up was impeccable, and the resolution in favour of the Colonial Office followed naturally, ending thus: 'I feel that we are not risking much by forgiving this rather doubtful debt.' The CDC was, therefore, allowed to transfer to a special fund certain of its liabilities to the Exchequer, totalling £20 million. Interest on these liabilities was waived, in so far as waiver did not already apply, and the £20 million was to be repaid by the Corporation to the Exchequer by instalments, calculated at 60 per cent of the amount by which its surpluses, if any, in any particular year exceeded £250,000. (Sir William Gorell Barnes told the author on 17 February 1976 that, in his recollection, this was settled at a meeting in the Treasury between the Secretary of State and the Chancellor, Mr Selwyn Lloyd, at which the latter overruled Sir Edward Boyle and Treasury officials. Sir William said that in the Colonial Office they were wholly uncertain whether the CDC could repay. He regarded the solution agreed with the Chancellor as a good one because its effect depended not on sentiments but on facts as they emerged.) A problem arose over the method of calculating the surplus for that purpose. The

CDC argued that capital gains and losses arising from the sale of investments, and any amounts which they put to reserve against prospective capital losses, should be taken into account, even though the decision by the Lord Chancellor was taken by reference to estimates provided by the CDC of their surplus/deficit over the following fifteen years on current account, i.e. ignoring capital gains and losses, or deeming them to cancel out. The Treasury objected to the large subjective element that would be brought into the calculations, and feared that it would reduce , or even nullify, the amount it might hope to receive under the formula approved by the Cabinet.[109] However, the Secretary of State discussed the matter with the Chancellor, and it was agreed that it would be right not to exclude provision for capital items.[110] The acceptance was on the understanding that the Corporation would not take advantage of the flexibility so provided to seek to minimise the amount of its annual payments to the Exchequer. Even so, it was not possible to foresee how the arrangements would work out and HMG, therefore, proposed to carry out a full review of the position in consultation with the Corporation after three years. The financial changes were announced by the Secretary of State for the Colonies, Mr Macleod, in the House of Commons on 27 April 1961.[111] The proposals did not require amendment of the ORD Act, 1959.

VI. INTEREST-FREE LOANS, 1965

On 30 July 1963, the Chairman raised three issues with the Permanent Secretary to the Treasury.[112] They were as follows. First, while accepting the general position as regards the servicing of Exchequer advances, the Chairman asked if two special cases could be considered for providing loans free of interest during the fructification period. The cases were (a) where the Corporation was assisting a scheme for smallholders in agriculture, and (b) where the CDC contributed funds to local development corporations. Secondly, he enquired whether the procedure for capital sanction could be expedited and, thirdly, enquired whether, as the CDC's results had improved, it was necessary strictly to match the CDC's borrowing from the Exchequer with corresponding CDC lending. Later the General Manager of the CDC elaborated on the three points, and the Permanent Secretary put it on record that he was not absolutely convinced that it would be against the interests of the Treasury to give the CDC, and other similar quasi-commercial bodies, an element of 'equity' capital.[113] He asked for the matter to be considered, realising that anything done for the CDC would have repercussions on the nationalised industries and that the tail could not be allowed to wag the dog in the matter.

In January 1964 the Chairman and General Manager explained to the Colonial Office official directly involved with CDC matters that the results for 1963 would show a deterioration compared with those for the previous two years, because of the rapidly rising amount of annual interest which the Corporation had to pay to the Exchequer,[114] which was expected in 1963 to absorb most of the Corporation's operating surplus, and to put the Corporation in the red by 1967. The Chairman and General Manager accepted the Treasury view that, while there was much in the CDC's case for equity capital, the CDC could not be dealt with in isolation from the other nationalised industries. So they sought relief elsewhere, particularly in having loans free of interest in the fructification period. However, their immediate interest was the precise procedure for the review of the 1961 financial agreement. It was agreed that the memorandum which the CDC proposed to submit would be sent in draft to the Colonial Office for comment. The immediate reaction in the Office to the news of the financial deterioration in 1963 and the possibility of an operating deficit in 1967 was that the 1961 settlement had had no significant effect, because the Sinclair Committee had concluded that 'after providing for all interest actually payable on Government Loans, the Corporation would, on the present basis of accounting, have an apparent surplus on Profit and Loss Account in each year up to 1966. Thereafter, however, a loss of a gradually increasing amount would emerge in each year up to 1978.'[115] If the CDC really could not pay its way, fundamental questions reaching beyond mere arithmetical and accountancy juggling would have to be faced at the review stage.[116] However, in the first place, the figures were surprising, as earlier information on cash flow had suggested that the Corporation would be able to finance itself within the £130 million ceiling and, in the second place, the outturn for 1961 and 1962 had suggested that the prospects were satisfactory.[117] In so far as neither inference was true, it was felt that, as before 1959, there was again legitimate cause for complaint that the Corporation tended to over-paint the picture in its Annual Reports. Pertinently, though perhaps belatedly, it was felt that it had to be established 'whether or not what they speak of happening in 1967, is likely to continue and, if so, for how long'.[118] Doubt was expressed as to whether the Corporation was likely to be relieved altogether of interest in the fructification period, but a calculation was made to illustrate the long-term result of the arrangement, and the difference to the Corporation came to a 2 per cent return on the investment. On a strict annuity basis, the CDC had to earn $6\frac{1}{2}$ per cent in order to service a loan of $5\frac{3}{4}$ per cent. When overheads were added, a return of something like 10 per cent was required on the bulk of its projects to break even overall. In fact, few projects available to the CDC were likely to be so profitable, while adding interest after a fructification period made even a 10 per cent return insufficient. It was concluded that, even if the CDC was given some equity capital, the dividend returned on it would be below the rate for Exchequer advances:

> We should therefore either have to accept that the Corporation was 'subsidised', or that HMG was, at one remove, in business. But HMG does not like being in business and might prefer that these activities should be wound up. The Corporation has a number of successes to its credit, and it has, in a number of cases, been very useful to HMG but, as was pointed out in 1959, does the development of one or two hundred acres in a particular Colony really make all that difference to its economy? That comment may well be unfair to the Corporation. So far as loans are concerned, it is arguable that there is little to be said for the interposition of any entity who requires an additional percentage between HMG and the ultimate recipient. We are therefore faced with the fundamental issues over again.[119]

Letters, which had been discussed and changed in the draft stage, were received promptly at the end of the three-year period by the Parliamentary Under-Secretary of State for Commonwealth Relations, Mr J. Tilney, who was responsible for the CDC at the ministerial level, and by the Colonial Office official directly involved. In his letter of 27 April 1964 to the Minister,[120] the Chairman claimed that the Corporation had become successful: 'In 1962, for the first time, it provided over half its gross investment from its own self-generated funds and, in 1963, it financed the whole of that investment from these funds. Its activities in 1962 benefited Britain's balance of payments by £6 million and promoted £7 million of direct exports. In 1963, it benefited the balance of payments by £12.9 million and generated £9.3 million of direct exports.' Much of the success was said to be due to the Corporation's flexibility. Yet there was one rigidity: 'We have *all* our money on loan but, for the development of tropical agriculture, share capital is far more suitable.' The reasons given were, first, the long gestation period for three crops, and, second, the greater fluctuation of the prices of tropical products than of those for other products. Of the several development corporations in existence, only the CDC was financed entirely by loan, with the resulting burden of interest, and the check on smallholder schemes and on developments in the smaller Colonies. It was realised that the CDC could not be treated separately from other nationalised industries, but relief short of a block of equity capital would be sought. The General Manager went into more detail in his letter of the same date.[121] He stated that over £1.5 million would have been paid to the Exchequer in the three years 1961–63, and claimed that the CDC had fulfilled the purposes for which it was established while earning 5.2 per cent for the taxpayer. The sharp rise of both interest rates and administrative costs was explained and, short of an allocation of equity capital which the CDC still regarded 'as being the real answer to the financial problem attaching to the undertaking of risk projects', the following were put forward to relieve the situation: (i) HMG might accept a ceiling on the average rate of interest that the CDC was required to pay in any year; (ii) fructification interest might be waived, instead of being deferred; (iii) the CDC's central administration could be used to supervise other forms of aid for HMG at small cost; (iv) the CDC should receive recoupment for management training and welfare expenditure, because it was expected to undertake projects in a fairly low profit range. Otherwise, it was concluded, operations unable to meet progressively stiffer financial terms would have to be rejected or discarded.

With the concurrence of the Commonwealth Relations Office, a letter was sent to the Treasury on 9 July 1964.[122] The letter was exploratory, because it was feared that what would help the CDC would not be acceptable and what would be acceptable would hardly help the CDC.[123] It was felt that further financial easement was both necessary and in HMG's interest. The four proposals made by the General Manager were commented upon in turn. In respect of the first, it was thought that a concessionary rate of interest was being sought and that the CDC should participate in any move in that direction arising from the deliberations of the Committee on Development Policy concerning the terms of aid loans.[124] The second proposal was thought particularly relevant to the extension of the CDC's operations in agriculture, especially peasant agriculture, and had found its place in the paper contributed by the Commonwealth Relations Office to the Committee on Development Policy.[125] The third proposal had attraction for the CRO, which thought that the CDC might be employed in a managerial capacity in some independent Commonwealth countries.[126] The Colonial Office thought that this might apply to Colonial territories also. On the fourth point, it was suggested that the Department of Technical Co-operation should treat the CDC equally with the private sector in regard to training schemes, but there was no justification for allowing the CDC to recoup expenditure on welfare services.

As the result of the discussions in the Committee on Development Policy, it was decided, in principle, that some of United Kingdom's aid should be by way of interest-free loans, and the question arose of applying the concession to the CDC's borrowing. However, after the General Election of 1964, the Ministry of Overseas Development (ODM) was set up. As from 1 January 1965 all matters affecting the CDC became the responsibility of the Minister of Overseas Development.[127] Consequently, both the review started by the Colonial Office and the application of the new principle were taken up by the new Ministry. In its memorandum to the Official Committee on Overseas Development, the ODM agreed that some alleviation of the terms on which it received funds would be needed if it was to continue to operate on the existing basis.[128] The proposal that the average rate of interest should be lowered to, say, 4 per cent was contrary to previous Ministerial discussions of the general question of soft lending, on the one hand, and, as the average was then around $5\frac{7}{8}$ per cent, would involve substantial interest-free lending to get the average rate down, on the other hand. The proposal that interest should be waived, rather than deferred in the fructification period, was more attractive as it did not involve a concessionary rate of interest as such, and the beneficiaries would be largely agricultural schemes and local development companies, in which the CDC invested alongside local Governments. It was realised that the case for the waiver involved acceptance of the view that the CDC's activities were only quasi-commercial and included an element of aid. Otherwise, it was concluded that neither the functions nor the resources of the CDC required revision. In the agreed report of the Official Committee,[129] it was pointed out that the CDC had not entirely distinguished between (a) the easing of their overall financial position and (b) facilitating their undertaking of marginal and less remunerative projects, but that the Chairman had agreed that the time had not arrived when a subsidy could be shown to be necessary. The Committee concluded that the interest concession should be directly related to projects, and was not intended to ease the Corporation's financial situation as such. It was for that reason that the ODM was prepared to carry the cost of the concession on its Vote. It was also the reason why the Treasury refused to extend the concession to schemes already finalised.[130] However, the Chairman raised with the Minister the problem of the increasing interest burden, which meant that the CDC had either to curtail its operations or to face a deficit. The Minister wrote accordingly to the Chief Secretary to the Treasury, Mr J., later Lord, Diamond, to say that perhaps in the following year she would wish to consider the CDC's financial situation.[131] In his reply, the Chief Secretary said that he was glad that the Minister and, though reluctantly, the Chairman had agreed that the concession on the waiving of interest should be limited to appropriate projects in the future, and not made retrospective. Concerning the possibility of holding a review of the Corporation's financial position, he was sceptical of the need for early consideration and concluded: 'But if next year you decide that a review of the Corporation's general position is called for, I would like to suggest that the basis for it should be not the Corporation's fears of what may prove on certain assumptions to be its position at some future date, but a factual assessment of what is actually happening at the current time.'[132] There could be no better sentence on which to conclude the great marathon debate. It is much to be regretted that this had not been both clearly stated and accepted five or six years earlier. The Annual Report of the CDC for 1965 declared that it was 'an historic occasion for the Corporation when the first loan was approved by the Treasury free from interest during the first seven years.'[133]

SOURCES

1. Treasury file IF 580/01, Part H, pp. 72–5, minute of 21 Mar 1952.

2. Ibid., pp. 80–1, letter of 31 Mar 1952 from the Chancellor of the Exchequer to the Secretary of State for the Colonies.

3. Treasury file IF 580/01, Part K, pp. 101–2, minute of 25 May 1954.

4. Confidential file EGD 81/161/02, 1957–1959, item E/8, minutes of meeting on the capital structure of the CDC held on 9 Dec 1957.

5. Treasury file IF 580/01, Part M, pp. 112–13, note of 19 Nov 1958 on the CDC.

6. Confidential file EGD 81/69/01, 1954–1956, items 4 and 5, discussions of 23 and 27 Nov 1956 between the Secretary of State and the Chairman.

7. File EGD 81/013, 1954–1956, item 1, letter of 23 May 1956 from the Chairman to the Secretary of State.

8. Confidential file EGD 81/161/02, 1957–1959, item 1, Confidential Memorandum of 22 Oct 1957.

9. Idem, para. 16(g).

10. Confidential file EGD 81/161/02, 1957–1959, item 12, United Kingdom Aid to the Colonies: Role of the CDC: Preliminary Draft Memorandum.

11. Ibid., item 13, United Kingdom Aid to the Colonies: Role of the CDC: Memorandum of 22 Oct 1957, by the Colonial Office.

12. Ibid., minute of 14 July 1958 on a second meeting held at the Colonial Office on 9 July with the Treasury and CDC.

13. Ibid., item 22, letter and enclosure of 22 Aug 1958.

14. Ibid., items 30A and B, Colonial Office comments on the Treasury Memorandum.

15. Idem.

16. Ibid., item 35, letter of 5 Nov 1958, from the Minister of State for Colonial Affairs to the Financial Secretary to the Treasury referring to the debate of the previous day.

17. Ibid., item 41, note on meeting of 20 Nov 1958.

18. Ibid., item 44, note of meeting of 4 Dec 1958.

19. Ibid., item 54, minute of 19 Jan 1959 by the Minister of State.

20. Ibid., item 63 and minute of 16 Feb 1959.

21. Ibid., item 64, letter and enclosure of 22 July 1959 from Lord Sinclair of Cleeve to the Secretary of State.

22. Secret file EGD 81/161/07, 1957–1959, item 16, CDC: Sinclair Committee Report: Note by the Colonial Office (26 Oct 1959).

23. Cmnd. 786, Appendices III and IV.

24. Idem, Appendix III.

25. Idem, para. 76.

26. Secret file EGD 81/161/07, 1957–1959, item 14, letter of 19 Oct 1959.

27. Ibid., item 16, CDC: Sinclair Committee Report: Note by the Colonial Office, para. 32.

28. Treasury file IF 580/01, Part M, p. 147H, 28 Aug 1959. The Potara Electricity Scheme was started under Lord Reith's chairmanship in 1953 to provide electricity for the dredgers under the Goldfields scheme. The cost rose because of unsatisfactory work by contractors and delays. While CDC had only a 45 per cent shareholding its substantial debenture holding gave it an equal representation on the Board of Directors. CDC had control of the parent British Guiana Goldfields Co. and so were responsible.

29. Secret file EGD 81/161/07, 1957–1959, items 17 and 19, minutes of 27 and 29 Oct 1959.

30. Ibid., item 20, note of 30 Oct 1959 by the Minister of State to the Secretary of State.

31. Ibid., item 22, minute of 11 Nov 1959 by the Secretary of State to the Minister of State. The minute was prefaced by the two lines from Macbeth: 'If it were done when 'tis done, then 'twere well/It were done quickly'.

32. Ibid., item 23, minute of 19 Nov 1959 by the Minister of State.

33. Ibid., item 24, minute of 20 Nov 1959 to the Minister of State.

34. Ibid., item 30, note of a Meeting in the Minister of State's Office on 15 Dec 1959.

35. Ibid., item 32, letter of 23 Dec 1959 from the Minister of State to the Financial Secretary to the Treasury.

36. Secret file EGD 81/161/07, Part C, 1960–1962, item 1960, Prime Minister's

Personal Minute Serial No. M 98161 of 21 Mar 1961 to the Lord Chancellor.

37. Ibid., item 167, minute of 27 Mar 1961 by the Lord Chancellor and also Treasury file 2–CF 9/01, Part F.

38. Secret file EGD 81/161/07, Part A, 1960–1962, item 3, letter of 27 Jan 1960 from the Chancellor of the Exchequer to the Secretary of State for the Colonies.

39. Ibid., item 7, letter of 19 Feb 1960 from the Secretary of State to the Home Secretary.

40. Ibid., item 11, letter of 7 Mar 1960 from the Secretary of State to the Home Secretary.

41. GEN 708/1st Meeting, 17 Mar 1960.

42. GEN 708/1, 14 Mar 1960, Annex B.

43. GEN 708/1, Annex D.

44. GEN 708/2, 30 May 1960.

45. Treasury file 2–CF 9/01, Part A, minute of 13 May 1960 and Brief of 27 May 1960.

46. Ibid., brief of 27 May 1960.

47. Ibid., minute of 30 May 1960.

48. Secret file EGD 81/161/07, Part B, 1960–1962, item 58. In his letter of 27 June 1960, the Financial Secretary to the Treasury made this point strongly to the Minister of State for Colonial Affairs.

49. GEN 702/2nd Meeting.

50. Secret file EGD 81/161/07, Part A, 1960–1962, item 54, letter of 17 June 1960 from the Minister of State to the Financial Secretary.

51. CC 39(60) item 6, 5 July 1960.

52. Secret file EGD 81/161/07, Part B, 1960–1962, minute of 11 July 1960.

53. Treasury file 2-CF 9/01, Part B, minute of 13 July 1960.

54. Ibid., minute of 14 July 1960.

55. Secret file EGD 81/161/07, Part B, 1960–1962, item 67, letter of 15 July 1960 from the Chancellor of the Exchequer to the Secretary of State for the Colonies.

56. Ibid., minutes of Meeting on 18 July 1960 on CDC's Capital Structure and also item 68 in Secret File EGD 81/161/07, Part B, 1960–1962.

57. Ibid., item 70, letter of 25 July 1960, and also in Treasury file 2-CF 9/01, Part B.

58. Treasury file 2-CF 9/01, Part C, minute of 7 Dec 1960.

59. Secret File EGD 81/161/07, Part B, 1960–1962, items 74 and 75A, letters of 30 Aug and 16 Sep 1960, and minute of 28 Sep.

60. Treasury file 2-CF 9/01, Part C, letter of 29 Sep 1960 from the Secretary of State for the Colonies to the Chancellor of the Exchequer. The Secretary of State for Commonwealth Relations wrote to the Chancellor in support of the Colonial Office view – letter of 6 Oct 1960 in idem.

61. Ibid., minute of 3 Oct 1960.

62. Ibid., minute of 6 Oct 1960.

63. Ibid., note of a meeting held at the Treasury on 18 Oct 1960.

64. Ibid., letter of 19 Oct 1960. The invitation was put in the draft minutes to call the bluff of CDC if it was bluffing.

65. Ibid., letter of 31 Oct 1960 from the Chairman to the Permanent Secretary to the Treasury.

66. Secret file EGD 81/161/07, Part B, 1960–1962, item 92, minute of 2 Nov 1960 to the Minister of State.

67. Ibid., item 95, Department's comments on the Chairman's letter of 31 Oct 1960.

68. Treasury file 2-CF 9/01, Part C, letter of 10 Nov 1960 from the Permanent Secretary to the Treasury to the Chairman of CDC.

69. Secret file EGD 81/161/07, Part B, 1960–1962, item 101, letter of 30 Sep 1960 from Lord Howick.

70. Ibid., item 102, minute of 3 Oct 1960 to the Secretary of State and Minister of State.

71. Treasury file 2-CF 9/01, Part C, minute of 18 Nov 1960. In a minute of 29 Nov 1960 it was pointed out that as Sir Nutcombe Hume was Chairman of the National Film Finance Corporation, which was also grumbling about its repayment burdens, any concession to the CDC would create an embarrassing precedent for dealing with the NFFC.

72. Ibid., note of a meeting at the Colonial Office on 21 Nov 1960.

73. Ibid., minute of 29 Nov 1960.

74. Idem.

75. Treasury file 2-CF 9/01, Part D, minute of 27 Feb 1961. The Minister of State for Colonial Affairs was most anxious to announce a new scheme to Parliament when it reassembled, as questions were frequently asked about such an announcement. See his minute of 22 Dec 1960 in Secret file EGD 81/161/07, Part C, 1960–1962.

76. Treasury file 2-CF 9/01, Part D, attached to minute of 7 Dec 1960.

77. Secret file EGD 81/161/07, Part C, 1960–1962, item 113E, draft note of a Meeting at the Colonial Office, 23 Nov 1960.

78. Ibid., item 114, letter and enclosures of 15 Dec 1960.

79. Ibid., item 120, letter of 9 Jan 1961.

80. Ibid., item E/123, meeting between the Minister of State and the Chairman of the CDC on 11 Jan 1961. Lord Howick was appointed Chairman and Mr Prideaux Deputy Chairman on 1 Dec 1960 on the retirement of Sir Nutcombe Hume, Chairman from 1 April 1959 to 30 Nov 1960.

81. Treasury file 2-CF 9/01, Part D, minute of 16 Jan 1961.

82. Idem.

83. Ibid., minute of 23 Jan 1961 to Sir Thomas Padmore.

84. Idem.

85. Ibid., minute of 24 Jan 1961, by the Treasury Officer of Accounts.

86. Idem.

87. Ibid., minute of 31 Jan 1961 by the Chancellor, agreeing to the memorandum of 30 Jan 1961 submitted by the Financial Secretary.

88. Ibid., letter of 31 Jan 1961, from the Financial Secretary to the Minister of State for Colonial Affairs. The second item was modified to read 'in excess of (say) £$\frac{1}{2}$ million' instead of £1 million, as in the submission to the Chancellor.

89. Secret file EGD 81/161/07, Part C, 1960–1962, item 144, letter of 3 Feb 1961 from the Minister of State to the Financial Secretary.

90. Ibid., draft new Treasury proposals of 16 Feb 1961. On the basis of the CDC's estimates of the level of prices of tropical products, it estimated that the surplus earned over the period 1961–1970 would average £200,000 a year, though ranging from roughly £1,000,000 in the earlier years to a deficit of £800,000 in 1970. The proposal was explained in the letter of 21 Feb 1961 from Sir Ronald Harris to Sir William Gorell Barnes in ibid. and item 155 in Secret file EGD 81/ 161/07, Part C, 1960–1962.

91. Ibid., item 154, letter of 20 Feb 1961 from Sir William Gorell Barnes to Sir Ronald Harris, and Treasury file 2-CF 9/01, Part D.

92. Ibid. According to a minute of 24 Feb 1961, CDC had 'since admitted that they gave a deliberate slant to the figures which they put to the Sinclair Committee'.

93. Treasury file 2-CF 9/01, Part E, brief for meeting between Colonial Secretary and Chancellor on 1 March 1961.

94. Treasury file 2-CF 9/01, Part D, minute of 24 Feb 1961.

95. Ibid., minute of 24 Feb 1961 on the letter of 23 Feb by Sir William Gorell Barnes.

96. Treasury file 2-CF 9/01, Part E, letter of 28 Feb 1961 from the Secretary of State to the Chancellor of the Exchequer.

97. Secret file EGD 81/161/07, Part C, 1960–1962, revised brief of 28 Feb 1961 for the Secretary of State's discussion with the Chancellor on 1 Mar 1961, at para. 14.

98. Treasury file 2-CF 9/01, Part E, brief of 27 Feb 1961 for meeting between Colonial Secretary and Chancellor of 1 Mar 1961, at para. 11.

99. Ibid., note on meeting between the Chancellor and the Colonial Secretary on 1 Mar 1961.

100. Ibid., minute of 10 Mar 1961 by Sir Ronald Harris.

101. Ibid., minute of 14 Mar 1961 by the Chancellor of the Exchequer.

102. Ibid., Annex to minutes of 16 Mar 1961.

103. Ibid., minute of 20 Mar 1961 from the Financial Secretary to the Treasury to the Chancellor of the Exchequer.

104. Secret file EGD 81/161/07, Part C, 1960–1962, item E/162.

105. Treasury file 2-CF 9/01, Part E, letter of 23 Mar 1961 from the Minister of State to the Lord Chancellor.

106. Secret file EGD 81/161/07, Part C, 1960–1962, item E/162.

107. Ibid., item. 164A and E/164A.

108. Ibid., item 167, CDC: Financial Reorganisation, para. 7(2), and also in Treasury file 2-CF 9/01, Part F.

109. Treasury file 2-CF 9/01, Part F, minute of 20 Apr 1961 from the Financial Secretary to the Treasury to the Chancellor of the Exchequer. The Financial Secretary said he was 'perturbed at the unsatisfactory way in which the Corporation approaches its dealings with the Exchequer' – para. 6 of minute.

110. Secret file EGD 81/161/07, Part C, 1960–1962, item 195, letter of 25 Apr 1961 from the Secretary of State to the Chairman of CDC.

111. H. of C. Deb., Vol. 639, cols 627–31, 27 Apr 1961.

112. Treasury file 2-FD 36/01, Part A, minute of 2 Aug 1963 by Sir William Armstrong.

113. Ibid., minute of 12 Sep 1963 by Sir William Armstrong on the previous day's meeting.

114. Confidential file EGD 81/161/012, minute of 8 Jan 1964.

115. Cmnd 786, para. 37, While the Report showed a deficit on Profit and Loss account in 1967 of only £110,000, the Chairman anticipated a deficit of £200,000 in that year. But, as the 1961 agreement had provided relief, why should the prospective situation be worse than that foreshadowed in the Sinclair Report? See draft letter of 10 Jan 1964 – item 1 in Confidential file EGD 81/161/012, 1963–1965.

116. Confidential file EGD 81/161/012, 1963–1965, minute of 10 Jan 1964.

117. Ibid., minute of 20 Jan 1964.

118. Idem.

119. Idem.

120. Ibid., item 9, letter of 27 Apr 1964 from the Chairman to the Parliamentary Under-Secretary of State for Commonwealth Relations.

121. Ibid., item 8, letter of 27 Apr 1964.

122. Ibid., item 12, letter of 9 July 1964. Original in Treasury file 2-FD 36/01, Part B.

123. Confidential file EGD 81/161/012, 1963–1965, minute of 28 May 1964.

124. DP(64) 27, 7 July 1964: The terms of aid loans.

125. DP(64) 23, 26 June 1964: Aid for Agriculture.

126. Confidential file EGD 81/161/012, 1963–1965, item 7, letter of 6 Apr 1964.

127. DTC/ODM file CF 370/821/01, item 2, letter of 12 Jan 1965 from the Permanent Secretary to the Chairman, enclosing a copy of the Ministry of Overseas Development (No. 2) Order.

128. WPL(65) 1 of 1 Jan 1965 – in Treasury file 2-FD 36/01, Part B. On the proposal of the CDC that it should be given some equity capital, the memorandum stated: 'This could hardly be equity capital in any real sense. From the facts of three cases, it is unlikely that the Corporation could earn a real equity return, and if private money was invested in its projects, pressure would almost certainly build up on the Treasury to underwrite a "dividend"' (para. 22).

129. Secret ODM file CF 370/819/01, Part B, item 40, DVO(o) (65) 12, 15 Apr 1965.

130. Ibid., item 65, letter of 18 June 1965.

131. Ibid., item 95, letter of 25 Aug 1965 from the Minister of Overseas Development to the Chief Secretary to the Treasury.

132. Ibid., item 95, letter of 28 Sep 1965 from the Chief Secretary to the Treasury to the Minister of Overseas Development.

133. CDC: Annual Report for 1965, para. 8.

7 From Colonial Development Corporation to Commonwealth Development Corporation, 1963

1. THE ISSUE IS RAISED

The issue of the CDC's role in newly independent Commonwealth countries was raised over the independence of Ghana and has been discussed up to, and including, the enactment of the ORD Act, 1959, in Chapter 5, Section vii, above. The general policy was set out in paragraphs 29–34 of the White Paper on Commonwealth Development (Cmnd 237, July 1957) and the Secretary of State's Circular Savingram No. 422/58 of 14 April 1958 explained the purport of the ORD Act, 1958 (later consolidated in the ORD Act, 1959), which gave legislative effect to the policy. The position was that the CDC might continue with any undertakings begun before independence, and complete any investment approved prior to independence; it might also, with the agreement of the local Government, undertake managerial and agency functions in new enterprises in ex-Colonies on a repayment basis, but without commitment of funds; it might not invest in new projects after independence. (Up to 16 July 1963, at least, managerial and agency services had not been asked for: see H. of L. Deb., Vol. 252, col. 154, of that date for a statement by the Minister of State for Colonial Affairs, the Marquess of Lansdowne.) This policy was endorsed by the Cabinet in July 1960,[1] prior to the Debate of 7 July 1960 on an Opposition Motion, which was principally aimed to empower the Corporation to extend its activities in territories which had already been granted independence.

The matter was next raised by the Chairman of the CDC with the Joint Permanent Secretary to the Treasury, Sir Frank Lee, in March

1961.[2] The latter enquired of both the Colonial Office and the Commonwealth Relations Office whether the Chairman might be told that

> if the time should ever come when the Corporation is, in fact, faced with the prospect of becoming a dwindling concern, because of insufficient suitable opportunities for investing the funds at its disposal in the dependent territories, the Government would be willing to re-examine the present limitations on the Corporation's freedom to invest in countries of the independent Commonwealth, with a view to some relaxation, if possible, of these limitations, at any rate in respect of some territories, e.g. the poorer ones.[3]

While the Colonial Office was willing to consider the need for a review of policy,[4] the CRO was firmly against a change, observing, somewhat tartly, that if there was so much scope in the newly-independent territories it was surprising the Corporation was not already more involved in some of them.[5] The Joint Permanent Secretary felt that the CDC might be able to play an important role in assisting continued private investment in some of the poorer independent Commonwealth countries, but did not consider, in the circumstances, that the Treasury should champion the extension of the CDC's scope[6] and, as the Chairman was content that the point be placed on record, the matter could rest.[7]

But it did not rest for long. The CDC asked, in a comment on its Annual Report for 1960, for reconsideration of its scope,[8] a suggestion which the *Financial Times* took up editorially on 18 May 1961, with the admonition that 'It was about time that the groundnuts were forgotten.' At the same time, the United Kingdom High Commissioner in the Federation of Nigeria, Lord Head, urged that, suitably renamed and adequately financed, the CDC would be an organisation as acceptable to independent Nigeria as it was desirable for United Kingdom interests, and the resistances to its continuance in Nigeria should be overcome.[9] Consequently, the Minister of State for Colonial Affairs, Lord Perth, asked for an official memorandum on the question, with special reference to activities in Colonies immediately prior to independence, and to the possibility of working through local Development Corporations, which might provide 'an instrument of expansion, without changing the basic policy of wishing the CDC to devote its greatest attention to the remaining Colonies'.[10] In the note prepared, it was suggested that arguments raised earlier for continued participation on the grounds of lack of entrepreneurial skill and experience were exaggerated when applied to Ghana, Malaya and Nigeria, but were becoming more relevant with the coming independence of Colonies like Sierra Leone, and territories like Tanganyika where the CDC might also become the instrument for United Kingdom aid. Two other arguments for a change of policy were, first, that otherwise the regional controllers would find the role of the CDC too limited and be likely to leave and, secondly, that, with the encouragement of Commonwealth countries to seek sources of capital in third countries, United Kingdom exports would be likely to suffer, and the participation of the CDC in local development corporations would, with a relatively small expenditure of funds, be likely to offset that result.[11] However, the re-examination of overseas expenditure going on at the time was not solely related on balance of payments considerations. The Chancellor of the Exchequer's statement of 25 July 1961, which indicated that overseas aid was not to rise much above the current level of £180 million a year, related largely to the need to restrain public expenditure so as to lighten the overload on the economy.[12] While CDC expenditure for 1961/62 was expected to fall within the desired limit of around £11 million gross, it was hoped to reduce the estimated figure for 1962/63 from £18 million to £15 million.[13]

In a draft letter to the Minister of State, the Chairman argued that (i) the sizeable stimulus to exports and (ii) remittances from the CDC and its staff helped the balance of payments, while (iii) the CDC was largely a revolving fund, owing to the regular repayments of investments and the occasional sale of projects, and (iv) the CDC had considerable usefulness during the transition to independence when projects were likely to need extra attention and finance. Furthermore, (v) the CDC could operate alongside any international or national institution in territories concerned, and this was a useful bridge between the United Kingdom, European Common Market countries and Commonwealth countries and (vi) otherwise more top level staff would leave.[14] But when the Minister of State put these points to the Financial Secretary to the Treasury, Sir Edward Boyle, the proposals were regarded as raising issues of policy which officials should first thoroughly consider and, in the meantime, any expression of opinion was to be avoided.[15] Officials immediately met to consider the position which, to the regret of the Colonial Office in particular, was found to involve legislation.[16] While inter-departmental discussions proceeded, the CRO having come round to the view that the issue required a fresh look,[17] pressures were maintained from several quarters, including Malaya,[18] Tanganyika[19] and Parliament. Thus, in the course of the

Second Reading of the Jamaica Independence Bill, Mr James Griffiths, a former Secretary of State, said he thought 'it is time to change the name of the Corporation, to enlarge its functions, and to use it as, perhaps, the most important instrument we have of channelling aid to the newly independent countries.'[20] Others took up the point,[21] and the Under-Secretary of State for the Colonies, Mr Hugh Fraser, said that he was 'completely convinced that "Commonwealth Development Corporation" will become the name of the Colonial Development Corporation. I think that this will be an inevitable development, but we have, of course, to look further at the details. I am speaking today only as a junior Minister, but I am sure that that must be the trend.'[22] By June 1962 the Secretary of State for the Colonies, Mr R. Maudling, was anxious to press ahead as quickly as possible,[23] and the Secretary of State for Commonwealth Relations, Mr D. Sandys, was in agreement.[24]

II. THE PROPOSED CHANGES

Accordingly, the following proposals were submitted to the Treasury as the basis for a recommendation to Ministers[25]:

(i) as soon as the necessary time could be made available, a Bill should be introduced to amend the ORD Act, 1959, so as to:

(a) remove the ban on the Corporation's embarking on new projects in a Colonial territory after it became independent within the Commonwealth;

(b) remove this ban in respect of those territories in which the Corporation was able to operate while they were dependent territories but which had become independent, viz. Ghana, the Federation of Malaya, the Federation of Nigeria, Tanganyika, Sierra Leone and Cyprus; and of others that would be added to the list before the new Act was passed, i.e. Jamaica, Trinidad and Uganda [this could not, of course, apply to Somaliland and the Southern Cameroons, which had meantime left the Commonwealth];

(c) change of the Corporation's name to Commonwealth Development Corporation.

(ii) these changes would *not* involve any increase in the ceiling of Exchequer lending to the Corporation and this was not contemplated;

(iii) until a Bill on these lines could be introduced, the matter should be the subject of an announcement of HMG's intention to proceed along these lines.

The Commonwealth Relations Office wrote to the Treasury in support. After acknowledging earlier resistance to the idea that the CDC should operate in independent Commonwealth countries, it was felt that circumstances had changed with the transition to independence of several poor Colonies, which still needed the kind of help the CDC could provide – a point which some newly-independent Commonwealth countries had already made.[26] The Secretary of State wrote urgently to the Chancellor of the Exchequer, as he felt he had to make a firm statement before the House rose for the Recess.[27] Officials agreed that the proposals should be put to the Cabinet.[28] The Cabinet paper was short, merely asking the Cabinet to agree to (i) the change in scope of the CDC, (ii) the change of name of the CDC, (iii) the introduction of legislation the following Session, and (iv) to authorise that the changes be announced before the House rose.[29] There was general agreement in the Cabinet that the Corporation's terms of reference should be widened, and the Commonwealth Secretary was invited to bring before an early meeting of the Future Legislation Committee the proposal to include such a Bill. He was invited to consider further, in consultation with the Chairman, the need for an early announcement of the Government's decision.[30] The Chairman was anxious that HMG should make such an announcement for three reasons in particular, namely (a) the need to reassure staff, who were showing signs of drifting away; (b) the desirability of pressing ahead with negotiations with Eastern Nigeria and Malaya; and (c) Parliamentary questions on the extent to which the CDC would be able to invest in Jamaica and Trinidad after independence. The announcement was made in both Houses on 31 July 1962.

The Oversea Policy Committee considered on 28 November 1962 whether a new CD & W Act should come into force on 1 April 1963, i.e. a year before the existing Act expired. The Future Legislation Committee suggested that both the CDC and the CD & W proposals should be covered in one Bill. The suggestion led to further delay of the CDC changes, because it was not until 4 January 1963 that the First Secretary of State, Mr R. A. Butler, who had pursued certain points arising from the discussion in the Oversea Policy Committee, was able to inform the Ministers concerned that he was satisfied there should be a new Act. The Colonial Office had then to obtain Treasury agreement on the amount of CD & W assistance for 1963/66, on which the two Departments differed at first by £28 million.[31] At this place, only the half of the Bill concerning the CDC requires treatment.

III. THE POSITION OF SOUTHERN RHODESIA

When the Secretary of State, Mr Duncan Sandys, made the announcement in the House of Commons on 31 July 1962, he was questioned about the position of Southern Rhodesia. The 1959 Act did not permit the CDC to operate in Southern Rhodesia *per se*, but only when it would be to the benefit of the Federation of Rhodesia and Nyasaland as a whole. (The Annual Report of the CDC for 1962 showed (pp. 69–70) that the Federal Government received assistance in three forms: (i) a loan in 1954 of £1.75 million for purchase of Vickers Viscount aircraft and spares for Central African Airways Corporation, which was repayable by annual instalments, 1959–67; (ii) a loan of £15 million in 1956 for Stage I of the Kariba hydro-electric undertaking, which was repayable by annuities over 36 years starting 1965; and (iii) the purchase of 50,000 shares in 1962 in the Industrial Promotion Corporation of Rhodesia and Nyasaland Ltd, which were £1 shares of which 15/- per share was paid up at the end of 1962.)

The position had not been considered when the Cabinet discussed the matter, but it was only realised later that amending legislation on the lines proposed would not enable the Corporation to operate in Southern Rhodesia for the benefit of that territory alone, as it would have had the more limited effect of extending the powers of the Corporation to those territories originally included within the terms of the ORD Act, 1948, i.e. territories which, at that time, were eligible for CD & W assistance, which Southern Rhodesia was not. Following the statement of 31 July officials of the Colonial Office discussed the matter with officials in the CRO and Central African Office, and it was agreed that the restriction of the CDC's powers in Southern Rhodesia should be removed. The main argument against this step was that the earlier decision to define the new scope of the CDC in terms of (a) those countries, then independent members of the Commonwealth, in which it had been previously empowered to operate, and (b) territories which would become independent Commonwealth countries at some future date, was intended to provide a logical basis for continuing the exclusion of the Old Dominions, India, Pakistan and Ceylon, whose exclusion was necessary because of the enormity of the demand for capital in the Indian sub-continent. At the Committee Stage, Mr G. M. Thomson (Dundee, East) proposed to omit '11th

February, 1948' and insert '15th August, 1947' in Clause 1 in order to include India, Pakistan and Ceylon. The Under-Secretary of State for Commonwealth Relations, Mr J. Tilney, said that

> the deputy chairman and the managing director told me in conversation yesterday that, if given the opportunity, the CDC would welcome the inclusion of India, Pakistan and Ceylon within its area of operations, although they would not expect, in the early stages, to be able to use any of the powers extensively. But I should also tell the Committee that the Corporation never put forward that suggestion in the conversations which we had with the Corporation during the past weeks, and I repeat that it has never as yet used its powers of management which it could have used in any of these three territories [H. of C. Deb., Vol. 679, cols 1897–8, 28 June 1963].

The amendment was negatived. However, the initial position had already been modified as a result of the recent decision that the loan assistance being given for Southern Rhodesia's development plan should take the form of Exchequer advances under the CD & W Acts. So there was little basis in logic for perpetuating the restriction on the powers of the CDC to invest in Southern Rhodesia, and it would have been anomalous if the CDC was empowered to embark on new projects in all independent Commonwealth countries in Africa, but was restricted in its operations in a territory of Africa for which HMG had still a measure of responsibility. Such discrimination would have been difficult to justify in Parliament or in Southern Rhodesia, especially as the Governments of the Federation and of Southern Rhodesia had asked informally for the amendment. These arguments were put to the Treasury, with the proposal that Southern Rhodesia be included in the extended field of operation of the CDC.[32] The Treasury was not happy to extend the Corporation's scope more than was strictly necessary, as the ceiling on the CDC's advances was not to be raised. However, it was agreed that Southern Rhodesia should become *eligible* for help from the CDC, though Ministers would have to be consulted before any assurance could be given that Southern Rhodesia could count on getting a share of available funds.[33]

iv. THE COMMONWEALTH DEVELOPMENT ACT, 1963

The question was submitted to the Secretary of State,[34] Mr Sandys, who agreed with the recommendation that Southern Rhodesia be included.[35] As a result, Clause 1(1)(a) of the Bill had to be somewhat awkwardly drafted to include: 'any overseas country or territory within the Commonwealth which is not a Colonial Territory as defined by that Act [ORD Act, 1959], not being a country which had become an independent sovereign country before February 11th, 1948, or a territory administered by the government of such a country.' Clause 1(1)(b) named the New Hebrides as a territory to which there should also be an extension of the CDC's powers. Here again the territory, being an Anglo-French Condominium, was originally excluded as not being a 'Colonial Territory' within the meaning of the 1948 Act. In 1955 the New Hebrides was brought within the scope of CD & W, and so it was thought logical that it should be brought within the scope of the CDC also.[36] Clause 1(2) renamed the CDC as the Commonwealth Development Corporation, while Clause 1(3) enabled the Secretary of State to give directions to the Corporation requiring it to obtain his approval when he so specified before it performed functions in any independent country. The purpose of this latter was to enable the Secretary of State to satisfy himself that the CDC's operations would be acceptable to the Government of the independent Commonwealth country concerned.[37] Presumably such approval might be revoked in exceptional circumstances, though there was no explicit statement to that effect in the Bill.[38] Clauses 1(4) and 1(5) were consequential. The Commonwealth Development Bill passed through the remaining stages in the House of Lords on 26 July 1963 and received the Royal Assent on 31 July 1963 (11 Eliz. 2, Ch. 40).

SOURCES

1. CC 39(60) item 6, 5 July 1960.

2. Treasury File 2-CF 9/01, Part E, minute of 21 Mar 1961 by Sir F. Lee.

3. Confidential file EGD 81/67/01, Part A, 1960–1962, item 26, letter of 24 Mar 1961 from Sir F. Lee to Sir W. Gorell Barnes.

4. Ibid., item 29, letter of 29 Mar 1961 from Sir W. Gorell Barnes to Sir F. Lee; and in Treasury file 2-CF 9/01, Part F.

5. Ibid., item 30, letter of 29 Mar 1961 from Sir A. Rumbold to Sir F. Lee, and Treasury file 2-CF 9/01 Part F.

6. Treasury file 2-CF 9/01, Part F, minute of 30 Mar 1961 by Sir F. Lee.

7. Confidential file EGD 81/67/01, Part A, 1960–1962, item 31, letter of 17 Apr 1961 by Sir F. Lee to Sir W. Gorell Barnes.

8. Ibid., item 35. The Chairman wrote to the Secretary of State for the Colonies about the matter on 22 June 1961.

9. Ibid., item 33, CRO Print, 16 May 1961: Federation of Nigeria – Tools for the Job. In his reply, the Secretary of State for Commonwealth Relations mentioned the balance of payments problem, and the more pressing needs of territories like Tanganyika: letter of 26 July 1961 – item 42/E1 in ibid.

10. Ibid., item 34, minute of 18 May 1961 by the Minister of State for Colonial Affairs. The Minister expressed this view after reading the letter from Sir F. Lee – see minute of 27 Mar 1961: item 27 in ibid. In replying to the Debate on CDC in the House of Lords on 27 June 1961, the Minister drew particular attention to the extent of existing CDC activities via Development Corporations in independent Commonwealth countries: H. of L. Deb., Vol. 232, col. 1007.

11. Confidential file EGD 81/67/01, Part A, 1960–1962, item E/46, note of 18 Aug 1961 on the Operations of the CDC in Independent Commonwealth Countries.

12. Ibid., item 48, note of 10 Oct 1961 for the Minister of State.

13. Ibid., item 51, minute of 25 Oct 1961.

14. Ibid., item 50, letter of 24 Oct 1961 from the Chairman to the Minister of State.

15. Ibid., item 59, letter of 5 Dec 1961 from the Financial Secretary to the Treasury to the Minister of State.

16. File EGD 81/67/01 Part B, 1960–1962, item 74, letter of 13 Mar 1962, and minute of 30 Mar 1962.

17. Ibid., item 76, letter of 16 Mar 1962 by Sir J. J. Saville Garner to the Chairman.

18. Ibid., item E/71, letters from Minister of Finance, Kuala Lumpur; Governor, North Borneo – item 77 in ibid.; Governor, Sarawak – item 83 in ibid.; Lord Selkirk, High Commissioner, Malaya – item 78/E/2 in ibid.

19. Ibid., item E/85A, letter from Minister of Finance, Dar-es-Salaam.

20. H. of C. Deb., Vol. 660, col. 1622, 31 May 1962.

21. Including Miss Joan Vickers (col. 1625), Mrs Eirene White (col. 1634) and Mr Charles Royle (col. 1638).

22. Idem, col. 1643. The matter was raised again during the Second Reading of the Trinidad and Tobago Independence Bill: H. of C. Deb., Vol. 662, cols 541–75, 4 July 1962.

23. Confidential file 81/67/01, Part B, 1960–1962, item 88, minute of 7 June 1962 by the Secretary of State.

24. Ibid., minute of 21 June 1962.

25. Ibid., item 90, letter of 22 June 1962 from the Permanent Under-Secretary of State to the Joint Permanent Secretary to the Treasury.

26. Ibid., item E/96, letter of 25 June 1962 from Sir H. A. F. Rumbold to Sir F. Lee.

27. Ibid., item 105, letter of 13 July 1962 from the Secretary of State for the Colonies to the Chancellor of the Exchequer. The letter was written after the Secretary of State discussed with the Chairman of CDC: see items 106 and 107 in ibid. It was his last day as Secretary of State for the Colonies as the Colonial Office became merged with the CRO and the Secretary of State for Commonwealth Relations, Mr Sandys, also became Secretary of State for the Colonies as from that date. Mr Maudling became Chancellor of the Exchequer.

28. Ibid., minute of 23 July 1962. The meeting of Colonial and CRO officials at the Treasury was on 18 July 1962.

29. C (62) 123, 20 July 1962.

30. CC 49(62) item 5, 24 July 1962.

31. Confidential file EGD 81/150/01, 1963–1965, item 36, memorandum of 11 Mar 1963 to the Secretary of State.

32. Confidential file EGD 81/67/01, Part B, 1960–1962, item 136, letter of 23 Aug 1962.

33. Ibid., item 138, letter of 31 Aug 1962. The point was made orally that any scheme put up by the CDC for Southern Rhodesia would have to be looked at in the light of the requirements of other territories whose economic status showed a greater need for CDC assistance–minute of 31 Aug 1962 in ibid.

34. Confidential file EGD 81/67/01, Part C, 1960–1962, item 145, minute of 3 Sep 1962.

35. Ibid., minute of 10 Sep 1962 by Secretary of State.

36. H. of L. Deb., Vol. 252, col. 154, 16 July 1963, Minister of State for Colonial Affairs in the Debate on the Second Reading.

37. Idem, col. 154.

38. Confidential file EGD 81/150/01, 1963–1965, item 27, Brief of 25 Feb 1963 for the Under-Secretary of State for Commonwealth Relations. See also items 30 and 31 of 5 and 11 Dec respectively in Confidential file EGD 81/67/06, 1963–1965.

8 The Changing Pattern of the Colonial Development Corporation's Activities, 1959–1968

1. THE POSITION TO 1958

As was shown earlier, there were changes of both scope and emphasis over the years 1948–1958. These may be briefly recapitulated with the help of the successive Annual Reports of the CDC. Under the Trefgarne regime, which continued to 31 October 1950 – Lord Trefgarne became Chairman-designate in July 1947, and Chairman when the ORD Act received the Royal Assent on 11 February 1948 – a total of 49 schemes became operational. By the end of 1950, the total was 50, spread over 20 territories, or 22 territories if the two Dependencies of Jamaica are separately counted. Capital sanctioned totalled £31,354,000, of which £10,175,962 had been committed; 64 per cent of the total was intended for primary production and processing. There was a wide variety of schemes, which included a building society – Federal and Colonial Building Society Ltd – to help with the housing shortage in Singapore and Malaya; loans to a public utility – Central Electricity Board, Federation of Malaya and Singapore – and to a statutory development board – Lagos Executive Development Board, Nigeria; development companies in three Colonies – Bahamas Development Undertaking, Dominica Grouped Undertaking and Tristan Da Cunha Development Co. Ltd; and two hotels – Fort George Hotel, Belize, British Honduras, and Lake Victoria Hotel, Uganda. In eight undertakings the Corporation was in partnership with governmental or statutory bodies, and in ten with private enterprise. So the majority of schemes were direct projects, and necessarily so if the Corporation was to develop Colonial resources quickly on a wide front both in terms of products and of territories. Not surprisingly, after the first fourteen months of the Reith regime – Lord

Reith became Chairman on 1 November 1950 and his term of office expired on 31 March 1959 – it was said that one of the lessons learned was 'that too much was attempted in the past by way of direct executive management – the Corporation all on its own.'[1] As shown earlier, the Minister of State, Mr John Dugdale, was doubtful as early as September 1950 whether any single organisation could effectively handle such a variety of projects in so many territories, and this view was shared by the new Secretary of State, Mr Oliver Lyttelton. It is not surprising, therefore, that the Annual Report for 1951 declared that 'Other things being equal, deliberate policy is to look for experienced private enterprise partners to share in investment and in management.'[2] Inspection of the charts in the Annual Reports for 1961 and for 1964 show that investment of CDC funds in direct projects and subsidiary companies rose from an average of some £17 million for 1948–52 to a peak level of some £24 million in 1958, falling to around £22 million by 1962. Investment in 'Associated companies and other investments (shares and loans)' rose from an average of about £1 million for 1948–52 to around £13 million in 1958 and £37 million in 1964. The third category shows, 'loans to Governments and statutory bodies,' reached an average of around £5 million for 1948–52, rose to £19 million by 1958 and was £39 million by 1964. (In 1956 a loan of £15 million was guaranteed by the Federal Government of Rhodesia and Nyasaland for Stage I of the Kariba hydro-electric undertaking. £2.95 million was drawn in 1960 and the remainder in 1961, and largely explains the rise in 'loans to Governments and statutory bodies' between 1958 and 1964.) Already in the Annual Report for 1952 it was stated that the Corporation was 'investing materially in loans for public utilities under government guarantee',[3] and two years later it was reported cryptically that 'CDC continues to put considerable sums on loan into provision of power, communications, housing; its money well directed in supplementing other funds going into such basic development till ground has been prepared for undertakings widely regarded as being more suitable for CDC.'[4] The controversy aroused by this cautious policy has been examined earlier, where it was shown that it was decided in 1958 that, save in exceptional circumstances, the Corporation would no longer be in the market for straight loans to Governments or their statutory boards.

The year 1958 has been selected in quoting CDC investment because it was the last full year of the Reith regime. By the end of that year, there were 77 continuing projects. Two projects, the British Guiana Consolidated Goldfields Ltd and the associated Potaro Hydro-electric Co. Ltd., had ceased operations and been placed in the hands of a Receiver, while the West Indies Navigation Co. Ltd had ceased to operate its ship around the West Indies. Capital sanctioned totalled £81.7 million, while capital committed came to £56.2 million. It was mentioned that the CDC was seeking to establish development companies in association with regional Governments in West Africa, and that preliminary discussions concerning co-operation had taken place with the International Bank for Reconstruction and Development and its affiliate, the International Finance Corporation. The contribution made by the CDC was summed up in this way by the Chairman:[5]

CDC doings have added to Colonial production of:

(a) food: rice, citrus, pineapples, bananas, palm oil, cocoa, coffee, tea, margarine, flour, meat, fish;
(b) other products: gold, silver, copper, timber, cement, manila hemp, wattle extract, rubber, hides, tobacco, tung oil, copra, electricity, houses, factories, roads and bridges..

Productive assets created directly or with CDC help include:

(a) hydro-electric installations in Dominica, St Vincent, Rhodesia and Kenya;
(b) plantations in Dominica, Borneo, Malaya, Tanganyika, Nyasaland, Swaziland and Nigeria;
(c) mines in Uganda, Kenya and Tanganyika;
(d) factories in Trinidad, Singapore, Malaya, Kenya, Tanganyika, Northern Rhodesia and Nigeria;
(e) sawmills in British Guiana (largest in South America) and Nigeria;
(f) irrigation canals in Swaziland;
(g) abattoir and ranches in Bechuanaland;
(h) new and better houses in Jamaica, Malaya, North Borneo, Singapore, Kenya, Nyasaland, Southern Rhodesia and Nigeria;
(i) hotels in British Honduras, Kenya and Sierra Leone;
(j) roads and bridges in Ghana and Nigeria.

Over half a million acres of idle land have been made productive. Wage-earning employment for over 16,000 workers is at present provided by CDC direct projects; employees have benefited from good health and welfare arrangements.

The Hume regime was short and essentially transitional in character. Sir Nutcombe Hume was a member of the Board of CDC from its inception, becoming Deputy Chairman on 1 November 1953, and Chairman on 1 April 1959. He retired on 30 November 1960, being succeeded by his Deputy Chairman, Lord Howick of Glendale, who, as Sir Evelyn Baring, was Governor of Southern Rhodesia, 1942–4; High Commissioner for the United Kingdom in the Union of South Africa and in Basutoland, the Bechuanaland Protectorate and Swaziland, 1944–51; and Governor of Kenya, 1952–9. In the Annual Report for 1959, the commercial and local association of the CDC was explained thus [6]:

(1) Opportunities have continued to be taken for partnership with private enterprise and association with local interests whenever it has been practical to do so.

(2) By supplementing private commercial investment, CDC funds are sometimes able to make possible development that would not otherwise be undertaken. The enlistment of private capital is also frequently the means of introducing experienced management.

(3) Private enterprise participation is not however invariably the best or most appropriate for all projects at every stage; development opportunities sometimes occur where investment and direction by CDC alone is the only way to get the development started. Later, when the projects have become established, the chance may come to enlist private enterprise association.

(4) There are now 24 direct projects with no significant outside participation and there are several outstandingly successful projects, notably Borneo Abaca Ltd, British Guiana Timbers Ltd, Swaziland Irrigation Scheme, Malaya Borneo Building Society Ltd and Usutu Forests, which were started, and in some cases continued after considerable reorganisation, under sole CDC control.

(5) The association of local interests with projects is achieved in a variety of ways according to circumstances. In some cases, there is financial participation by local governments or statutory bodies, as well as or as an alternative to local private enterprise; in others local representative persons have been invited to serve on the boards of subsidiary companies.

(6) Much thought and study have been given to smallholder schemes attached to nucleus estates as a means of providing close association with the local people. The Corporation hopes to undertake or assist more of these in future.

As seen earlier, the point made in (3) had, in fact, been made by an official in the Colonial Office in November 1951, when he feared that a rigid adherence to the principle of participation proposed by the new Secretary of State, Mr Oliver Lyttelton, would not only have eliminated bad and doubtful projects, but also might have prevented the adoption of some projects that were not then in the doubtful category. This was allowed for in the letter the Secretary of State sent later that month to the Chairman of the CDC. It is sufficient here to note the confirmation of part of the initial strategy of the CDC. Concern is rather with the points made in (5) and (6) above, which might most conveniently be approached via the resumed tripartite meetings.

11. TRIPARTITE DISCUSSIONS, 1959–1960

It was noted earlier that the monthly meetings of the Colonial Office, the Treasury and the CDC of the Trefgarne period did not survive long once Lord Reith became Chairman. In 1958 the Minister of State, Lord Perth, considered that their resumption would provide a regular forum in which major difficulties between the Corporation and Government Departments could be discussed. The Chairman and the Financial Secretary to the Treasury, Sir J. Simon, agreed.[7] An incidental advantage to the Colonial Office was that the CDC could put its 'ceaseless string of complaints' about interest rates direct to the Treasury.[8] But it did not prove possible to hold the first meeting before April 1959, by which time Sir Nutcombe Hume had become Chairman. It appears that a total of five meetings were held, the fifth taking place on 29 February 1960, and then no more were called.[9] However, they pinpointed the main policy issues in the changing pattern of CDC activities and these will be considered briefly in turn.

(a) The Cameroons Development Corporation

The first issue was whether the CDC should invest in a territory likely to leave the Commonwealth, and whether it should withdraw when the territory did leave. The problem arose following the intimation by the Federal Government of Nigeria in April 1957 that both it and the Government of Southern Cameroons would welcome the participation of the CDC in the Cameroons Development Corporation (Camdev) by way of investment and association with management. The CDC was invited to investigate, which it did in June/July, 1957, prior to negotiating the terms of participation. It was agreed that the CDC would be appointed managing agents of Camdev, with effect from 1 January 1959, and that not later than 31 December 1961 Camdev would be reconstituted as a joint stock company. The necessary additional capital of £3 million was to be provided by the CDC, of which £1 million would be made available on the CDC becoming managing agents and the rest would become available after the end of the reorganisation period.[10] The CDC, therefore, applied on 8 August 1958 for approval by the Secretary of State for capital sanction for £3 million for the purpose. However, the approach of Nigerian independence complicated the matter, as it was thought possible that the Southern Cameroons would then cease to be administered by Nigeria, which in turn might wish to withdraw from Camdev.[11]

It is unnecessary for the present purpose to follow in any detail the resolution of the issue.[12] The main points were as follows. The Southern Cameroons became a mandated territory after the 1914–18 War, and was administered as part of Nigeria until Nigeria became independent in 1960. It was then administered direct from London until, as the result of a plebiscite in 1961, it elected to join the neighbouring, former French, but by then independent country of Cameroon. The two countries became the Federal Republic of Cameroon, of which the former Southern Cameroons became West Cameroon. Camdev was established as a statutory corporation in the Southern Cameroons shortly after the 1939–45 War to take over and develop estates which had belonged to German companies and individuals and had been taken over by the Custodian of Enemy Property. By 1959, Camdev was in need of further capital and, as stated, the CDC was invited to participate. Under a special termination clause in the agreement, the CDC was entitled to withdraw if a situation arose which materially altered the state of Camdev's affairs. However, it was agreed that this clause could only be invoked for major reasons of policy and not simply because Southern Cameroons joined the Cameroon Republic. The ORD Act, 1959, allowed the CDC to continue with an investment in an ex-colonial territory which subsequently left the Commonwealth, as the former Southern Cameroons had done. On that basis, the CDC was given formal approval in December 1959 to invest £3 million in Camdev. £750,000 of the first £1 million had been drawn by June 1962.[13] The Southern Cameroons joined the Cameroon Republic on 1 October 1961, and the agreement with the CDC had to be renegotiated as the Cameroon authorities did not wish to turn Camdev into a joint stock company.

The CDC considered the pros and cons of continued participation in Camdev and felt that (i) from the commercial standpoint, Camdev was as attractive an investment as African agriculture could offer, and there were no agricultural or commercial reasons for limiting investment to the first £1 million; (ii) a decision against further investment would be likely to lead to the termination of the management agreement with the CDC; and (iii) with the CDC's investment, Camdev was the largest single element in the West Cameroon economy, and for the CDC to prejudice Camdev's operations by a radical curtailment of its investment was likely to have unfavourable political consequences. (HM Government had agreed to extend up to 30 September 1963, the Commonwealth Preference on Cameroon products marketed in the United Kingdom. This continued the assistance to Camdev in marketing its bananas, though the CDC intended to diversify Camdev's production away from bananas.) So the CDC wished to invest a further £1 million, instead of the original further £2 million, and asked for Ministerial agreement for their proposal, which was supported, at the official level, by the Colonial Office, the Treasury and the Foreign Office. In addition to the arguments pressed by the CDC, officials mentioned that the termination agreement did not operate simply because the territory left the Commonwealth, and it was thought that, in view of our forty years' administration, HMG should act favourably towards the territory. One complication was that the West Africa Group of the Conservative Commonwealth Council (CCC), represented to the Secretary of State, Mr R. Maudling, that the CDC investment should be restricted to the first £1 million as the territory had left the Commonwealth and, despite the nature of the termination clause, they felt that the CDC should not support a project in a foreign country and that any aid to the Cameroon Republic should be channelled through more appropriate agencies.[14] Yet the submission was agreed by the Secretary of State for the Colonies, the Foreign Secretary and the Financial Secretary to the Treasury.[15] Later the CDC requested written confirmation that they might negotiate on the basis stated, which the Secretary of State provided.[16] The Chairman of the West Africa Group of the CCC was assured that any agreement with the Cameroon authorities would have to be acceptable to both the CDC and HMG and leave managerial control with the CDC.[17] Nevertheless, there was continued Tory backbench opposition to further CDC investment in a country which chose to leave the Commonwealth, although there was also some Opposition support for the continued investment in the Southern Cameroons during the Debates in June 1963 on the Commonwealth Development Bill.[18] Despite Foreign Office pressure, it was decided not to extend the preferences on bananas from the Cameroons beyond September 1963 – a decision which affected the profitability of Camdev and created a conflict between its commercial soundness and political expediency.[19] The Foreign Office view was earlier expressed in a letter of 30 October 1962 from Sir P. Reilly to Sir H. Poynton thus:

> We have now considered further the question of the Corporation's operations in the Republic of Cameroon and the Somali Republic, and agree that the CDC should not be empowered under the new Act to undertake new projects in these countries. We are glad to see that it is your intention to preserve the Corporation's power to carry on Camdev, as we attach great importance to this project. I think that similar criteria should be applied to the Gambia, if and when it unites with Senegal. . . . If Gambia chooses to leave the Commonwealth and unite with Senegal it will not be for any lack of sympathy with us but because independence within the Commonwealth would not offer her an economically viable future. As a union with Senegal is the obvious solution for Gambia's problems from the economic point of view, I think it is reasonable that we should try to provide her with as good a dowry as possible [item 169 in Confidential File EGD 81/G7/01, Part C, 1960–1962].

In the circumstances, it became unlikely that the CDC would increase its investment above the £1 million loan in a territory whose economy was becoming increasingly assimilated to that of the European Economic Community. Indeed, the CDC's stake could be reduced by redeeming, say, £750,000 of the loan, leaving £250,000, while the Corporation retained managerial control. It was against this background that it was suggested that the Federal German Government might make a loan to Camdev to enable it to repay a substantial part of its indebtedness to the CDC and that, as between the Federal German and the British Governments, the transaction be counted as a contribution under the development aid transfer section of the Stationing Costs Agreement.[20] However, the West Cameroon Government did not favour the proposal, which did not proceed.[21] Meanwhile, the arrangement with the CDC became politically objectionable in West Cameroon and alternatives were beginning to be explored in 1964.[22] Production of rubber, oil palms and bananas fell in 1964 compared with 1963 from what were expected to be temporary factors, while the profit of £36,603 for 1963 turned into a loss of £85,315 for 1964, partly owing to the steeply declining price of bananas in the United Kingdom due to the effect of the removal of

Commonwealth preference not being wholly offset by successful sales in France and Italy.[23] In 1964, an agricultural mission visited Camdev to appraise past and proposed future development, including plans for the association of Camdev with the West Cameroon Government in smallholder settlement schemes. The resulting report was intended to form the basis for applications by Camdev for long-term loans from IBRD and other agencies.[24]

(b) Activities in Nigeria

The CDC's activities in Nigeria were discussed at each of the five 'summit' meetings because the date of Nigerian independence, 1 October 1960, had been announced and the CDC was anxious (i) to postpone the 'cut-off' date, after which new projects could not be started, (ii) to receive capital sanction for as many of the schemes submitted as possible, and (iii) to obtain clearance for participation in development corporations in the Federation. All three raised policy issues. The first was resolved at the first meeting.[25] It was raised by the Minister of State, Lord Perth; and the Chairman of the CDC, Sir Nutcombe Hume, followed by saying that he thought 1 January 1960 was too early. The Financial Secretary to the Treasury, Sir J. Simon, said that the Treasury had proposed an early date so that the Corporation's activities would not spread over far into the period of independence. However, in the light of current discussions and of the new spirit of co-operation between the Corporation and the Departments, and with the proviso that there should be a real tapering-off of a number of new projects which the CDC submitted for approval before 1 April 1960, the Financial Secretary was prepared to agree that the 'cut-off' date might be six months before Independence. It was agreed that (a) the 'cut-off' date should be changed to 1 April 1960; (b) HMG would need to be satisfied that there were exceptional circumstances before accepting applications after that date; and (c) it would not normally be possible for schemes to be approved which would not be in effective operation before 1 October 1960.

During the eleven years to March 1959, the CDC had committed only £3.4 million on continuing projects in Nigeria plus £2.1 million on abandoned projects. While both the Minister of State and the Chairman were visiting Nigeria in August 1959, the Minister was rather surprised to hear from the Chairman that the Corporation had projects in the territory which totalled £5 or £6 million. Yet he readily supported the Chairman for three reasons. First, he felt that the Chairman would only put forward proposals which were sound and would, at least in large part, come into operation before Independence. Secondly, the CDC's investment had been small hitherto and some of the investment opportunities available should be taken up. Thirdly, if the Corporation had additional investments, it would justify the continuance of good management and staff, which would in turn provide potential help and guidance for British manufacturers who might wish to invest in the country, and so contribute to its economic development.[26] The figure of £5 or £6 million was overtaken on 1 October 1959 by that of £11.9 million given for a list of projects under investigation in Nigeria.[27] The major new item was in respect of nucleus plantations in the Western and Eastern Regions, against which a figure of £6 million was put. At the 'summit' meeting on 2 October 1959[28] the Minister of State said that he had already expressed sympathy with the CDC's desire to increase its investment in Nigeria, but he had not contemplated figures of the order proposed. The Treasury was surprised, because at the meeting of 23 April 1959 a tapering-off of investments in the territory had been promised. The Colonial Office undertook to study the proposals in the light of the undertaking of May 1959, which had been circulated to Governors and Ministers in Nigeria and to the CDC.[29] Particular attention was to be paid to the requirement that any project should be 'substantially operative before the independence date'.[30] Some projects, including the nucleus estates which were in the 'shopping list' of 1 October 1959, were thought not to satisfy the requirement.[31] At the 'summit' meeting of 23 November 1959 the Chairman asked the Colonial Office to say what scale of investment prior to independence would be regarded as reasonable, but both Ministers felt that the projects on the list should be examined individually. As a result, the project for nucleus estates, for a sugar plantation at Bacita, and for a large housing scheme at Moba Village, amounting together to between £6.5 million and £8.5 million, were not approved.[32] Seven projects totalling between £4.1 million and £4.6 million were approved, while one of £650,000 was deferred. The rubber plantation development in Eastern Nigeria was raised by the Premier of that Region, Dr M. I. Okpara, with the Prime Minister, Mr H. Macmillan, on his visit to Enugu in January 1960. The latter explained that it would not be appropriate for United Kingdom financial assistance to continue to be given to the Federal or Regional Governments of Nigeria, after independence, through the same channels as were customary before.[33]

On his return, the Prime Minister wished to consider what channels of economic aid should take the place of the CDC and CD & W, and a report was requested.[34] The Note prepared stated that the capital expenditure programmes of the various Nigerian Governments over the period 1955–62 provided for a total estimated expenditure in the public sector of some £330 million.[35] Of the total, some £276 million was expected to come from Nigeria's own resources, and the balance of £54 million from various external resources. Of the latter, CD & W funds would contribute about £17 million, Colonial Exchequer loans of £3 million to independence, and £12 million as a Commonwealth Assistance loan after independence. The IBRD had lent £10 million, and it was expected that the balance would come from France, the United States and various forms of 'contractor finance'. With current capital approvals amounting to between £4 million and £4.5 million, the CDC commitment was expected to be around £9 million by the date of independence. Clearly, it was rather marginal in relation to the scale of economic development afoot in Nigeria. Yet, even had there been no difficulty over the imminence of independence, the Colonial Office would have refused to allow the CDC to undertake a large plantation commitment in Nigeria unless it had been able to secure substantial risk capital from suitable private enterprise, which it had failed to do. In other words, it doubted whether there was any really genuine need for the CDC to meet.[36]

In a letter to the Governor-General, Sir James Robertson,[37] the Minister of State contended that the rules had been stretched very considerably in approving expenditure which would not be incurred until after independence, particularly in view of the United Kingdom's current balance of payments prospects and the mounting bill for overseas aid, so there was no point in devising new channels of aid, which would 'subject the economy to a strain which it simply could not stand'. The Governor-General's disappointment with the CDC's contribution was not reflected in the CDC's Annual Report for 1959, which stated that it had 'been possible with the active assistance of HMG to make a significant increase in the capital committed to projects in Nigeria in the last full year before independence'.[38] It is a fair comment that, as in the case of Ghana, the CDC only became anxious for projects in Nigeria when the imminence of independence meant the territory was about to be removed from its field of operations. As the Minister stated in his letter of rebuttal to the Governor-General, the rules had been stretched also 'in giving, exceptionally, block sanctions for the regional development companies in the East and North'. Here again policy issues had to be resolved.

In April 1958 the CDC submitted to the Colonial Office, for preliminary clearance, a scheme for regional development companies in Nigeria so that the CDC might meet the suggestion of regional governments that the Corporation be more closely associated with their statutory boards.[39] It was explained that the CDC could not associate directly with the statutory development boards as they were responsible for much grant and loan finance which the CDC could not endorse. So the intention was for the CDC and the statutory boards to form regional development companies which would investigate local investment opportunities.[40] However, already in November–December 1957 a mission from the Commonwealth Development Finance Company (CDFC) had visited Nigeria at the invitation of the Federal Government and discussed the idea of a Federation-wide development corporation. At a meeting at the Colonial Office in May 1958,[41] under the chairmanship of the Minister of State, the CDFC representatives stated that the proposed corporation was regarded as a unifying factor in Nigeria, a point strongly supported by the Minister, who felt that CDFC's view was compatible with the existence of regional companies as desired by the CDC. Some days later, the Minister told the Chairman, Lord Reith, that the Colonial Office preferred the CDFC idea of an institution operating on a pan-Nigerian basis rather than the CDC proposal for separate regional companies.[42] But the Chairman of the CDC had already complained to the Deputy Governor-General of Nigeria, Sir Ralph Grey, that the CDFC was confusing the CDC's own proposals although, in fact, it was apparently the first that had been heard in Lagos of the CDC's regional plans.[43] It seems that the CDC was sceptical of the whole idea of a private enterprise development finance company in Nigeria, especially in view of its experience with the proposed Malayan Industrial Development Finance Corporation, which had come to nothing.[44] The Colonial Office favoured the CDFC's Federation-wide proposal, partly because it was federal and partly because, being federal, it would act as a channel for external private investment.[45] However, no objection in principle was raised against the CDC proposal, providing it was agreed that further capital sanctions would not be possible after independence.[46] The Deputy Governor of the Western Region, Sir George Mooring, commented that: 'A duplication of organisations with substantially the same aims, competing for available expertise and investment opportunities, could well tend to confusion and waste.'[47] But his was a lone voice. The Governor-General was concerned to know what the CDC would be able to do in the way of continuing investment in the regions.[48] In reply to an enquiry from the Colonial Office,[49] the Treasury rejected, irrespective of Nigeria's approaching independence, the advance of £750,000 for the CDC's initial contribution to the Northern Nigerian Development

Company, because the application gave no details of the terms on which funds would be made available or of the likely result of the Company's operations. It was feared, not unreasonably, that, useful though they might be, development companies might be set up in order to evade detailed control of their activities, and individual submission of schemes for expenditure exceeding £50,000 was proposed.[50] The Colonial Office objected to this 'important new doctrine' on *ad hoc* capital sanction which, it was argued, would make the operation of a development company impossible.[51] Naturally, the Treasury did not want to surrender control to such an extent that the interests of the Exchequer were not safeguarded, and asked the Colonial Office to make counter-proposals.[52] There were suspicions enough already in the Colonial Office concerning the Chairman's intention of circumventing Government policy in regard to operations in independent countries through inflated estimates for capital sanction.[53] As the result largely of the persistence of the Minister of State, Lord Perth,[54] the Treasury eventually approved the application for capital sanction in respect of the Northern Nigerian Development Company and of the Eastern Region Development Company, after the CDC had assured the Colonial Office that it (i) would give HMG advance preliminary notification of any projects under consideration by the two companies, and would accept advice given by HMG on grounds of public policy; and (ii) recognised that the two companies were special cases which would not constitute a precedent for similar Companies outside the West African region.[55] The CDC was, therefore, permitted to borrow £750,000 for the purpose of investment in the Northern Nigerian Development Company, and £170,000 for investment in the proposed development company in the Eastern Region.[56] This initial capitalisation provided for estimated requirements up to the date of independence and so, given existing policy on the activities of the CDC in newly-independent Commonwealth countries, the original capital sanctions were to be regarded as final.[57]

(c) The Finance of Development Corporations

On 14 August 1958, the CDC submitted eighteen schemes requiring clearance in principle; among them were schemes for development companies in both Sierra Leone and The Gambia.[58] The objects were said to be (i) to provide the Government concerned with an inexpensive service to undertake preliminary investigation of projects which might prove of commercial merit, and to arrange for any necessary expert advice; (ii) to provide a simple commercial structure through which Government, the CDC and later others could participate financially, and in management and other services, in viable commercial projects; (iii) to channel CDC funds to the territory, unless the size, or other features, of any project made it undesirable or impracticable; (iv) to provide in the case of Sierra Leone a portfolio of shares in projects which, in time, might be sold to small local investors.[59] Initially, investment was to be limited to £20,000 in Sierra Leone against £15,000 from the Government, and £10,000 in The Gambia against an equal amount from the Government. The CDC was to undertake the management with, in the early stages, one manager for the two companies. The formation of, and the participation of the CDC in, such companies was within the terms of the ORD Acts and, indeed, was regarded as a welcome development in the two territories by the Colonial Office.[60] As prior capital sanction was not required for investments not exceeding £50,000, the sums of £20,000 and £10,000 were added to the list of capital sanctions, though it was noted that the authorised share capital of the companies might be large in order to cover further development, and this was to be borne in mind when the general issue came to be discussed.[61] A similar arrangement was made when a development company was formed in the Borneo territories, with an initial capital of £3000.[62]

The general issue was not taken up by the Departments, and the matter was raised by the Chairman of the CDC at the final 'summit' meeting on 29 February 1960. The Minister of State repeated the view of Departments that 'block' sanctions prevented them from carrying out their responsibilities. It was agreed to hold an early meeting of officials to consider possible ways of financing development corporations.[63] Already there was a proposal from the Sierra Leone Government that the capital of the Sierra Leone Development Company should be increased to £750,000, of which the CDC should subscribe £500,000 and the local Government the remainder.[64] The Corporation was to control the Board and manage the company; it argued that capitalisation of that order was necessary to make it worth while setting up a management organisation in Sierra Leone, that it was in practice impossible for the Corporation to operate on the basis of individual capital sanctions for projects as they arose, and that a development company on the lines proposed was often the only practicable way of initiating projects in smaller territories and of securing a commitment by other parties to participate.[65] The Treasury had, as seen earlier, strong objections to 'block' sanctions for development companies controlled by the Corporation. The main objection was that it thereby lost control over the uses to which large amounts of Exchequer money was put, and the establishment of several such companies by the CDC in different territories would defeat the object of the capital sanction procedure, which operated on an individual project basis. 'Block' sanctions meant that the CDC, through its local development companies, would have complete freedom of action in approving expenditure on new projects, and the Colonial Office would neither be able to consider whether there were any legal, or policy, objections to the use of Exchequer money, nor to form an opinion on the commercial soundness of the schemes, as the 'block' system was inconsistent with these requirements. Also, the Colonial Office was far from certain that a local Government contribution of £250,000 would be regarded as a desirable use of scarce resources when the overall financial requirements of the Colony came to be discussed with a Sierra Leone delegation. The Colonial Office brief to the Minister of State concluded firmly that: 'In our view, therefore, the Nigerian companies must continue to be regarded as a very special case, and the CDC must find ways and means of operating in Sierra Leone and in other territories, e.g. Tanganyika, where they would like to have "block sanctions" on the normal basis of approval for individual projects.'[66]

At the 'summit' meeting of 29 February 1960, it was agreed to hold an early meeting of officials to consider ways and means of financing development corporations. In fact, the CDC had on 18 December 1959 requested clearance in principle of a proposal made by the Government of Tanganyika for it to participate in the financing and management of a local development corporation.[67] The new corporation was expected to operate on commercial lines and be charged with assisting in the economic development of the territory by attracting overseas investment and management, primarily for projects in association with private enterprise. The local Government was expected to contribute by transferring to the new organisation its interests in existing commercial enterprises. As a first step, the Corporation was asked to advise on the appropriate capital structure, control and management of the new organisation, for which the Government had tentatively suggested an initial capital of £1 million with power to increase to £5 million. The CDC did not expect to take a minority interest in a Government-controlled organisation.

In accordance with the decision reached at the 'summit' meeting, there was a meeting of officials of the Colonial Office, the Treasury and the CDC. It was agreed not to take a decision on the Sierra Leone issue, but instead to consider it as part of the general financial picture in the course of the early negotiations on an independence settlement.

On the general issue, a compromise solution was reached whereby, in cases where the CDC showed that the setting up of a local development company was the right course, the Corporation would be given overall capital sanction for a total investment in the company, but would be required to obtain separate capital sanction within the overall limit for individual projects costing more than a given amount. The amount would vary according to circumstances, including the size of the territory and the strength of the local management, and would be decided when the overall sanction was given, possibly being as much as £50,000 or as little as £5000 or £10,000. A submission was made to Ministers accordingly[68] and, after clearance, communicated to the CDC, which agreed, albeit with some reluctance.[69]

This policy decision represented the form which assistance should take notwithstanding the system adopted in Nigeria. But Sierra Leone was, by the end of 1960, nearing independence, and so came closely to parallel the situation that had led to the substantial relaxation of normal capital sanction procedure in the case of Nigeria. The Treasury, therefore, conceded that the Nigerian pattern should be adopted in the case of Sierra Leone Investments Limited 'on the basis that it is firmly understood that the present arrangement is not available for use in the case of other Development Companies in any territory, whatever its size, unless possibly a territory is on the verge of independence'.[70] The qualification, necessary though it was, provided the CDC with its opening in connection with the proposed Tanganyika Development Company. Preliminary clearance for investment by the CDC of £500,000 in shares, to match the share subscription which the Tanganyika Government was contemplating, was requested in November 1960.[71] The Colonial Office had no objection, in principle, but expected to receive separate capital sanction applications for the projects to be undertaken, except for small schemes not exceeding a financial commitment 'at a figure to be agreed'.[72]

The CDC came up with two objections to that procedure. First, it stated that the Minister of Finance of the Government of Tanganyika, Sir Ernest Vasey, held that, in view of the imminence of independence, the Tanganyika Government would be reluctant to submit to capital sanction procedure imposed by HMG, and negotiations were suspended. Secondly, the German Federal Government was prepared to match the Tanganyika Government and the CDC subscriptions on the premise that the CDC would be involved in management. It was stated that, if the CDC had to receive capital sanction from HMG, the German partner would be required to apply to Bonn, and this would be regarded as a 'stumbling block', which could lead again to a suspension of negotiations. The CDC, therefore, asked for Nigeria-type treatment for the proposed Tanganyika Development Company.[73] The Colonial Office was sympathetic and wrote to the Treasury thus:

> By seeking to retain a formal United Kingdom power of veto on the eve of each project, and by insisting on receiving all the details which a capital sanction application contains, we will obviously be asking for political trouble, and accused of retaining imperialist interests unsuited to the new United Kingdom relationship with a sovereign country. Moreover, our view is that the United Kingdom can retain all the control it really requires by having an understanding with the CDC that they gave us the general details of a project when the planning stage has started, and make sure we have no objection in their going ahead on policy grounds. We could ask for any details we thought relevant at the time.[74]

The Treasury raised some general questions, in part it would appear in order to delay a decision at one level while the whole question of the CDC's participation in Tanganyika after independence was being discussed at another level, the same official being involved at each level. The Treasury wanted to be satisfied that there was the need for such a company, and also to consider the financial implications of a contribution by the Tanganyika Government at a time when it was dependent on Exchequer loan assistance to meet its capital requirements.[75] Nor did it wish to generalise the 'block sanction' method further, fearing that the CDC would establish such companies in each territory as it approached independence and expect 'block sanction' treatment as a rule rather than, as was intended over Nigeria, a special exception. Also, it was not convinced that participation by another Government rather than a private concern necessitated the avoidance of a procedure which the Corporation had suggested, and Ministers had agreed to, only a year earlier. The Colonial Office recalled that the IBRD's Report on Tanganyika had in 1960 supported the idea of an investigatory company, provided it drew on the assistance of the CDC, or an equivalent outside body, although the Colonial Office felt it was impracticable to explore investment opportunities before establishing the company, as the IBRD suggested, as there would be 'little incentive to seek the advice of an investigatory company unless it could also commit funds'.[76] It was felt that the continuance of the CDC in Tanganyika would help to maintain procedures, such as open tendering, which the United Kingdom wished to see continued. The Colonial Office wished to have the CDC's proposal to participate in the company taken into account as part of the United Kingdom's economic aid to Tanganyika. As regards procedure for capital sanction, the Colonial Office view was that 'the arrangements for securing agreement in principle in advance of any investment' provided all that was necessary, and this was especially so in the light of possible German participation, which otherwise would inevitably increase scope for delay and discord.

Among the papers submitted to the Conference on Financial Aid to Tanganyika after independence, which met in London on 28 June 1961, was one asking HMG to allow the CDC to make further investments, if necessary, in the concerns in which it was already committed, and to permit the CDC to make investments in projects under discussion, or at the exploratory stage, if firm proposals were agreed in principle prior to the date of independence, i.e., 28 December 1961. By June 1961 the CDC was concerned with eleven projects for which capital sanctions totalled about £8.5 million. The new investments proposed by the CDC came to around £1.5 million. It was regarded by the Treasury as contrary to normal practice, because it was so near the date of independence as virtually to circumvent the intention of the ORD Act 1959, which debarred the Corporation from new investment in independent Commonwealth countries.[77] As the CDC already had capital sanction totalling £8.5 million and was, in any case, approaching its borrowing ceiling, the relevant Division of the Treasury intended to resist the proposals, unless there were special reasons to justify an exception in any particular case. This view was endorsed because 'In practice, such investment involves a call on the United Kingdom balance of payments for purposes which are not really of first priority.'[78] At the time, Tanganyika was unable, without external assistance, either to balance her budget or to finance her minimum development requirements, and so needed generous treatment in other ways, e.g., CD & W, Exchequer loans for development, compensation and commutation of pensions. Accordingly, it was agreed by the Financial Secretary to the Treasury, Sir Edward Boyle, that proposals for new CDC investments prior to independence should be resisted.[79] The Secretary of State for the Colonies, Mr Macleod, raised the matter, along with others, with the Chancellor of the Exchequer, Mr Selwyn Lloyd.[80] The Secretary of State urged that more than the building society project, which was an essential part of the plan for avoiding a moratorium on the building societies in East and Central Africa, should be permitted. He mentioned the Development Corporation (£500,000), the scheme for tea planting or small-holder cocoa (£150,000 to £200,000) and possibly a pyrethrum scheme (£60,000). He thought that there was a good chance of all the schemes mentioned being well under way before Independence Day, and that 'it would be a big psychological mistake now to cut off all projects in an active state of consideration'. With the building society loan of £500,000, the total came to around £1.2 million, as against the original Colonial Office bid for around £1.5 million. On 10 July 1961 the Treasury was able, 'following the Ministerial decision regarding CDC investments in Tanganyika', to agree in principle to the project for a development corporation on condition that (a) at no time would there be a request to exceed £500,000, (b) Tanganyika would provide a matching contribution within available resources, including the aid promised by HMG; (c) CDC's contribution would be found within the £130 million limit to capital sanctions; (d) any expenditure incurred on that project in 1961–62 would be matched by postponement of some other CDC investment; and (e) separate capital sanction for each individual project within the sanction given for the overall investment would be sought.[81] The other schemes mentioned in the Secretary of State's letter were also agreed on the same conditions.[82] The CDC reverted to 'the only stumbling block' to German participation being the capital sanction procedure still required by HMG.[83] In view of the request of the Regional Controller for an immediate reply, and pressure by the Colonial Office, the Treasury made the third exception and agreed to the system of 'block' sanction, placing reliance on the system of preliminary clearance to veto, or defer, a project, should it be thought necessary to do so.[84] Not unnaturally, the Treasury thought 'that the next case, if any, should be decided against the background of a proper and timely consideration of the issues'. An application for capital sanction for £500,000, on long-term conditions, to finance the CDC's third share in the Tanganyika Development Finance Company (TDFC) was made on 14 November 1961, and agreed that month.[85] The company was registered on 17 December 1962. On 12 December 1962 the CDC reported that the Manager-Designate had taken up his appointment, and preliminary clearance was requested for a loan of £50,000 to assist in the erection of a tea factory at Idetero in 1963.[86] The proposal was readily supported, both for its own sake and because it was thought useful to have a tripartite stake in the industry.[87] The CDC's investment in the TDFC by the end of 1962 totalled £12,500.[88]

III. DEVELOPMENT CORPORATIONS IN AFRICA, 1962–1964

On 28 February 1962 the CDC requested preliminary clearance of a proposal for the formation by the CDC and the Uganda Development Corporation (UDC) of a joint development company in Uganda to operate on commercial lines.[89] The broad purpose was to further the economic development of the territory, 'with particular reference to the need to attract to Uganda capital and expert management from outside, primarily by investment in projects to be established in association with private enterprise'. No details of capitalisation, or management, had been decided, though it was stated that the CDC would not be a minority partner. The application was not unexpected in the Colonial Office, but seen to raise several issues. To begin with, there was a legal aspect, because the preliminary view of the lawyers was that development companies were *ultra vires* the ORD Act.[90] Then there was a capital aspect. It appeared that the main interest of the UDC was less with the long-term effects of the joint development with the CDC than with relieving itself of an immediate financial problem in relation to existing commitments. The proposal was that the UDC should transfer some of its existing investments and the CDC should contribute cash, so that the UDC's liquidity problem would be relieved. However, the CDC and the Chairman of UDC, Mr, later Sir James, Simpson, were advised that the time was not opportune to put the proposal forward, because (*a*) owing to the difficulties of getting a pre-independence financial settlement with Uganda, the Treasury was unlikely to entertain a proposal for a further £1 million for Uganda, *via* the CDC, which was not part of the independence settlement, (*b*) the Treasury would not favour a proposal where only the CDC subscribed cash and (*c*) even if the scheme were approved, it would not be in time to enable the CDC to invest £300,000 over the next few months in the new machinery due for delivery. So both Corporations agreed to hold over the idea for a while.[91] The CDC renewed its application just before the Chairman attended the independence celebrations, because it understood that the UDC's negotiations with German and American interests had progressed, and its own uncommitted position was becoming difficult to maintain. It was said also that progress was being made towards the establishment of a joint company in Kenya with both the Government and the West Germans as partners, although, in fact, the CDC's own request for preliminary clearance was not made until 12 November 1962.[92] The

Colonial Office supported the renewed application in a letter to the CRO, which was soon to become the Department concerned, and a copy of the letter was sent to the Treasury. Neither the CRO nor the Treasury were willing to commit themselves to the proposed joint development company in Uganda.[93] To the Treasury, it raised the familiar question of whether the rather loose form of control, which was exercisable over the projects financed from the CDC's money under the general umbrella of a Development Corporation in an independent territory, was compatible with its responsibility for the use of public money. The request of September 1961 for a discussion of this as a matter of general policy before another application was received had not been taken up, perhaps inevitably so as the *modus operandi* of Whitehall is essentially that of the particular, in which the general has less urgency, even though in this, as in some contexts, eschewing the general suited the CDC best, the Colonial Office next best and the Treasury least. Again the Treasury insisted: 'In general, we would much prefer to reach agreement on the principles governing new operations by the CDC in the independent Commonwealth and, incidentally, to wait until the necessary legislation is through before we allow the Corporation to be committed, even in principle, to any new scheme outside the Colonies.'[94] There were, according to the Treasury, two problems to consider, namely (i) the objections in principle to participation by the CDC in Development Corporations; (ii) what should be done to implement the agreed policy that the CDC's drawings upon the Exchequer should be controlled on an annual basis once it began to invest in new projections in the independent Commonwealth.[95] As regards the first of the problems, there was by that time not only the Uganda proposal requiring attention, but also a proposal for further investment in the development corporation in Northern Nigeria, and a request for clearance in principle of a proposal for a joint company in Kenya.

The Colonial Office disputed that there could be objections in principle,[96] as the Treasury had agreed in 1958 that development companies could perform useful functions and the Corporation might participate in them. The matter was, therefore, one of procedure for capital sanction, and the Colonial Office urged that there should be a move in the direction of accepting the 'exceptional' policy agreed over the Nigerian companies as the rule.[97] The Colonial Office letter was discussed at a meeting with the CRO and the Treasury on 1 January 1963, and its general line was accepted with little modification. After further comments by the Treasury and discussion with the CDC, all parties approved the terms of a letter setting out the procedure to be followed in the case both of investments in new development companies and of supplementary investment in existing development companies.[98] Where the Corporation proposed to invest in a local development company, the application for capital was to be submitted for the amount that was to be invested in the company. When that application was approved and the company proposed to invest in a project, the Corporation would supply, at as early a date as possible and in as much detail as possible, a description of the project and an indication of how the money was to be provided by the company, and on what terms. It was hoped as a rule to give an opinion on the general acceptability, or otherwise, of a project within ten days. Where the Corporation's investment in a development company did not exceed £50,000, or where the project as a whole did not exceed £50,000, the new procedure was not applicable. Quarterly reports of such investments were to be made for information purposes. It was stated that the initial application for capital sanction should 'be related to a reasonable assessment of the needs for foreseeable projects', being supplemented later 'if, and as, a further range of projects came into view'. It was noted earlier that the Corporation felt unable to assess investment opportunities before embarking on investment in a development company, and so the suggestion just quoted was an attempt to settle initial capitalisation less on political and prestige grounds and more on grounds of economic potentiality. The proposal had, however, come rather late in the day. Finally, where the development companies existed in independent Commonwealth countries, the CDC was expected to keep in close touch with the offices of the United Kingdom High Commissioners so that they were informed and might help to expedite subsequent consultations. The letter was accordingly circulated to the ten High Commissioners.[99]

In accordance with the agreed procedures, the CDC began notifying at quarterly intervals commitments of less than £50,000 by development companies. The first was for the quarter ending 30 June 1963,[100] and showed only one such investment. It was made by Northern Developments (Nigeria) Ltd in a firm to manufacture perfumes in Nigeria. The estimated capital cost was £63,000, of which the NDNL's contribution was to be £13,000, of which £3000 was to be in equity and the balance on loan at 8½ per cent. In the next quarter, ending 30 September 1963,[101] the NDNL was reported to have another project, namely a joint venture to construct a gas bottling plant in Kaduna and to organise a distribution system throughout Northern Nigeria, at an estimated capital cost of £65,000, of which the NDNL had agreed to provide £5000 in equity and £25,000 in an 8¼ per cent secured loan of which one-half was convertible into equity. The Eastern Nigerian Industrial and Agricultural Company Limited was reported to have two commitments. First, the regional Government had established a Fund for Agriculture and Industrial Development to provide loans to indigenous enterprises. It was to contribute up to £50,000, at an interest rate of 8 per cent and with repayment of the loan guaranteed by the regional Government. Secondly, a gas-bottling plant was to be built at Port Harcourt and distribution organised throughout the region, at an estimated cost of £60,000. The Fund was to provide £7000 in equity and £15,000 in 8½ per cent secured loan, of which up to £5000 would be convertible into equity. Sierra Leone Investments Limited had undertaken to provide £15,000 in 8½ per cent loan, part of which was convertible into equity, in a £40,000 factory in Freetown to produce plastic sandals. Neither the Tanganyika Development Finance Company nor the Borneo Development Corporation Limited had any commitments to report in either quarter.

Given the nature of the agreed procedure, it is not surprising that the General Manager of the CDC was pleased with 'such a satisfactory conclusion', though he observed that it would be necessary 'to arrive at the right sort of compromise between the need for early clearance, which means the submission of information at an early stage, with the desire of the Departments for as much information as possible'.[102] The letter went on: 'In particular, of course, the financial details tend to be worked out at a comparatively late stage in the working up of a new project, so we trust that it will be recognised that the information on finance will normally tend to be general rather than particular.' How, then, did the new procedure work out in practice?

Once the new procedure was in the main agreed, preliminary clearance was requested for an investment of £500,000 by the CDC in the Kenya Development Finance Company (KDFC). The capitalisation was to be as in the case of the Tanganyika Development Finance Company, i.e. a total of £1.5 million to be contributed in equal parts by the CDC, the Federal German Government and the Kenya Industrial Development Corporation, the contribution of the last being partly through the transfer of revenue-earning investments and the rest in cash. The Colonial Office strongly supported the proposal,[103] and the Treasury agreed that the scheme did 'not seem likely to give rise to difficulties'. When the CDC applied to borrow up to £500,000 as its contribution to the KDFC, it was noted that the initial authorised share capital had been raised to £2 million, with £1.5 million paid up. The question arose as to whether the initial capitalisation was related to economic potentialities. The Colonial Office dealt with the point in its letter to the Treasury.[104] It said, in part, that 'so far as we are able to assess the potential from here, a share capital of £2 million, to be called up as the needs arise, seems to be about right for Kenya', though the relevant file contains no evidence for this view. It went on to assert that, politically, 'the desirability of the Kenya company matching the Tanganyika company is obvious in the present political climate in East Africa'. For good measure, it added the telling point that it was desirable to bring in the maximum contribution 'and equal shares by the other main participants seems the right way of doing this'. The Treasury consented to the borrowing without more ado,[105] and the CDC was so informed on 18 July 1963, i.e. less than four weeks after the application was made.

In November 1963 details of six investments under consideration by the KDFC were sent by the CDC to the Colonial Office for clearance in principle.[106] They were (i) expansion of a canning factory at Thika, (ii) expansion of a hotel then under construction in Nairobi, (iii) proposed new hotel in Nairobi, (iv) factory for the dehydration of vegetables at Nairasha, (v) kraft pulp, paper and paper-board mill at Broderick Falls, and (vi) sugar factory at Kisumu. The Colonial Office saw no reason to object, although it mentioned in its covering letter to the Treasury that it wondered whether Nairobi could immediately support 200 more hotel rooms, and it noted that there was uncertainty about the level of the investment in the dehydration factory, though it would only slightly exceed the clearance-free limit of £50,000 in total in any case.[107] The Treasury was reminded of the promise to clear within ten days, and told of the desire to clear as many as possible of the proposed investments before Kenya became independent on 12 December 1963.[108] The Treasury obliged by clearing the first four. The remaining two, in which the CDC was expected to have shares of only 2 per cent and 2½ per cent respectively, were cleared after the High Commissions in East Africa had been consulted. The CDC was thus given clearance within three weeks of making an application. So, as far as the CDC was concerned, the new procedure was entirely satisfactory: whether the letter of 30 April 1963 setting out the procedure marked the coming of age of development companies, or of the CDC itself, or both is a matter of opinion. The certainty is that only a bare minimum of control was exercisable thereafter by Whitehall. The passage of the Commonwealth Development Act, 1963, cleared the remaining obstacle due to the restriction imposed by the ORD Acts.

When the application for clearance for participation by the CDC in a proposed Development Finance Company of Uganda (DFCU) was revived after the passage of the Commonwealth Development Act, it raised no objection of principle,[109] as had the previous application. Nor did the application from the CDC for approval to borrow the sum of £500,500 for investment in the DFCU raise issues: it went through in a month.[110] Similarly, the Treasury had felt unable to authorise a supplementary investment of £1,050,000 in the NDNL under Section 6 of the ORD Act, 1959, and was obliged to hold the application over.[111] The application arose directly from the development plan which the Government of Northern Nigeria had prepared in 1962. It envisaged the setting up of a development bank and two development corporations, one for agriculture and the other for industry, which would absorb the existing development institutions in the region. At the time, there were two main development agencies, namely Northern Region Development Corporation, a wholly-owned Government corporation which had undertaken both commercial and social welfare projects, and the NDNL. The Government proposed that NDNL should become its main agency for financing commercial development, leaving the NRDC to carry out projects of a social and welfare nature only, and the NDNL should take over from the NRDC such of its commercial investments as it was prepared to accept. At the same time, the CDC was asked to provide the NDNL with further capital – £3 million was suggested – which, with additional capital from the Government, was expected to suffice to meet the demands for commercial development finance in the region which could not be obtained from other sources over the following two or three years.[112] The CDC proposed that immediate approval should be given for £500,000, and later for a further £1,050,000, to bring the total equal to the contribution of the Government.[113] The United Kingdom Trade Commissioner in Lagos strongly supported the proposal,[114] and the CRO agreed that there were strong political and economic arguments in favour of a sizeable investment by the CDC in Northern Nigeria and, given the size of the population and the stage of its economic development, the sum proposed was reasonable.[115] The Treasury agreed in principle to the application for a further £500,000, on the understanding that there was no commitment to go beyond that figure as there were a number of quite difficult issues involved and the need to tread warily.[116] The issues concerned the appropriateness of further investment in the NDNL, owing to misgivings arising because the CDC's substantial existing investment in the company had failed to produce a profit, the question of control, and the possibility under the existing statute of sanctioning further capital. The proposal was agreed in principle on 31 December 1962, and the investment of supplementary capital of £500,000 was approved in May 1963.[117] Consent was made conditional upon the CDC's agreement to the new procedure set out in the letter of 30 April 1963. Further capital of £550,000 was applied for by the CDC on 29 April 1963, as the uncommitted balance of the NDNL was then only £283,000.[118] While the Colonial Office and the CRO were in favour of the application in principle, it was felt that to sanction it under Section 6 of the ORD Act, 1959, would strain over-far the meaning of that Section. The Corporation was asked to accept an assurance that the application would be approved as soon as the Commonwealth Development Bill was enacted, and the Treasury was asked to concur.[119] The Treasury felt that the proposal challenged the authority of Parliament, and so promised to give urgent and sympathetic consideration to the proposal for investing the remaining £1,050,000 to enable the NDNL to complete its reconstruction plan once the Bill was enacted.[120] At the same time, the Treasury complained of its inability to obtain information on which to base the control of the CDC's rate of investment. It was hoped to decide on the ceiling for investments before the new Bill became law and there were any further large investments in independent Commonwealth countries to consider. The CDC was informed of the Treasury's willingness to consider the application for the remaining £1,050,000 once the Bill was enacted without serious amendment.[121] The protest concerning the difficulty over information was not mentioned. Approval for the investment was given without delay; the Treasury was concerned only with the wording of the CRO letter to the CDC 'in order to make sure that it was in accordance with the law, as amended by the Commonwealth Development Act, 1963'.[122]

In its Annual Report for 1963, it was stated that the CDC then had commitments to invest more than £6 million in twelve overseas development companies, including the CDC's wholly-owned regional subsidiaries.[123] In the following year, it was reported that:

A feature of 1964 has been the expansion of the CDC stake in industrial development, and especially in secondary industries, through the continuing growth of the territorial development companies established in partnership with the Governments of the countries and other associates, both governmental and private enterprise. The largest and most advanced is Northern Nigeria Investments Limited, in which the Northern Nigeria Government (through its own development agency) and the CDC each owned half shares. It has played an active part in the striking industrial developments in the North, mainly around Kaduna and Kano. At the end of 1964 commitments came to a total of £3,841,250 in 26 projects, the industrial investments including factories making textiles, blankets, cigarettes, metal windows and leather goods . . .

Comments on some of the other development companies followed.

iv. FIELD EXPERIENCE OF THE CDC

It is not intended to attempt to assess in one way or another the participation of the CDC in development companies, because sufficient material for a meaningful evaluation cannot be found in the files on which this study is based. However, in addition to what has been used so far in this treatment of development companies, the applications of the CDC for approval in principle of projects, for initial capital sanction and, wherever relevant, for supplementary capital sanction, all provide pointers to motives, operational problems and degrees of achievement, and so shed light on Colonial development. The author acknowledges with gratitude the kindness of Sir Arthur Gaitskell, a member of the CDC, 1954–73, for showing him his own Notes on the Field Experience of the Corporation.

As regards motives, many emergent territories set up development corporations in order, in part, to stimulate development in various sectors, mainly industrial, of their economies and, in part, to have control of those sectors. Some were highly successful, notably the Uganda Development Corporation, but even the successful ones were handicapped by lack of capital, of managerial ability, and of ability to assess projects put up by interested parties, while expatriate businesses continued to invest independently of the local development corporation. The CDC entered as a partner in local development corporations, or their offshoots, contributing capital and management, and bringing in expatriate companies in joint ventures, thus enabling the local Government to participate without direct involvement. The Corporation was a pioneer in this field, but the IBRD and its affiliate the IFC followed suit later, taking part in, for example, the Nigerian Industrial Development Bank[124] and the Malaysian Industrial Development Finance Company.[125]

Experience differed from territory to territory, though the striking difference was found between African and Far Eastern participation. Whereas in Africa foreign ownership prodominated and local initiative came largely from Government institutions, in Malaysia the sponsors were mainly indigenous entrepreneurs. The record has been mixed, with failures or partial failures resulting from a number of causes. These were principally (a) political changes, including internal disturbances and confrontations with others, (b) faults in the project, or (c) shortcomings of the sponsors. As an example of the effect of political change, the effect on the efficient Borneo Aboca Limited might be instanced.[126] The estates lay along the Indonesian border and so were exposed to hostile action. Despite severe labour difficulties, planting had been extended and the shortage of rubber tappers, due to the confrontation with Indonesia, turned a prospective profit into a loss. Several examples might be given of projects going wrong. First, the Northern Nigerian Government was anxious to start a sugar industry and, although it was not approved in 1959, it was later started with a majority of Government capital. Soil surveys were satisfactory as were trial plantings, but in the first two years of full scale plantings yields were well below estimates. The main reasons were that (i) soils were more variable than the survey revealed, (ii) irrigation on a large scale was not as efficient as on small plots, (iii) field supervision was inadequate, and (iv) problems associated with an untrained labour force had been underestimated. So more capital was needed to avoid insolvency when low yields caused revenue to be below estimates. There was overmuch loan capital and deferred payments on factory machinery to be carried by three-and-a-half tons of sugar to the acre, instead of the forecast four-and-a-half tons. Thus, overoptimistic forecasts had to be pruned; the project and estate were otherwise found satisfactory. Secondly, the Kilombero Sugar Company Limited was incorporated in Tanganyika in 1960 to grow and mill sugar cane and refine sugar.[127] The CDC, the IFC, the Standard Bank and Dutch finance was involved, and the Managing Agents were Dutch. In the first phase, production was planned to reach 10,000 long tons of sugar in the year ending 30 April 1963, and to rise to 20,000 long tons in the following year. The second phase was to increase production to 30,000 long tons in the year ended April 1967. In 1962, the Managing Agents revised the estimates to 13,000 long tons, 24,000 long tons and 35,000 long tons respectively. In the first season, 11,028 long tons were produced but in the second only 12,690 long tons compared with an estimate of 22,152 long tons, and the company was immediately in financial difficulties. A Committee of Investigation reported in December 1963 that up to another £1.5 million would be necessary to enable the company to reach the target for the first phase and to expand eventually to 31,500 long tons. Kilombero was considered to offer an excellent opportunity from an agricultural point of view for successful sugar cane cultivation, but there had been a number of operational errors which had adversely affected the Company's position. The Managing Agency Agreement was terminated, technical consultants were appointed and the management was made responsible directly to the Board. The CDC's investment was raised from £1,385,605 to £1,914,605.[128] However, the land was not as suitable for sugar cane as had been declared earlier and the position did not become satisfactory, with the result that the CDC eventually withdrew from the project.[129]

Thirdly, the CDC invested in Kenya Canners Limited via the Development Finance Company of Kenya.[130] The company, which had been incorporated in 1952, proposed to mechanise the pineapple section of its plant, which was still manual, and to expand other sections. Although the profit record was disappointing up to the end of 1962, it was expected to improve with the new plant, and the DFCK was invited to invest up to £150,000 towards the new capital. However, supplies were affected by drought and the unreliability of deliveries by smallholders, with the result that forecasts were not realised and equity capital was lost. Fourthly, as mentioned earlier, the CDC sought clearance in principle in November 1963 for investment by the DFCK in a hotel in Nairobi then in process of construction so that it might be expanded from 60 to 100 bedrooms.[131] It was stated at the time that profitability had still to be demonstrated, and detailed figures were awaited. It was later found that the hotel could not make a significant profit unless further extended. Finally, a project for producing a pottery industry in Jamaica is illustrative in particular of operational problems. The scheme was submitted for preliminary clearance in May 1959,[132] and a company was incorporated in Jamaica the following year with share capital of £272,000. The Royal Worcester Porcelain Company Limited was to subscribe £160,000, Jamaica Development Finance Corporation £37,500 and the CDC £75,000.[133] The company was intended to manufacture a large range of earthenware products from local clays, for sale in the Caribbean and in North and South America. In its Annual Report for 1963, the CDC reported that the share capital was to be increased by £100,000, which would be contributed by the three partners in proportion to their initial holdings.[134] Substantial losses were reported for 1963. During tests in the pilot plant, local clays were found to be unsuitable and the plant required more electric power than was expected. Inexperienced labour led to faulty output and to a higher proportion of rejects than were expected. The parent company was unable to provide management to overcome these problems and continued losses soon exhausted the extra capital.[135] A technical investigation was undertaken by an expert procured through the United States Agency for International Development, but losses persisted and eventually the CDC withdrew.[136]

The list could be extended further, but the examples given illustrate the main problems arising, problems reminiscent of those encountered in the Trefgarne period when, as in the 1959–64 period, there was an attempt to launch rapidly a succession of varied projects in a number of territories. The transfer from the earlier solo projects to the later joint ventures was not always an improvement. Indeed, it sometimes introduced new problems, because the private sponsor was new to the territory, or to the precise kind of activity involved, or had divided interests, or employed less able managers than for its established production. As regards solo projects, the General Manager of the CDC argued in September 1963 that private investors from outside the territory

> were often willing to join in the project simply and solely because the CDC was already in it. In other words, it might well have been true in the past that the willingness of private investors to join in a project was a good touchstone of its profitability, but now the boot was tending to be on the other foot, and private investors often came in, without examining the project in detail, simply assuming that the CDC itself had looked into it.[137]

A comparison of the lessons of the Trefgarne period with those of 1959–64 suggests that the basic problem was not that of State versus private enterprise schemes, but simply one of adequate feasibility and market surveys, and of efficient management, which might be present, or absent, under either solo or joint ventures. In the Annual Report for 1964 it was stated that:

> Development companies with their functions of investigation, promotion, investment and after-care, are highly sophisticated projects which call for first-class staff trained in the requisite techniques. Such staff are expensive, and the development company must have prospects of an adequate level of business, reached reasonably quickly, if it is to be a commercially viable project. The more simple the economy and the greater the lack of local professional men, the more skills have to be specially imported and the more complex and expensive becomes the operation. It is, accordingly, important that markets among developing countries

should be as large as possible, and that as much as possible of the sound business coming forward should be channelled through the local development agency.[138]

Once the proliferation of such agencies is accepted, this conclusion follows. But there was a conflict between the apparent political necessity to be involved in so many agencies and the economic efficiency and viability of their operation, though it must be recalled that the CDC rested its case on grounds of maintaining trade and economic influence rather than on compelling political reasons. Earlier the Deputy Governor of the Western Region of Nigeria was quoted as warning that 'a duplication of organisations with substantially the same aims, competing for available expertise and investment opportunities, could well lead to confusion and waste'. The proliferation of agencies caused management to be less efficient, because the smallness of the scale of operations justified only 'second eleven' managers and because better managers tended not to stay. It also often resulted in a general overestimate of the range of likely viable investment opportunities, causing funds to be channelled as time went on increasingly into marginal and sub-marginal projects. The initial belief in a plenitude of suitable, viable projects died hard. The CDC's response to the forced realisation that such projects were, in fact, hard to come by was to seek further concessions on the terms on which they borrowed from HMG, so that other schemes might be considered. However, before turning to that aspect, there are two further aspects of the pattern of the CDC's investment which require treatment. The first concerns the activity of the CDC in initiating and participating in building societies, and the other concerns smallholders schemes in peasant agriculture. Both involved local participation, and eventual local ownership.

v. PARTICIPATION OF THE CDC IN BUILDING SOCIETIES

(a) Singapore and Malaya

To help with the housing shortage in Singapore and Malaya, the CDC set up the Federal and Colonial Building Society Limited early in 1950, with an initial capital of £375,000. This action followed an appraisal of the local situation which showed that there was a number of small Chinese contractors ready to build houses if the money was available for house purchase, and a large middle-income group in steady employment able to finance their own housing, but without the funds for outright purchase. A manager, Mr J. Burgess, was recruited by the CDC, who not only organised mortgage procedures, but advised also on the organisation of the contracting side so that unit costs were kept down. Initially, advances at 6 per cent were made of up to 75 per cent of the Society's valuation, repayable over a maximum period of fifteen years, and 100 per cent could be advanced if the applicant's employer guaranteed 25 per cent.[139] According to the Annual Report for 1953, the Society had helped about 1900 families of modest incomes to own their homes, assisted in reducing costs and improving building standards, made profits and was managed with efficiency and initiative.[140] In that year, the CDC applied for capital sanction for an additional investment in the Society of 10 million Straits dollars, equivalent to £1,166,667, because the existing capital of £2,333,333 was virtually committed by the end of 1952. The additional capital was contingent upon the Federal Government putting up a similar sum, which was regarded in the Colonial Office as a move in the right direction, although a contribution from private savings would have been preferred.[141] However, the Treasury had, in the past, serious misgivings about the CDC's rapidly increasing investment in the project, partly because it was doubtful whether the ORD Act covered the activity and partly because it was felt that there should be some local contribution of funds, backed up by the Government of Malaya if necessary. In addition, following the conclusions of the Commonwealth Economic Conference of 1952, a strong balance of payments emphasis was to be given to policy, so that it was necessary to 'be all the more convinced that purely social projects are really worthwhile'.[142] The Colonial Office was, consequently, asked to make a case on the basis of the past performance and the future plans of the Society. The Colonial Office official who wrote to the Treasury after the Secretary of State, Mr Lyttelton, had personally approved the application, minuted that 'In all fairness, it must be admitted that, apart from the fact that this is a profitable investment for the CDC, the grounds for it as a desirable piece of Colonial development are slender.'[143] Colonial Governments were asked to supply the detailed information which the Colonial Office lacked. Much statistical information was not available, but it was clear that (a) there was little chance of public contributions to the Society, (b) 1600 families had been housed, mostly in Singapore, (c) 280 houses had been completed, and a further 55 started in the Federation at an average cost of £1750, (d) the proposed extension of the Society was complementary to the Government's plan to develop the Malayan

Housing Trust. This was passed on to the Treasury, with the recommendation that, despite the misgivings, which the Colonial Office shared, capital sanction be allowed.[144] Meantime, the CDC, which had asked the reasons for the delay and then objected to the telegrams to Malaya and Singapore, was told firmly, in a letter drafted by the Permanent Under-Secretary, that the Colonial Office could 'certainly not accept any implication that the Secretary of State is in a position of accountability to the Corporation'.[145] Still the Treasury felt unable to concur:[146] basically, it did not like the scheme as a CDC project; it felt it should be financed by local subscription, and it used the Commonwealth Economic Conference as a peg on which to hang more fundamental objections.[147] It was decided to ask the CDC to take the matter further locally, with a view to arranging to raise money locally from private sources or, if that was not managed, to secure a larger direct participation from Government funds.[148] On the basis that most of the money was to be used for new houses and all spent in Malaya, the contribution of the CDC being matched by an equivalent investment by the Government of Malaya, the Treasury agreed to the sanction, using the 'other grounds' criteria of the Commonwealth Economic Conference to do so.[149] The CDC was asked to keep the possibilities of obtaining private capital under continuous review.[150] It was by then nearly five months since the original application had been submitted, and it was clearly highly unlikely that any further capital provision for the Society would be approved by HMG.[151] The commitment of £3.5 million to the Society was by far the biggest that the CDC had made when, in the autumn of 1955, doubts had first arisen over the legality of housing projects under the ORD Act, 1948. The position up to the end of 1955 for the CDC's participation in building societies is shown in Table 8.1.

TABLE 8.1 CDC Finance for Housing Development: Commitments and Advances to 31 December 1955[152]

	Commitment	Advances
S. Rhodesia Housing Loan	£1 million	Nil
Federal and Colonial Building Society	£3.5 million	£1,975,000
Kenya Housing Loan	£2 million	670,000
Works Contracts:		
Nigeria	£295,000 ⎱	275,000
Gold Coast	£350,000 ⎰	
Other West African	£821,000	500,000
	£7,966,000	£3,420,000

To return to the Federal and Colonial Building Society: it had become active in the Federation in 1953 and, by the beginning of 1957, had lent 20 million dollars and committed a further 11 million dollars. In 1956, loan applications just exceeded 2000, and were from places as widely separated as Alor Star and Kota Bahru in the North to Johore Bahru in the South. As the result of the Society's efforts, low-cost houses were being built and sold for 8000 dollars at a minimum. By direct building of low-cost housing estates on behalf of local authorities, the selling prices of brick and tile houses, including the cost of sanitation and land, was brought down to 4800 dollars at a minimum and 8000 dollars at a maximum.[153] With the co-operation of the Federal Government, loans of up to 90 per cent of valuation could be obtained for houses selling below 8000 dollars, and the result of the Society's direct building thus brought ownership within the means of those able to provide up to 500 dollars towards the purchase and a monthly repayment of 40 dollars. Loan facilities were available in all major towns in the Federation.

By 1958 it was evident that the Singapore registration of the F & C Society Limited, which by then had become the Malaya Borneo Building Society Limited (MBBS), and the participation by the Government of the Federation in its capital structure were obstacles to participation by Borneo local finance, particularly by the Government of Sarawak, in operations in Borneo territories (Sarawak, North Borneo and Brunei). At the same time, there were objections to Malayan and Singapore investment in Borneo operations. So the CDC proposed the formation of a separate company, to be called Borneo Housing Development Limited, entirely independent of the MBBS, though accepting its advisory services.[154] The CDC was given capital sanction to invest a total of £234,000 in the new company, a quarter of which was represented by a transfer from the MBBS.[155]

No policy issue was involved. This was not the case with applications of the same year for investment in regional building societies and housing development in Nigeria. The application was submitted in April 1958[156] and a more detailed statement was made in May 1958.[157] It was felt to be necessary to consult the Treasury which, it was realised, did not regard housing as the type of development which the CDC was primarily intended to undertake. Hitherto, two housing schemes had been sanctioned in Nigeria, namely the Nigerian Housing Development Society and the Kaduna Housing Company, and preliminary clearance had been given to two more, namely the Kano African Housing Scheme and the Western Region Housing Scheme. According to the letter from the Colonial Office to the

Treasury, 'the plain fact is that the Regions do not want their need for building societies to be met by extending the scope of the Nigeria Housing Development Society: they want to have their own Regional societies. The CDC hope to achieve a reasonable compromise by setting up Regional societies which would in practice be managed and so co-ordinated by the Federal society.'[158] The justification was thus, essentially and openly, political rather than economic. The project for housing development was an adjunct to the proposed building societies, made necessary owing to the lack of local enterprise to undertake housing construction. The Treasury view was that the projects were likely to meet with objections, and possibly rejection, unless (a) the balance of housing with other activities was not upset and (b) the CDC contributed no more than 50 per cent of the capital required.[159] The Colonial Office felt that the maintenance of a 'proper balance' was primarily a matter for the CDC, although it agreed that the trend of the CDC's investments should be watched. The suggested 50 per cent rule was felt to be arbitrary rather than a matter of principle and should not be raised in each and every case.[160] While the Treasury's doubts were due to its concern with the long-term effect of housing activities on the Colony's external resources, it did not wish to risk another disagreement with the CDC and agreed, providing the CDC accepted the need to preserve a proper balance overall, that it was unnecessary to impose arbitrary requirements on projects.[161] The CDC were informed accordingly.[162]

(b) East and Central Africa

Earlier on, the Secretary of State, Mr Macleod, was quoted as urging, in his letter to the Chancellor of the Exchequer, Mr Selwyn Lloyd, *inter alia*, that more should be permitted by the CDC than 'the building society project, which is an essential part of the general plan for avoiding a moratorium on the building societies in East and Central Africa'. The explanation of the reference is as follows. In the second half of 1960, it became clear that, unless financial support were provided, one or more of the building societies in Kenya would have to declare a moratorium. The situation resulted from a loss of confidence on the part mainly of East African investors, who sought to withdraw their money. It was feared that a financial crisis would be precipitated in East Africa and, because of the link between the building societies of East and Central Africa, have repercussions in Central Africa. At the strong request of the United Kingdom and Kenya Governments,[163] the CDC agreed to hold discussions with the three building societies operating in East Africa, and with other interested parties, to establish whether a satisfactory scheme could be worked out whereby the Corporation might assist in meeting the excess of withdrawals over mortgage repayments and new deposits. As a result the CDC applied for capital sanction for a sum not exceeding £2 million in order to meet the estimated net withdrawals in the period to 30 June 1961.[164] The scheme of support was successful in keeping the three societies concerned afloat until 30 June 1961. The three societies were the Kenya Building Society, which operated only in Kenya, the Savings and Loan Society, which operated mainly in Kenya but also to a lesser extent in Tanganyika and Uganda, and the First Permanent Building Society, which was registered in Northern Rhodesia and had expanded into Nyasaland and East Africa, where it had branches in all three mainland territories and Zanzibar. The liabilities of the three Societies to East African investors totalled some £8.5 million, of which the First Permanent's liabilities were about £4.5 million and the Savings and Loan's liabilities were about £2.5 million. The latter Society was a wholly-owned subsidiary of the Pearl Assurance Company, which had an equity interest in the Society. The Kenya Building Society had been helped by the Norwich Union which, however, had no obligation towards the Society. The First Permanent in Northern Rhodesia had liabilities to investors of about £7 million, while the other four building societies in Northern Rhodesia had liabilities of about £9 million, making £16 million in all. After July 1960 all the Societies had experienced withdrawals, a trend which became serious at the time of the Federal and Northern Rhodesia constitutional discussions in January and February 1961. Apart from the First Permanent, which the Government of Northern Rhodesia had to assist with over £1 million, the position was not critical at that time.

According to the report on the position in East and Central Africa by Mr J. Burgess, the CDC's consultant on building societies, so far as Kenya was concerned the position of the Kenya Building Society and the Savings and Loan Society was manageable, provided they were supported. However, the position of the First Permanent was critical by mid–1961 and likely to lead to closure. It was, therefore, recommended that further assistance to the First Permanent – and it was estimated that £900,000 would be required for the year ending 30 June 1962 – should be on condition that the Society should be divided into separate units for Central Africa, on the one hand, and East Africa, on the other.[165]

The matter was discussed between the CDC and the Colonial Office in August 1961, and a Note was drawn up setting out the financial arrangements as between the CDC and HMG in the United

Kingdom, under which the Corporation was prepared to operate a Society in East Africa which was formed to take over the assets and the liabilities in East Africa of the First Permanent Building Society.[166] Subject to the arrangements being accepted locally, the CDC applied for approval to borrow up to £4,610,000 in respect of further possible investment in building societies in East Africa.[167] A sum of £190,000 remained from the earlier sanction of £2 million. It was estimated that the maximum commitment to the First Permanent would be £4,350,000, but the CDC wished to advance a further £450,000 to the other two Societies in Kenya in order to preserve the building society movement in East Africa so that, in time, it would be able to develop. No one knew for how long the CDC, or rather its subsidiary, the East Africa Development Company, would have to support the Societies.[168] The application was quickly agreed by the Treasury,[169] and arrangements were accordingly made for the transfer of assets and liabilities.[170]

Following these arrangements for the management and support of the First Permanent, the CDC received a similar request from the Kenya Building Society. The CDC proposed that the assets and liabilities of the KBS should be transferred to a new company, which would be a wholly-owned subsidiary of the CDC.[171] Hitherto, capital sanction approved for building societies in East Africa amounted to £6,610,000. A further £363,100 was requested in respect of possible further investment in the KBS, and readily agreed.[172] This was the result of the operation of the arrangement over the First Permanent, which arrested the withdrawal of public deposits, restored confidence and led to the restoration of public deposits, which, in turn, had adversely affected the KBS, which lost deposits and asked for assistance.[173] Both were 'run-down' operations, where mortgage assets were reducing as capital repayments were received as no new loans were granted. It was reported in March 1964, that both Societies were being satisfactorily run down, in accordance with the original intention, as the CDC did not wish to allow either Society to borrow from the general public in order to lend on house purchase mortgages.[174] While some organisation would have to be kept in being for perhaps twenty years to collect repayment on mortgages, otherwise there was no phoenix in the ashes. Nevertheless, the rightness of the policy of supporting the run-down operations was amply proved.[175] A crisis, whose political effects at the time were incalculable, had been avoided, at very little cost to HMG.[176] The CDC's considerable expertise in the matter was an essential ingredient in carrying out that policy.

VI. SMALLHOLDER SCHEMES IN PEASANT AGRICULTURE

The second aspect of the pattern of investment by the CDC requiring attention is that concerning smallholder schemes in peasant agriculture. During 1961 the Chairman of the CDC, Lord Howick, discussed several times with the Minister of State, Lord Perth, the possible role that the Corporation might play in Colonial territories which had become independent. In the final draft of his letter of 14 December 1961 to the Minister, Lord Howick listed three ideas for further consideration. They were, first, the possibility of making fuller use of the various territorial development corporations as channels for further finance after independence; secondly, the possibility of ploughing back the profits and capital repayments arising from existing projects and investments, perhaps in association with the territorial corporations; and, thirdly, whether the CDC should be able, in partnership with others, to undertake important new projects with fresh capital in cases where local development corporations had insufficient funds.[177] The letter was written in readiness for high-level talks when the Chairman returned from a visit to the Far East.[178]

On returning from his tour, the Chairman wrote to the Secretary of State, Mr R. Maudling, to make one further suggestion as to how the CDC might help a former Colony.[179] In the countries about to form the new State of Malaysia, there was a pointer to the type of help which would be acceptable and useful, not only in Borneo and Singapore but also in Malaya itself, nationalist, independent and rich in natural resources though it was. The proposal that had been put to the Chairman was that the CDC should 'manage' the Malayan Government's oil palm settlements. He was told that the establishment of prosperous smallholders was Malaya's main bulwark against Communism, the typical terrorist being the Chinese villager rather than the Chinese townsman. So, the settlement scheme was politically important in rural Malaya, from whence many Ministers derived their support and, at the same time, would help to diversify from rubber to oil palms, which would provide a useful hedge against fluctuations in rubber prices as, of all the oils and fats, palm oil was expected best to maintain its price. The Chairman felt that the CDC was well equipped to provide the management involved because the Regional Controller, Mr D. Fiennes, was the first chairman of the Government's Federal Land Development Authority (FLDA), a statutory body set up in 1956 to promote and carry out agricultural development and land settlement schemes in association with State Governments, and the CDC had already made a loan of £600,000 to the Authority. Also, the Corporation had itself made a success of growing oil palms on an estate named Kulai, within a few miles of the first oil palm settlement of the FLDA. It was proposed that Kulai should be used as a demonstration estate, more of the FLDA managers should be trained there, other oil palm settlements should be supervised on something like a managing agency basis, and factories should be built and operated on the basis of a management charge. The Chairman did not feel that these proposals in connection with rural settlement schemes in Malaya, together with proposals connected with managing the Government of Sarawak's smallholder rubber scheme and expanding trading estate activities in Singapore, would involve substantial new investments if money deriving from the area could be redeployed there. While he found the proposal attractive, the Secretary of State regretted that it was legally impossible under the ORD Acts, 1958–59.[180] The removal of the legal restriction on the operations of the CDC in newly-independent Commonwealth countries has been discussed already. Attention will be focused at this point on the CDC's activities in connection with smallholder schemes.

The Chairman elaborated his ideas in a letter to the President of the IBRD, Mr G. D. Woods.[181] The argument for participation in smallholder schemes ran along the following lines. Industrialisation alone would not solve the problem of the very poor, and so the land must be made to support a large population on a better standard of living than their existing standard. In both Asia and Africa, if the standard was to rise in the countryside, success would have to be made of smallholder farming in at least part of the rural areas. Three reasons pointed to the importance of the task: (a) it was right to help where the greatest poverty of the greatest number existed; (b) many African countries had, for political reasons, become independent after a short period of transition, and the educated men in charge of the governments could not reasonably be expected successfully to accomplish the extremely difficult task of raising the standards of a mass of small peasants without help; and (c) it was among the really poor who lived on the margin of existence that the Communist appeal of the short cut to prosperity made most progress, certainly in Asia. Failures with smallholder farming was usually due, in the Chairman's view, to a lack of organisation. When the Chairman was Governor of Kenya, an experienced agricultural officer who visited Ceylon had found that attempts to develop smallholder tea there had failed, because of lack of careful supervision. When the Kenya Government embarked on smallholder tea in the high-altitude areas, it did so under conditions of close supervision. The first smallholder tea reached the auction floor in Nairobi in 1959 and fetched good prices. The lesson was that the smallholder needed three types of help: (i) credit and, in some cases, physical assistance with his cash crop; (ii) help in the processing and marketing of the crop, otherwise he would be a weak seller, compelled to sell at harvest time; and (iii) stimulus from one or two larger units, which could afford to try new methods – hence the importance of the nucleus plantation system. The Chairman believed that 'bringing efficient management into tropical smallholder farming, notably through nucleus plantation schemes, is the most valuable contribution that the CDC can make to the rural welfare of underdeveloped countries'.[182]

The emphasis was new rather than the idea itself. The original nucleus scheme, according to the CDC,[183] was the Kulai oil palm estate, which was purchased in May 1950 and had had to be rehabilitated following war time neglect.[184] Guthrie and Company Limited acted as managing agents. The estate was in an area notorious for terrorist activity and in July 1954 both the manager and the regional Controller were murdered.[185] In 1957 a new factory was completed and transferred to a new company, Johore Palm Processing Limited, which was formed to process, at cost, the fruit not only of Kulai but also of neighbouring growers who would participate, as shareholders, in the company in proportion to their planted acreage.[186] The ultimate objective was to run the factory on a co-operative basis, meantime encouraging the growing of oil palms in South Johore by providing processing facilities. In 1959, Kulai prepared a 15-acre nursery for the first 1000 acres of Johore State Land Development Board's 4000-acre smallholder scheme, which was financed by the FLDA.[187] In 1963, application was made for the borrowing by the CDC of up to £90,000 to install three 4½-ton automatic presses to bring the factory up to its maximum capacity of about 120,000 tons of fruit per annum, which would be required when the 10,000 acres of oil palms in the Kulai complex were all mature.[188] At the same time, a net sum of up to £151,000 was sought for Kulai to cover the cost of replanting 1287 acres, the yield from which was falling as planting had taken place initially in the period 1929–36.[189] The applications were strongly endorsed by the High Commissioner and readily approved.[190]

Thus, the CDC had built up and run a plantation and factory first, and then encouraged smallholders to come in. Probably that was the most desirable ordering, though not one that could always be followed.

In the case of the Eastern Nigeria nucleus estate and smallholders' scheme, the two parts had to be established together. The project was mentioned by the Premier of the Region to the Prime Minister of the United Kingdom in January 1960, but had to await the passage of the Commonwealth Development Act before it could be sanctioned. The project was for the establishment of a 4000-acre nuleus rubber estate and of an associated settlement scheme for 500 smallholders, with a total of 4000 acres planted to rubber, 2500 acres of food crops and 500 acres of village areas, together with a rubber factory to serve both nucleus estate and smallholder developments.[191] The intention was to spread the planting over seven years, with smallholder development following one year behind the estate. The nucleus estate was to be owned by a company formed by the CDC and the Eastern Nigerian Government on an equal financial basis. The smallholder scheme was to come under a statutory Smallholder Board of Management while the rubber factory was to be owned by a separate company, initially wholly financed by a loan from the Estate Company, in order to provide an efficient processing and marketing service for both developments. It was intended that the loan would be repaid by the estate out of the share capital in the factory company and by smallholders through a levy on rubber sold by the factory on their behalf. The CDC was to develop and manage the estate and run the factory. Both the CDC and the Government were to provide £200,000 in equity and £300,000 in loan finance; the CDC was to make a loan of £400,000 for the smallholder scheme, if the Government was unable to raise the required £900,000 from other sources. The High Commissioner supported the application, albeit with some slight reservation over the smallholder scheme,[192] and the CDC was given capital sanction of £900,000 as requested.[193]

Just as Kulai dated from the Trefgarne period, so did a somewhat different kind of smallholder assistance provided in the West Indian island of Dominica. As part of the Dominica Grouped Undertaking, which was taken over in 1949,[194] two estates were purchased to grow citrus and coconuts, with bananas as a quick cash crop. It was thought that the citrus grading and packing station would be used by local growers, but it was found that it would be necessary for the CDC to buy and market if the station was to be used to capacity.[195] At first, only the Melville Hall Estate was developed. By 1952, it was the largest producer of bananas on the island,[196] and, by 1956, the largest producer in the whole of the Windward Islands of Grenada, St Vincent, St Lucia and Dominica. The example set had, it was claimed, stimulated development, particularly in north-east Dominica.[197] With the building of an access road, the Castle Bruce Estate was taken in hand again in 1961, thus spreading overheads. A scheme was started in that year to encourage local agriculture by processing and marketing other growers' cocoa and met with a satisfactory response, 69.5 tons being processed in 1962.[198]

Smallholders with a cash crop, living in crowded conditions, needed help of a different kind. The African tea growers of Kenya provide an example. The Swynnerton Plan of 1954 for intensifying the development of African agriculture in Kenya included the development of tea growing by African smallholders. The CDC's interest in smallholder tea development began with an invitation in 1958, from the Government of Kenya, to consider the provision of finance for a programme of fourteen tea factories to be set up over a number of years to process green leaf from some 9300 smallholders, each growing one acre of tea on their holding. In 1959, joint missions from the CDC and tea companies visited Kenya and, with representatives of the local Department of Agriculture, visited a number of African tea-growing areas. As a result of their reports, the CDC informed the Government of Kenya that, subject to the satisfaction of certain conditions as to the planting, the general progress and the standards of supervision, and subject also to commercial prospects remaining favourable at the time the decision was required, it would, in association with commercial partners, be willing to invest in up to five factories for processing African-grown tea in the period to 1964. The proposal was agreed in principle by the Colonial Office on 24 February 1959.[199] The missions emphasised the importance of ensuring that smallholders were adequately financed and supervised and, in October 1959, a Working Party was set up by the Minister of Agriculture in Kenya to examine the question. The CDC, which had initiated the discussions leading to the enquiry, was represented on the Working Party, which reported in November 1959 on 'the need to set up a new Authority to promote, finance and control the development of cash crops, particularly tea for smallholders'. Its two main functions were to be 'the provision of adequate funds to carry through an agreed development programme to completion, and the direction of tea growing so that it may be properly co-ordinated with the factory development'. Such funds and direction were then lacking. Consequently, the Government of Kenya proposed the establishment of a Special Crops Development Authority (SCDA), replacing the existing Tea Marketing Boards, to control developments of cash crops and, in the first place, of tea for smallholders in existing native land units. The CDC submitted a proposal for preliminary clearance, in which it was stated that the

SCDA would plant some 7800 acres and provide services and supplies to African tea growers, recovering its costs by a cess from the sale of the smallholders' green leaf.[200] The Department of Agriculture was to administer the scheme and provide field supervision on a fee basis. Of the £600,000 thought to be necessary, the CDC was asked to provide a loan of £500,000 to the SCDA under guarantee by the Government of Kenya. The CDC felt it would have influence on the Authority, via its member on the Board, though the Department of Agriculture would, in fact, administer and supervise the programme. This latter, however, made the loan fall within the 'finance-house' category. The Colonial Office asked that the proposal should be considered on its general merits as 'whatever Ministers may shortly decide on the broad CDC question, it is clear now that the 1956 "finance-house" policy is really out of date'.[201] The Treasury and the Minister of State were asked to treat the project as an exception to the 'finance-house' rule.[202] The Treasury replied at first that, if it was agreed that no further risk projects would be submitted, the project would be approved,[203] but later withdrew the condition.[204] The Minister of State readily approved,[205] and the CDC was so informed.[206]

When the formal application for capital sanction was received, it was found that the CDC wished to borrow £900,000 to lend to the Authority whose peak financial requirement, expected to be reached by June 1968, would be £960,000.[207] The proposals included (a) the taking over of the existing development, (b) the taking over and extension of the functions of the Central Province and the Nyanza and Rift Valley African Grown Tea Marketing Boards, and (c) the responsibility for further planting. Existing development under (a) included 1520 acres of smallholder tea planted before 1960, the planting of about 800 acreas during April/May 1960, the establishment of tea nurseries, and the taking over of the Government tea factory at Ragati in the Central Provinces. The functions of the Authority under (b) were to finance, control and supervise all aspects of tea growing up to the sale of the green leaf to the processing companies. Existing services were to be extended, including the formation of a green leaf buying and transport organisation, and agreements with tea companies to ensure the smallholder could market his crop; the Department of Agriculture instructors on field supervision were to continue under a managing agreement. The planting programme under (c) provided for a further 6700 acres in the Central, Nyanza and Rift Provinces and the establishment of two additional nurseries. A thousand acres of tea was expected to provide an economic output for one tea factory, and the planting programme was based on that requirement, reaching an early peak in 1962, and ceasing after 1967. The field services were to be built up *pari passu* with the planting programme, the buying and transport services not reaching their peak until the planted areas reached maturity in 1971– 72. Ten areas were envisaged, each under a senior and specialist Tea Officer. Their development depended on securing satisfactory market- ing arrangements with a tea company, and had to be suited to local conditions, such as roads and nearness to existing tea estates. Apart from a contribution of £60,000 towards the necessary capital, the Government of Kenya undertook to (i) finance the Department of Agriculture staff housing requirements arising out of the scheme (some £65,000), (ii) provide the necessary roads (£110,000), (iii) transfer assets of the Tea Boards, including the Ragati factory (£80,000), and (iv) transfer other developments to date. It was estimated that the Authority would recover not later than 1984 its capital costs by charging a capital levy on the production of green leaf at the rate of 7 cents per pound weight – the East African shilling, divisible into 100 cents, was at par with the United Kingdom shilling, i.e. one-twentieth of a pound. The continuing costs of the Authority was to be recovered after the tea matured by a cess of 10 cents per pound weight, subject to revision if circumstances altered. In due course, six tea factories would be necessary, costing around £100,000 each. The CDC expected to have to contribute 50 to 70 per cent of the cost. The scheme was planned to give a small, but sufficiently attractive, income to the greatest number of smallholders. The actual income per acre of tea at maturity was planned to be not less than £50 per annum, and the income of smallholders was expected on the basis of ability, soil types, etc., to be between £30 and £100 per annum. The CDC asked that repayment should not begin until the eleventh year, because it took about eight years to get a full crop from new plants and planting would continue until 1967.[208] The Treasury agreed 'as an exceptional case, the moratorium of ten years on repayment of principal in view of the length of time which it takes for tea to come into full bearing', but no commitment for the factory finance could be undertaken at that time.[209] Two members of the Corporation staff were appointed to the Board of the Authority, and one of them, the Regional Controller, Mr Peter Wise, became chairman.

In April 1962 the CDC sought capital sanction for £160,000 (£51,000 in equity and £109,000 in loans) towards the £240,000 needed to build two factories, the remaining £80,000 being contri- buted for the SCDA by Messrs Arbuthnot, Latham and Company Limited, who would manage both factories, and Messrs Dalgety and

New Zealand Loan Limited, which would act as tea brokers in East Africa.[210] The application was approved. It was followed, two years later, by an application to borrow up to £1,070,000 so that the CDC might subscribe to the equity and loan capital of fourteen further companies to be formed in Kenya to own and operate tea factories for processing leaf produced by smallholders, under what was by then called not the SCDA, but the Kenya Tea Development Authority (KTDA).[211] The application was strongly supported by the British Trade Commission in Nairobi and approved. Messrs James Finlay and Company Limited and George Williamson (Africa) Limited agreed to provide the capital along with the CDC for the first three of these factories.[212] The application of April 1964 mentioned that the KTDA had, in July 1963, invited the CDC to consider participation with the IBRD in financing a further 14,399 acres of smallholder tea that was estimated to cost £1.5 million. After an IBRD mission had visited Kenya in September 1963 to investigate existing and proposed developments, the matter was discussed in Washington between the Kenya Government, the KTDA, the CDC and the IBRD. It was proposed that the IBRD's affiliate, the International Development Association (IDA), would contribute £1 million and the CDC would use the £200,000 unspent from the original capital sanction of £900,000, IBRD's contribution being contingent on the CDC's undertaking to provide its share of the finance required for factory development.

At 31 December 1964, 19,928 smallholders had planted 10,922 acres, of which 2,254 acres were planted in 1964. By the same date, the KTDA had drawn a total of £780,000 from the CDC, as against £500,000 at the end of 1963. The marked success of smallholder tea in Kenya has been due to a combination of circumstances. (The author discussed the question at length with the late Mr P. M. Wise, then Regional Controller of CDC and the Chairman of KTDA, on 16 April 1969 in Nairobi, and records his gratitude for Mr Wise's helpfulness.) In the first place, it began at a time of buoyant tea prices, when some large firms wished to diversify away from India and Ceylon, and so the climate was propitious. Secondly, the operation was fully supported by the Ministry of Agriculture, both technically and by exhortation, though at the same time politics was rigorously excluded by the Government of Kenya in its dealings with the KTDA. Thirdly, the KTDA's contribution provided for the election of growers' representatives to the Board through a three-tier structure of Divisional, District and Regional Committees. This pyramidal structure of committees allocated supplies of planting material and disciplined growers effectively and with consensus. Fourthly, on processing, a close grass-roots connection was maintained, as smallholders could buy shares in the factories. Problems arose, e.g. the inadequacy of the system of feeder roads for the volume of traffic, and required research and expenditure to provide solutions; but the basic organisation was sound. Where it was copied, as in Malawi, where in 1967 a Smallholder Tea Authority was set up following the recommendations of a CDC mission, it has worked well, but where certain ingredients, such as the committee system and the grass-roots connection, were omitted, as with the Uganda Tea Growers' Corporation, there was a less successful outcome.

VII. INTEREST-FREE LOANS AND THE ROLE OF THE CDC IN 1965–1968

Just before the three kinds of assistance that the CDC provided to smallholders were examined, the views of the Chairman as expressed in his letter to the President of the IBRD were noted. On his return from Africa, the Chairman was shown a copy of a letter received by the Chancellor of the Exchequer, Mr Maudling, from Mr Woods, who feared that collaboration between the CDC and the IBRD's private investment affiliate, the International Finance Corporation (IFC), would be inhibited unless the CDC, like the IFC, could repay its borrowings to the extent that profits were realised from equity investments, instead of under the existing system of fixed interest and amortisation.[213] In his reply, the Chancellor merely noted that there was an element of the IFC practice in the arrangements made in 1961 with the CDC, whereby debts arising from past losses were paid off out of profits, though new borrowings continued to pay interest.[214] However, the Chairman of the CDC, Lord Howick, was more concerned with the President's claim that, as the funds of the IFC carried no obligation to pay interest or dividends, 'the IFC management is primarily concerned with the maximum ultimate development results, and not with immediate return'. The Chairman's concern was due to his belief that, if the financial requirement of the best possible return were removed, management would deteriorate.[215] In his view, that would be fatal, because 'it is management almost more than money which we can and do bring to a new country and, notably, to small farmers in that country'. Managers were expected both to run the nucleus farm on strictly commercial lines, and also to train managers for smallholding bodies and assist the smallholders. The Chairman concluded:

> If we do not try to earn at least a dividend, that same manager would become like a civil servant and the country would not obtain as efficient help for their smallholders from him, nor as effective training for the educated young men who must manage future smallholder settlements, as he does at present. The Malayan Government have been particularly impressed by the results of training these young men on a commercially successful plantation, as distinct from those of training other young men on a government experimental farm.

Nevertheless, the Chairman, when he called on the Permanent Secretary to the Treasury, Sir William Armstrong, at the end of July 1963, while accepting the general position as regards the servicing of Exchequer advances, asked if two special cases where he thought there were grounds for giving loans free of interest during the fructification period might be considered.[216] The two cases were, first, when the Corporation was assisting a scheme for smallholders in agriculture and, secondly, where it was making money available to local development corporations. The General Manager of the CDC later explained to the Permanent Secretary that in many of these projects, particularly where finance was provided for smallholders, a rate of interest sufficient to cover the Treasury rate plus the CDC's 1 per cent simply could not be afforded.[217] If such projects were to be launched, he urged that cheaper funds should be brought in and averaged with the CDC's money so that a rate could be levied that was payable, though even so some smallholders would be able to pay very little in the long run. It was admitted by the CDC that some of the projects adopted were not viable by existing standards, and only if standards were sufficiently eased could such activities be extended. This raised a crucial question concerning the purpose of the Corporation, though, for the moment, the Treasury view was that, if a project was viable as a whole, it was perfectly reasonable for the Exchequer to be compensated in later years for agreeing to a moratorium in earlier years. However, it was clearly the assumption of viability in the longer run that was in question. For, as the Chairman explained, managers on nucleus estates were expected to operate both as commercial farmers and as technical training and assistance workers. While the former activity directly affected viability, the latter did so only in the long run and, meantime, was a form of aid. The Corporation was, therefore, wishing both to lower the margin at which it operated, and also to provide services from which an early return was not to be expected.

The CDC was not alone in seeking concessions at that time, for the CRO submitted in June 1964 a Note to the Cabinet Committee on Development Policy which was discussing whether steps should be taken to maintain the proportion of British bilateral aid that was available to finance local costs by increasing the flow of such aid to the independent Commonwealth.[218] The CRO set out, in its Note, the policy considerations which led it to propose that the aid given for agricultural development in Africa should be increased. Here it is sufficient to repeat the five conclusions drawn, which were:

(i) Settlement schemes (fully worked out from the land-use survey to the point of economic occupation), schemes for agricultural education, particularly in extension services aimed at the farmer; drainage and irrigation and water supply projects, pilot crop projects, nucleus estates combined with smallholdings, agricultural credit, marketing and processing schemes, offer the best scope for the application of external financial assistance to agricultural development in Africa;

(ii) Such schemes should apply to the improvement in the quality and type, not only of export crops, but also of crops for the domestic market;

(iii) External financial assistance should be provided, as need is found, upon other than commercial terms, and should extend to local costs;

(iv) The fullest use should be made of the experience of the CDC, as offering not only the managerial skills which the recipients cannot themselves provide, but also a way of ensuring some reasonable control over the disbursement of British aid;

(v) The British Government should participate to the fullest possible extent, either directly or through the CDC with the IBRD/IDA, in projects for agricultural development.

It was recognised in the Note that the adoption of these proposals would not involve any dramatic shift in the emphasis of the United Kingdom's aid programme 'if only because the number and size of the projects in respect of which we are likely to be able to devise adequate measures of supervision will be limited'. Though the Treasury wished to consider the implications for manpower and the Foreign Office was reluctant to have the concessions confined to independent Commonwealth countries, the conclusions were endorsed by the Committee, which invited Departments to put the propositions to their Ministers individually as they considered necessary.[219] There was pressure also at the time, i.e. mid-1964, from the United States in particular, for the softening of the terms of lending. It was in this context that the Economic Policy Committee took note that the Chancellor of the Exchequer, Mr Maudling, would arrange for officials to reconsider the arguments for and against the use of low interest rates for overseas aid loans.[220] It was recognised that any concessionary rates on aid loans would have to be extended to the CDC, which would inevitably lead to increased drawings from the Treasury.[221] The climate of thinking had, in fact, so changed that a Treasury official was 'inclined to argue a case for conceding some equity capital, limited to investment in agricultural projects. This would encourage investment in what is probably the most important aspect of development aid, and could be defended against any extension in the United Kingdom, because, manifestly, British agriculture does not need further development.'[222] A colleague agreed that 'there certainly does seem to be a case for allowing equity investment for agricultural projects if HMG does decide to undertake equity investment in the nationalised industry field. Since this is essentially a question of establishing basic agriculture, it should not raise difficulties on the home front.'[223]

However, the whole question of the CDC's borrowing rights had to be postponed until after the 1964 General Election when it was considered by the newly-responsible Department; the Ministry of Overseas Development (ODM).[224] The matter was treated in Chapter 6, Section vi, above. The Minister of Overseas Development, Mrs B. Castle, it will be recalled, decided to waive the payment of interest by the Corporation on part of its borrowings from the Exchequer for certain projects. At the time, the CDC's equity investments were receiving 40-year advances, interest during the seven-year fructification period being postponed, and compounded and paid over the remaining 33 years. For loan investments, the Corporation received terms which matched the terms on which the money was made available to the project. Under the proposed waiver, while the Minister would, with the consent of the Treasury, approve individual projects for the application of the concession, the CDC was given for its guidance the categories in which projects would normally qualify.[225] They were: (a) agricultural and forestry projects, nucleus estates, smallholder and land settlement schemes; (b) territorial development companies, each company being treated as a single project, and

(c) low-cost housing schemes. Other projects could also be submitted, including, for example, public utilities in the poorer territories and, though more rarely, industrial companies, including companies engaged on the processing of agricultural and forestry products. In the case of any project, whether it came within a category or not, it had to be shown (i) that it would be generally desirable for the development of the country, or region, in which it was to be located, and (ii) that, as far as could be foreseen, it would not be profitable enough to enable the CDC to pay the full Treasury rate of interest over the whole period of Treasury advances for the project and also to cover the CDC's own margin. The waiver of interest was available for both equity and loan investments in approved projects provided that, in the case of loans, the CDC granted an identical waiver of interest to the project concerned. The maximum period for which interest would be waived for any project was seven years; the actual period, in any case, would, for a loan, be the period for which the CDC had waived interest to itself and, for equity investment, the fructification period. The waiver was not retrospective.

The general climate of opinion of 1963–64 which facilitated the waiver of interest was noted above. Yet, it still might be asked whether the CDC, established in the very different circumstances of 1948, would be relevant to the circumstances of the last third of the twentieth century, even with the waiver. The ODM gave some consideration to the question in its Memorandum to the Official Committee on Overseas Development.[226] Apart from the obvious political difficulty of letting the Corporation run down, it was felt that a case for its continued support could be made on its merits which, as the following extract shows, were put in terms of the 1948 'gap' (housing and electricity), technical assistance (smallholder schemes), joint participation (expatriate private capital) and as a channel for aid. The argument ran as follows:

> Some of the CDC's projects undoubtedly make a vital direct contribution in a territory, e.g. African housing schemes in Zambia and elsewhere, and electricity in the smaller West Indies. Its agricultural projects make a contribution to economies, not only directly, but by way of demonstration and linked small-holder schemes. It also helps to bring in outside capital, which almost certainly would not otherwise come in. On the other hand, it would have to be said that some of its projects are marginal to territorial economies, although most of these territories are at a stage of development where almost any development is useful. It is able to

provide management for projects, and has now quite a large staff of skilled advisers (some drawn from the old Colonial services); this is of considerable value in some of the new independent countries where entrepreneurial skills are often particularly deficient. It combines a number of safe projects (among which housing can be included) with others in which there is a fair degree of risk, and the one class helps to carry the other.

In short, the Corporation is now identified as a channel for the expenditure of aid (advances to it count in the Aid Programme), and it has become an effective means of doing this. It is doubtful whether the Government machine itself is entirely appropriate for the sponsoring and running of commercial type projects such as the Corporation carries through. While it could certainly be said that some of the Corporation's projects are more useful than others, the aid money which passes through the Corporation can certainly be said to be usefully spent: in fact, now probably more usefully than ever.[227]

No attempt was made to improve the CDC's general financial position, e.g. by an indirect, or hidden, subsidy. The purpose was to enable the Corporation to undertake certain kinds of project which were possible only with cheap money.[228] The concessions to the CDC were recommended because softer terms of aid for loans granted directly to developing countries were then in prospect. There was no question of changing the terms of reference of the Corporation, which were felt to be sufficiently wide for it to pursue all the desirable functions which fell within its field of activity, and there had, in any case, been no suggestion that the field should be widened to include new kinds of development.[229] Nor, within its existing resources, could its sphere of operations be extended to include the Indian sub-continent or foreign countries, though the resources were judged to be adequate for some time for the existing kinds of activities in the territories in which it was operating.[230] The CDC was then able to have a total £150 million outstanding; at the end of 1964, it had outstanding some £88 million from the Treasury, and about £1 million from other sources. The ceiling of £150 million on its borrowing was not likely, therefore, to impose a limit on its activities for some years.

This, then, was the upshot of the triennial review of the Corporation's financial structure which the Corporation had requested in April 1964. The aid element in the activities of the CDC was recognised, though the CDC realised that the impact of the waiver would be small for several years while the investment in eligible projects was built up. According to the Annual Report for 1965:

> At the end of 1965 CDC carried outright responsibility for direction and management, or shared in that responsibility, for fifty commercial/industrial projects. These projects included estate companies producing between them most of the better-known tropical products and smallholder schemes producing almost as wide a range of crops, forests and plantations with processing factories for sugar, palm oil, pulp, wattle extract, etc.: they included mines, hotels, power supply undertakings, industrial development companies and house mortgage companies. By virtue of the personal positions built up locally by CDC's regional controllers in Central Africa and Southern Africa, one might also include a major airline and the most modern abattoir in the Southern Hemisphere. The aggregate investment in all these undertakings totals tens of millions of pounds: they are spread throughout Commonwealth Africa, the Far East and the West Indies. Gradually, a management team has been built up competent and experienced to handle the problems which arise in developing countries. As time goes on, the local peoples occupy an increasing number of the more responsible posts by deliberate policy and training. In support of the managers, CDC has also built up technical sections with expertise in particular lines such as tropical agriculture, house mortgage finance and local industrial development companies for which there is strong demand in the CDC area of operations. Increasingly, there have been requests for CDC help with surveys and investigations in Africa and elsewhere to which every effort is made to respond within the capabilities of a hard-worked staff. The Corporation staff can also help in the seminars, teach-ins, etc., which in the Western world are an increasing feature of development aid. It is, however, most important that, owing to calls for this type of assistance, they should not be diverted from the practical end of trying to make two blades of grass grow where one grew before.[231]

The year 1965 was an eventful one for the Corporation. Apart from the waiver on interest charges, much happened in the Commonwealth. In East Asia, the 'confrontation' of Indonesia and Malaysia continued and Singapore left the Malaysian Federation. In Africa, Southern Rhodesia made a 'Unilateral Declaration of Independence', which in turn caused disturbances in other parts of the continent. It led to the break of diplomatic relations between the United Kingdom, on the one side, and Tanzania and Ghana, on the other. Early in 1966 the regimes in Ghana and Nigeria were suddenly changed.

Against this background and that of economic stringency in the United Kingdom, the CDC undertook new commitments of £13.5 million in 1965 as compared with £12 million in 1964. At the same time, the CDC was able to report a large expansion in the operating surplus after charging all revenue items except interest due to HMG and before any capital adjustments. On that particular basis, the operating surplus rose by £625,729 from £5,002,593 in 1964 to £5,628,322 in 1965. However, interest charges due to HMG rose from £4,449,681 to £4,781,240 over the two years 1964–65. What remained on revenue account together with sundry capital profits and re-alisations enabled a capital loss of £275,000 on the disposal of the CDC's interest in the Worcester Porcelain Company (Jamaica) Ltd to be written off, and the provision against the book value of projects and investments to be increased by £997,000 to £2,997,000. This provision was said to be earmarked against particular investments and to conceal no free reserve.

The expansion in the operating surplus was attributable in large measure to the high prices prevailing for copper and palm oil. The Annual Report commented rather curiously: 'Had the Corporation invested in some other primary products of the tropics such as sisal or cocoa, the result would have been different. The Corporation can, therefore, hardly yet be considered to have stultified by its own efforts the complaints which it voices about the unsuitability of its capital structure.'[232] Yet there was an inconsistency. It arose from the inclusion in the forecasts prepared for Lord Sinclair of Cleeve of deliberately pessimistic export earnings by plantations. The forecasted deficits had not emerged, and the CDC suggested that it was because investments had been in those products that were enjoying buoyant prices rather than others! However, the direction of the CDC's interest in primary products had not changed: it had an interest in palm oil from the early years. It was the poor expectations with respect to prices which had turned out to be wholly unjustified. The gloss on the increased surplus was rather specious, suggesting a certain Bourbonesque element in the Corporation which was prepared neither to forget nor to learn despite the flexibility shown by HMG. The Corporation still hankered after the receipt of capital without the obligation to pay the going rate for Government finance, because it wished to indulge freely in ventures which from the outset were not expected to pay their way, as in the case of smallholder schemes in peasant agriculture.

For the immediate future, the Chief Secretary to the Treasury's ruling was wholly appropriate, namely that

> if next year you decide that a review of the Corporation's general position is called for, I would like to suggest that the basis for it should be not the Corporation's fears of what may prove on certain assumptions to be its position at some future date, but a factual assessment of what is actually happening at the current time.[233]

However, if the CDC should find so-called 'gap' projects really hard to come by and wished increasingly for that, and possibly also for other, reasons to participate in uneconomic projects of the kind which Lord Howick favoured, the question would naturally arise whether the CDC was the most appropriate organisation to become so involved.

At the time when the formation of the CDC was being discussed, there was no suggestion that the role of CD & W would be affected. They were parallel organisations. The projects that came under CD & W fell conveniently into three categories: welfare, self-supporting schemes and indirect economic schemes. The first two were clearly not relevant to the task envisaged for the CDC. Nor were the indirect economic schemes, such as road-making and bridge-building, where the benefits were diffused and long-term and there was never any question of introducing, for example, a turnpike system in order to obtain a direct return on roads and bridges. However, schemes for which the Corporation was to receive interest-free capital came close to CD & W's indirect economic schemes, being virtually identical in so far as it became impossible to recoup the capital investment involved. In such cases, the CDC would be acting as an aid organisation. If, in time, the CDC enlarged this sector appreciably, it might well be asked whether it was an appropriate role for a statutory corporation to play. The sector might be thought to be more suitably a part of the ODM, just as the Export Credits Guarantee Department (ECGD) has always been part of the Board of Trade and its successor, the Ministry of Trade.

By 1965, as the result of the waiver of interest charges on certain types of scheme, on the one hand, and of the persistence of the CDC on the need for a change in its capital structure, on the other, two questions were arising which merited serious consideration by HMG before any further concessions, or other changes, were made in the constitution or role of the CDC. The narrow question was whether the interest-free sector of its operations should remain with the CDC or be absorbed into the ODM. The wider question was whether there remained a sufficient 'gap' sector to justify the continuance of the CDC as a separate statutory corporation. In this connection, it is instructive to note the views expressed by the CDC on its twentieth anniversary in 1968 on the interest-free concession and the 'gap' sector. On the first of these it was reported that

it was also decided to establish a committee at official/executive level to consider future financial arrangements for the Corporation. As a result of discussions in this inter-departmental committee, with a representative of the Corporation also present, a decision was taken to allow the Corporation a sum within the annual allocation to be drawn on the new 'waiver' terms each year. In 1968 the amount qualifying for waiver was raised to £5 million from £2 million in the previous year. This was most valuable since the rate at which the Corporation drew from the Treasury during the calendar year 1968 varied between $7\frac{3}{8}$ per cent and 8 per cent and in the last few months has reached $8\frac{7}{8}$ per cent. The existence of 'waiver' money in accordance with the new arrangement made it possible for the Corporation to join with the World Bank in financing the Third Plan for the development of smallholder tea in Kenya and an important expansion to village settlements in Malaya. Without the new arrangements it would have been impossible for the Corporation to have invested in any agricultural schemes which help smallholders.[234]

The enlargement of the aid element thus raised the narrower question already posed. The Report went on to state that

Since December 31, 1968, interest rates have been progressively increased to the present level of $8\frac{7}{8}$ per cent. It is now almost impossible for CDC to undertake new projects profitably without either a significant increase in its allocation of waiver money over the 1968–69 figure or some more fundamental alteration in its capital structure. Few projects in the developing territories can expect to be able to service their capital at rates in the 9–10 per cent bracket and CDC has therefore asked Government to give urgent consideration to the problems with which it is faced.

This raised the wider question, as 'gap' projects were already few and far between. The CDC was beginning to see its future in the field of aid, where it quoted with understandable pride the view of others that its work was 'as effective a form of aid as any in the world'. It concluded:

'With the double financial easement of a considerable sum of money received on "waiver" terms, and reasonably low interest rates, the field of true "effectiveness" might at some future date be substantially increased.'[235] However, in that case, the question arises whether the CDC should continue as a statutory corporation rather than merged into the Ministry of Overseas Development.

VIII. A COMMENT

What has been written so far about the CDC, its working, its rather tedious debates with Whitehall, and its possible future arises directly from the files. The author, in his visits to the Caribbean and to East and Central Africa, was fortunate to be able to discuss the working of joint ventures with the Regional Controllers and other staff of the CDC and also with the staffs of the local development corporations. The visits stretched over the period 1955-69 and so overlapped with the independence of several Colonies and Mandated Territories and with the change of the Corporation's name from the Colonial to the Commonwealth Development Corporation. There was not as much enthusiasm in the independent Commonwealth countries visited about the change in the CDC's area of operations as there was in London. This is an aspect which deserves comment.

As was shown in the treatment in Volume 2, Chapter 6, of the CDC over the early years, the purpose of the proposed Corporation was seen as that of operating big *ad hoc* development schemes in the Colonies and Mandated Territories on a 'break-even' basis. In the Colonial Office it was felt that, on grounds of general policy, big industrial developments in the Colonies ought not to be exploited by private enterprise and, in any case, private enterprise was unlikely to show the degree of activity in such matters as was considered desirable. Treasury officials concurred, believing that the proposal was on the right lines and represented a necessary stage in Colonial development. Doubts came in the early 1950s with the early failures and the unexpectedly difficult attitude of Lord Reith. Mr Oliver Lyttelton questioned whether the Corporation could be expected satisfactorily to operate so many different kinds of projects in so many Colonies. Mr John Dugdale wondered whether there should be two complementary Corporations. It also came to be questioned whether there were sufficient of the so-called 'gap' kind of project to warrant the rather top-heavy Corporation.

Matters looked rather different from the Colonial end. There was generally a preference for public rather than private enterprise in the

Colonies of Africa and the Caribbean. There was also – and this became clearer when the change of title of the CDC was being discussed – a widespread preference for local rather than British public enterprise. It would appear, therefore, that it would have been a more appropriate stage in Colonial development if from the outset reliance had been placed on local efforts. Instead of establishing a statutory Corporation, a Colonial Enterprises Act could have been passed, enabling HMG to channel funds via duly constituted local development corporations for the purposes for which CDC was established. It is true that in time the Corporation adopted a regional approach, channelled funds through local development corporations, set up local building societies and was substantially involved in schemes for peasant agriculture, notably the outstandingly successful joint ventures in tea in Kenya and Malawi. All this is to the credit of the Corporation and is not to be underestimated. Indeed, it rather supports the author's view that the whole effort should have been locally based from the outset.

When the possible winding-up of the Corporation was being considered, not, it seems, very seriously, in March 1960, Mr Iain Macleod recognised, as is recorded in Chapter 6, Section iv, above, that Colonial Governments would welcome the transfer of the unspent allocation of the Corporation's capital and of repayments due to the Corporation to their development projects. He believed that there would be an outcry in Parliament if it was proposed that the Corporation should be wound up because of the mystique associated with the Corporation. This might well have been so. The alternative of devolution to local development corporations was never contemplated. This is rather curious as many in the field, both CDC staff and others, realised that independent Commonwealth countries were unlikely to wish to continue, much less to increase, their reliance on an official British organisation directed from London for public enterprise schemes.

If from the beginning, or at some later stage, it had been decided to work through local development corporations, there would have been many advantages in addition to that of making public enterprise a local matter. Some of these might be gauged when the two phases of the East African Groundnuts Project are compared. The many avoidable errors of the phase when the project was the responsibility of the Ministry of Food gave way to the phase where the attempt to bustle Nature was abandoned in favour of an attempt to provide a viable pattern for African agricultural development. This latter was successful and, as shown in Chapter 4, the project was in time taken over gladly by the Government of Tanganyika. It is suggested that what Sir Stuart Gillett managed to do in Tanganyika could have been managed throughout the Colonies and Mandated Territories via local development corporations and that there was, therefore, no need for a statutory Corporation. As with the Groundnuts Project in its second phase, the whole of Colonial public enterprise would have had the benefit of the expertise of the advisory staff of the Colonial Office. Much tiresome paperwork would have been avoided also, especially that of the Reith years, the tediousness of which has been shown above.

Essentially, public enterprise would have been a local concern, with local control and full scope for local initiative. The Advisers to the Secretary of State would have been available for consultation on schemes submitted, if not when the schemes were being mooted. Especially in the smaller Colonies but not exclusively so, there would have been a shortage of qualified and experienced staff to run the development corporations and expatriates would have been required. There would be nothing unique about that: local churches, universities and the administrations themselves developed on that basis. It would have been better, in the long run, for both HMG and the Colonies if public enterprise had been allowed to follow their example.

However, these suggestions arise from a study of the Corporation as it operated. The civil service does not work by careful study and preparation but very largely on the basis of immediate solutions. The CDC originated in this way. At the end of the war, Colonial Governments wished to promote industrial development and enquired of the Colonial Office how this might best be undertaken. Mr J. Rosa prepared a paper on the subject which was circulated in the Office. Lord Portal, the chairman of the Colonial Economic Development Council, saw the scope for something more positive, namely a statutory corporation to promote both industrial and agricultural development in the Colonies and drafted the Note, which, as is related in Volume 2, Chapter 6, Section i, his Council considered on 10 March 1947. It is possible that he thought of himself as chairman of the new corporation, though this was not to be as the Prime Minister offered the appointment to a former Labour Member of Parliament, Lord Trefgarne. As is shown in the same chapter, the idea caught the imagination of Ministers and, in due course, the Corporation was created. From the outset, it gained the allegiance of many members of both sides in Parliament. Lord Reith sedulously fostered the mystique that surrounded the Corporation, but he did not create it. Despite its chequered career, particularly in the earlier years, it seems that it was never really on the cards to wind it up or radically to alter its functions or methods. It was endowed with a permanence, because it was thought of having an essential role in Colonial development, though it was not easy to define that role.

The Treasury was convinced that the Corporation had no role and that it could not satisfactorily be controlled. It was, therefore, always sceptical and always anxious. It insisted – as it had over the CD & W operations – on having a copy of virtually all the information available to the CDC on each of its projects. But this led not to better control but instead to frustration. In the first place, Treasury officials were not equipped to make the intuitive judgements from the data which businessmen have to make. In the second place, the judgement of the commercial potentiality of a project was entirely within the discretion of the CDC. As Sir David Serpell told the author on 25 November 1975, the Treasury's greatest fear was that discretionary power would lead to the bad use of funds, and the Treasury was never assured until the CDC adopted the scheme basis which operated under CD & W. This was seen as the way to prevent indiscreet expenditure. If the check should be eluded, with this procedure the damage was limited in time, place and size.

The Earl of Perth, who was directly responsible for the CDC when he was Minister of State for Colonial Affairs between January 1957 and April 1962, told the author on 14 November 1975 that, because of its conviction that the Corporation had no role to fulfil and could not adequately be controlled, the Treasury tended to be unreasonable in their dealings with the CDC. For other reasons, including his aggressiveness, Lord Reith was also often unreasonable, and so could not be helped as much as would otherwise have been possible. Nevertheless, he was strongly of the opinion that the Corporation had an important contribution to make in Colonial development. He saw its function as basically those listed in the Corporation's Annual Report for 1959 and quoted on p. 194 above. It could recruit appropriate people for the schemes in hand; it could participate in joint ventures; it could, largely by example, educate local people in modern business methods; and it could do all this without arousing the suspicions of motives, which the direct involvement of HMG would have done. Nevertheless, the capital structure was inappropriate for an organisation with these functions and Lord Perth welcomed the changes made during Lord Howick's period as chairman. If, instead of dwelling wholly on the losses made, the repayments of advances and the payments of interest were totalled, Lord Perth felt it would be realised to what a considerable extent the Treasury had received its money back. At the same time, despite the inflexible conditions under which funds were made available, the Corporatiom operated in fields where private enterprise was unwilling to become involved on its own. With an appropriate capital structure and a happier relationship with the Treasury, Lord Perth was of the opinion that the CDC still had an important part to play in the Third World.

SOURCES

1. CDC: Report and Accounts for 1951, p. 5.

2. Ibid., p. 5.

3. CDC: Report and Accounts for 1952, p. 6.

4. CDC: Report and Accounts for 1954, p. 5.

5. CDC: Report and Accounts for 1954, p. 11.

6. CDC: Report and Accounts for 1959, p. 10.

7. File EGD 81/69/01, 1957–1959, items 7, 4, 6, 9 and 11 respectively: minute of 1 Aug 1958 by the Minister of State after a discussion with the Chairman; letter of 7 Aug 1958 from the Minister of State to the Financial Secretary to the Treasury; letter of 21 Aug 1958, from the Financial Secretary to the Minister of State; letter of 2 Sep 1958 from the Minister of State to the Chairman; and letter of 5 Sep 1958 from the Chairman to the Minister of State.

8. Ibid., item 13A, minute of 12 Sep 1958.

9. Ibid. The Meetings were held on 23 Apr, 9 July, 2 Oct and 23 Nov 1959 – see items 27, 34, 51 and 58. The fifth meeting was on 29 Feb 1960 – item 14 in file EGD 81/69/01, 1960–1962.

10. Confidential file EGD 81/14/012, 1957–1959, item 1/E, CDC: Application for Capital Sanction – £3,000,000: Cameroons Development Corporation.

11. Ibid., item 3, letter of 5 Sep 1958.

12. See ibid. and also Secret file EGD 81/14/012, 1960–1962, Parts A and B.

13. Secret file EGD 81/14/012, 1960–1962, Part B, item 86, submission of 21 June 1962 to Ministers: Cameroons Development Corporation.

14. Ibid., item 75, letter of 31 May 1962 from Mr Norman A. Pannell, MP, to the Secretary of State.

15. Ibid., minute of 21 June 1962.

16. Ibid., item 101, minutes of 25 sep 1962 by Sir Hilton Poynton to the Secretary of State and the latter's minute of 4 Oct 1962.

17. Ibid., item 106, Brief of 22 Oct 1962 for the Parliamentary Under-Secretary.

18. Secret file EGD 81/14/012, Part A, 1963–1965, minute of 2 July 1963.

19. Ibid., minutes of 3 and 12 July 1963.

20. Secret file EGD 81/14/012, Part B, 1963–1965, minute of 31 Jan 1964 and paper of 11 Aug 1964 on Camdev – item 90/E(ii).

21. Ibid., item E/94(ii), record of a meeting between the Minister of State for Foreign Affairs, Mr P. Thomas, and the Minister of Finance in the West Cameroon Government on 28 Aug 1964.

22. Ibid., items 80 and E/80, letter and enclosure of 9 Mar 1964.

23. CDC: Report and Accounts for 1964, para. 119(4).

24. CDC: Report and Accounts for 1963, para. 129(6).
25. File EGD 81/69/01, 1957–1959, item 27, note of a meeting on 23 Apr 1959, para. 4.
26. File 81/14/031, 1957–1959, item 2, letter of 10 Aug 1959 from the Minister of State for Colonial Affairs to the Permanent Under-Secretary of State.
27. Ibid., item 3, 'Projects under investigation in Nigeria for which CDC has not applied for capital sanction'.
28. Ibid., item 4, note of a meeting on 2 Oct 1959.
29. Ibid., item 1, Aide-Memoire on the Position of CDC in Nigeria after Independence.
30. Ibid., item 7, letter of 6 Nov 1959.
31. Ibid., item 6. The Minister of State told the Chairman on 29 Oct, that he believed the plantation business would be a non-starter. On 20 Nov 1959 the CDC submitted a reduced project for three rather than six plantations, costing between £3 million and £4 million instead of £6 million – item 12 in ibid.
32. Ibid., item 19, letter of 21 Dec 1959 from the Minister of State to the Chairman of CDC.
33. Confidential file EGD 81/14/031, 1960–1962, item E/1A, letter of 19 Jan 1960 from the Prime Minister, Mr Macmillan, to the Premier of the Eastern Region, Hon. Dr M. I. Okpara.
34. Ibid., item 1A, letter of 19 Jan 1960 from the Secretary of the Cabinet to the Permanent Under-Secretary of State.
35. Ibid., item 11, Economic Aid to the Federation of Nigeria after Independence.
36. File EGD 81/14/031, 1957–1959, minute of 7 Dec 1959.
37. Confidential file EGD 81/14/031, 1960–1962, item 22, letter of 12 Apr 1960 from the Minister of State to the Governor-General, Federation of Nigeria.
38. CDC: Report and Accounts for 1959, para. 89(4).
39. File EGD 81/14/04, 1957–1959, item 1, Scheme under investigation 23 Apr 1958: Regional development companies, Nigeria.
40. Ibid., item 4, letter of 20 May 1958.
41. Ibid., item 6, note of a meeting held on 9 May 1958.
42. Ibid., item 7, note of a meeting held on 6 June 1958.
43. Idem.
44. Ibid., item 8, Aide-Memoire of talks with CDC on 18 and 23 June 1958.
45. Ibid., item 11, letter of 30 July 1958 from Sir Hilton Poynton to the Governor-General.
46. Idem and letter of 30 July 1958 from Sir Hilton Poynton to the CDC – item 12 in ibid.
47. Ibid., item 17, letter of 15 Aug 1958 from the Deputy Governor of the Western Region to Sir Hilton Poynton.
48. Ibid., item 23, letter of 17 Sep 1958 from the Governor-General.
49. Ibid., item 24, letter of 7 Oct 1958.
50. Ibid., item 42, letter of 26 Nov 1958.
51. Ibid., item 44, letter of 8 Dec 1958.
52. Ibid., item 48, letter of 23 Dec 1958.

53. Ibid., minutes of 11 Aug and 9 Sep.

54. Ibid., minute of 2 Mar 1959.

55. Ibid., items 69 and 68 respectively: letter of 10 Mar 1959 in reply to letter of 9 Mar.

56. Ibid., item 74, letter of 18 Mar 1959.

57. Ibid., items 84–7, Despatches Nos 949, 190, 226 and 237 of 6 May 1959 from the Secretary of State to the Governor-General and Regional Governors, Nigeria.

58. File EGD 81/016, 1957–1959, item 66, letter and enclosures of 14 Aug 1958.

59. File EGD 81/15/01, 1957–1959, item 2, letter of 1 Sep 1958. The Gambia correspondence on EGD 81/12/06, 1957–1959, mainly duplicates that of the Sierra Leone file.

60. Ibid., item 4, letter of 22 Sep 1958.

61. Ibid., items 6 and 7, letters of 30 Sep and 2 Oct 1958.

62. Ibid., item 2, letter of 1 Sep 1958.

63. File EGD 81/69/01, 1960–1962, item 14.

64. File EGD 81/69/01, 1960–1962, item 9, letter of 17 Feb 1960.

65. Idem.

66. File EGD 81/69/01, 1960–1962, items 5, para. 11.

67. File EGD 81/016, 1957–1959, item 105, letter and enclosure of 18 Dec 1959.

68. File EGD 81/015, 1960–1962, item 4A, submission of 11 Mar 1960.

69. Ibid., item 7, letter of 25 Mar 1960.

70. File EGD 81/8/016, 1960–1962, item 5, letter of 5 Dec 1960.

71. Ibid., item 4, letter of 18 Nov 1960.

72. Ibid., item 6, letter of 14 Dec 1960.

73. Ibid., item 7, letter of 25 Apr 1961.

74. Ibid., item 8, letter of 28 Apr 1961.

75. Ibid., item 9, letter of 5 May 1961.

76. Ibid., item 10, letter of 9 June 1961. A minute of 23 May 1961 accepted that, as the IBRD thought in terms of £500,000 from all sources, 'While therefore the International Bank's report gives encouragement to a small Development Corporation, we could scarcely argue from its authority for something which is clearly more than an investigatory body.'

77. Treasury file 2-CF 425/101/01, Part A, minute of 27 June 1961.

78. Ibid., minute of 28 June 1961. It was again endorsed in the minute of 29 June 1961 by Sir Ronald Harris to the Financial Secretary, in ibid.

79. Ibid., minute of 30 June 1961.

80. Ibid., letter of 30 June 1961 from the Secretary of State for the Colonies to the Chancellor of the Exchequer.

81. Ibid., item 11, letter of 10 July 1961.

82. Ibid., item 13, letter of 23 Aug 1961. The building society project was dealt with separately as it concerned the whole of East and Central Africa.

83. Ibid., item 14, letter of 14 Sep 1961.

84. Ibid., item 16, letter of 26 Sep 1961.

85. Ibid., items 20 and 24, letters and enclosure of 14 Nov 1961 to the Under-

Secretary of State, Colonial Office; letter of 30 Nov 1961.

86. Ibid., item 28, letter of 12 Dec 1962.

87. File EGD 81/8/016, 1963–1965, item E/1, letter of 10 Jan 1963.

88. CDC: Report and Accounts for 1962, p. 64.

89. File EGD 81/9/05, 1960–1962, item 1, letter and enclosure of 28 Feb 1962.

90. Ibid., minute of 14 Mar 1962.

91. Ibid., items 7 and 2 respectively: letter of 28 Sep 1962; Note of Meeting on 4 Apr between Chairman of UDC and the Legal Adviser to UDC.

92. File EGD 81/016, 1960–1962, item 59, letter and enclosure of 12 Nov 1962.

93. Ibid., items 10–12, letters of 5 and 16 Oct and 13 Nov 1962.

94. Ibid., item 10, letter of 5 Oct 1962. On a subsidiary point the reply stated: 'So far as the United Kingdom trade argument is concerned, I do not at the moment see how CDC participation will help to divert procurement away from American sources – unless, that is, CDC participation is in substitution for American participation. And I think we would all agree that it would be wrong to do anything which might discourage American aid.'

95. Ibid., item 13, letter of 20 Nov 1962.

96. Ibid., item 20, letter of 14 Dec 1962.

97. File EGD 81/015, 1960–1962, item 20, letter of 14 Dec 1962.

98. File EGD 81/015, 1963–1965, item 15, letter of 30 Apr 1963.

99. Ibid., item 18, Confidential savingram of 8 May 1963 from CRO to High Commissioners.

100. Ibid., item 19 and 19/Ei, letter and enclosure of 7 Aug 1963.

101. Ibid., item 22 and 22/E, letter and enclosure of 12 Dec 1963.

102. Ibid., item 14, letter of 24 Apr 1963.

103. Ibid., item 2, letter of 5 Apr 1963.

104. Ibid., item 7, letter of 5 July 1963.

105. Ibid., item 8, letter of 15 July 1963.

106. Ibid., items 10, 11 and 13, letters and enclosures of 18, 20 and 28 Nov 1963.

107. Ibid., item 12, letter of 26 Nov 1963.

108. Ibid., item 14, letter of 3 Dec 1963.

109. Confidential file EGD 81/9/05, 1963–1965, items 1 and 4, letters of 9 Aug and 2 Sep 1963.

110. Ibid., items 5 and 7, letter and enclosure of 21 Oct and letter of 20 Nov 1963.

111. File EGD 81/14/042, 1963–1965, item E/25, letter of 1 July 1963.

112. Confidential file EGD 81/14/042, 1960–1962, item 22/E/1, memorandum of 16 Nov 1962 by CDC.

113. Ibid., item 25, letter of 29 Nov 1962. There was no commitment on the part of CDC to contribute a further £1 million in cash, although the Government had proposed it. That would have raised the total on either side to £3.3 million.

114. Ibid., item E/26, letter of 1 Dec 1962.

115. Ibid., item E/28, letter of 14 Dec 1962.

116. Ibid., item 33, letter of 27 Dec 1962.

117. File EGD 81/14/042, 1963–1965, item E/17, letter of 24 May 1963.

118. Ibid., item 13, letter and enclosure of 29 Apr 1962.

119. Ibid., item E/16, letter of 21 May 1963.

120. Ibid., item 22, letter of 14 June 1963.

121. Ibid., item E/25, letter of 1 July 1963.

122. Ibid., item 33, letter and enclosed draft for CDC of 12 Aug 1963.

123. CDC: Report and Accounts for 1963, p. 4, para. 6.

124. CDC: Report and Accounts, 1964, p. 117, para. 112.

125. Ibid., p. 60, para. 34.

126. Ibid., pp. 54–5, para. 21.

127. Confidential file EGD 81/67/07, Part A, 1963–1965, item 115/EC(ii), letter and enclosure of 5 Mar 1964.

128. Confidential file 81/67/07, Part B, 1963–1965, item E/123, letter of 15 Apr 1964 to Controller of Finance CDC.

129. CDC: Report and Accounts, 1968, states on p. 93, para. 80, that the Government of Tanganyika acquired the interests of the oversea investors, involving a capital loss for the CDC.

130. Confidential file EGD 81/67/07, Part A, 1963–1965, item 40, letter and enclosure of 18 Nov 1963.

131. Ibid., item 42, and E/42(i), letter and enclosure of 20 Nov 1963. The hotel was the Panafric.

132. File EGD 81/016, 1957–1959, item 88, letter and enclosure of 25 May 1959.

133. CDC: Report and Accounts for 1960, p. 33, para. 33.

134. CDC: Report and Accounts for 1963, p. 38, para. 27. CDC's share was £27,523 and was approved on 2 Dec 1963 – see letter of that date to Controller of Finance, CDC: item 8 in Confidential file WID 20/224/2, 1963.

135. CDC: Report and Accounts, 1964, p. 48, para. 15.

136. File 2-WID 20/202/1, 1964–1966, item 17, letter of 4 Nov 1964.

137. Treasury file 2 FD 36/01, Part A, minute of 12 Sep 1963 by the Permanent Secretary to the Treasury, Sir William Armstrong.

138. CDC: Report and Accounts, 1964, p. 2, para. 8.

139. CDC: Report and Accounts for 1950, p. 22, para. 40.

140. CDC: Report and Accounts for 1953, p. 33, para. 30(8).

141. File SEA 36/37/01, 1951–1953, item 25, letter of 16 Mar 1953.

142. Ibid., item 26, letter of 20 Mar 1953.

143. Ibid., minute of 23 Mar 1953.

144. Ibid., item 37, letter of 28 Apr 1953.

145. Ibid., item 39, letter of 15 Apr 1953.

146. Ibid., item 46, letter of 22 May 1953.

147. Ibid., minute of 5 June 1953.

148. Ibid., item 47, letter of 12 June 1953.

149. Ibid., item 58, letter of 27 July 1953.

150. Ibid., item 60, letter of 5 Aug 1953. As stated in the Annual Report for 1963, in August 1963 the CDC made an offer for sale to the Malayan public and others of M $5 million of its holding of ordinary stock, in accordance with its long-term

policy of gradual disposal of its investments in established projects. The offer, at a premium of 7 per cent, was oversubscribed 29 times and, as a result, by the end of 1963 there were some 5000 shareholders.

151. Ibid., minute of 24 Aug 1953.

152. File EGD 81/228/01, 1954–1956. Table prepared for Parliamentary Answer No. 1, 18 Apr 1956.

153. File EGD 81/23/06, 1957–1959, item 7, letter of 27 Nov 1956 from the General Manager of the Society to the Building Research Station.

154. Ibid., item 13, letter of 26 Aug 1958.

155. Ibid., item 35, letter of 2 Jan 1959.

156. File EGD 81/14/02, 1957–1959 (duplicated on EGD 81/14/03, 1957–1959), item 1, letter of 28 Apr 1958 and enclosure.

157. Ibid., item 4, letter of 27 May 1958.

158. Ibid., item 5, letter of 13 June 1958.

159. Ibid., item 8, letter of 18 June 1958.

160. Ibid., item 9, letter of 23 July 1958.

161. Ibid., item 10, letter of 5 Aug 1958.

162. Ibid., item 11, letter of 18 Sep 1958.

163. File EGD 81/6/04, 1960–1962, item 17, letter of 13 Apr 1961 from the Chairman of CDC to the Minister of State.

164. Ibid., item 1, letter and enclosure of 15 Dec 1960.

165. Ibid., unnumbered item, Brief of 18 July 1961 by Colonial Office on Building Societies in East and Central Africa.

166. Ibid., item 21A, letter of 25 Aug 1961.

167. Ibid., item 22, letter and enclosure of 31 Aug 1961.

168. Ibid., item 24, letter of 8 Sep 1961.

169. Ibid., item 26, letter of 14 Sep 1961.

170. Ibid., item 41, letter of 22 June 1962.

171. File EGD 81/6/04, 1963–1965, item 1, letter and enclosure of 14 Jan 1963.

172. Ibid., item 6, letter of 19 Mar 1963.

173. Ibid., item 30, letter of 23 Dec 1963.

174. Ibid., item 35, letter of 2 Mar 1964.

175. Ibid., minutes of 13 and 20 Apr 1964.

176. Ibid., item 39, letter of 27 Apr 1964.

177. Confidential file EGD 81/67/01, Part A, 1960–1962, item 63, letter of 14 Dec 1961 from the Chairman of the CDC to the Minister of State.

178. Ibid., minute by the Minister of State on item 63 above.

179. Confidential file EGD 81/67/01, Part B, 1960–1962, item 67, letter of 27 Feb 1962 from the Chairman to the Secretary of State.

180. Ibid., item 72, letter of 9 Mar 1962 from the Chairman to the Permanent Under-Secretary of State.

181. Treasury File 2 FD 36/01, Part A, letter of 25 July 1963 from the Chairman to the Permanent Secretary to the Treasury, enclosing a copy of a letter he had sent on 22 May 1963 to the President of IBRD.

182. Idem, letter of 22 May 1963 to the President of the IBRD, para. 13.

183. CDC: Report and Accounts for 1963, p. 3, para. 5.

184. CDC: Report and Accounts for 1950, p. 23, para. 42.

185. CDC: Report and Accounts for 1954, p. 34, para. 37.

186. CDC: Report and Accounts for 1957, p. 37, paras 41 and 42. Johore Palm Processing Limited was a subsidiary of Kulai Oil Palm Estate Limited, which was a wholly-owned CDC subsidiary. They had a joint manager.

187. CDC: Report and Accounts for 1959, pp. 42–3, paras 42 and 43.

188. Confidential file EGD 81/67/07, 1963–1965, item 27, letter and enclosure of 30 Oct 1963.

189. Ibid., item 28, letter and enclosure of 30 Oct 1963.

190. Ibid., items 60(ii) and (iii), letters of 2 Dec 1963.

191. Confidential file EGD 81/67/07, 1963–1965, item 1, letter and enclosure of 31 July 1963.

192. Ibid., item 8A, Confidential telegram No. 974 of 22 Aug 1963 from the High Commissioner, Lagos, to the CRO.

193. Ibid., item 59, letter of 29 Nov 1963.

194. CDC: Report and Accounts for 1949, p. 5.

195. CDC: Report and Accounts for 1950, pp. 13–14, para. 28.

196. CDC: Report and Accounts for 1952, p. 33, para. 26.

197. CDC: Report and Accounts for 1956, p. 31, para. 30.

198. CDC: Report and Accounts for 1962, p. 35, para. 22.

199. File EGD 81/7/010, 1957–1959, letter of 24 Feb 1959. Doubts in the Colonial Office concerning the commercial viability of coffee factories, in view of the growing world surplus of coffee, were not referred to in the letter, which agreed in principle to both the tea and coffee factories proposed in the submission.

200. File EGD 81/7/017, 1960–1962, item 1, letter and enclosure of 1 Feb 1960.

201. Ibid., item 3, letter of 3 Feb 1960. No exception was allowed in reply – item 4.

202. Ibid., item 5, letter of 5 Apr 1960; and Submission of 13 Apr 1960 to the Minister of State, item 7.

203. Ibid., item 6, letter of 11 Apr 1960.

204. Ibid., minute of 13 Apr 1960.

205. Ibid., minute of 13 Apr 1960 by the Minister of State for Colonial Affairs.

206. Ibid., item 8, letter of 20 Apr 1960.

207. Ibid., item E/9, letter and enclosure of 19 Aug 1960.

208. Ibid., item 11, letter of 31 Aug 1960.

209. Ibid., item 12, letter of 28 Sep 1960.

210. Ibid., item 31, letter and enclosure of 5 Apr 1962.

211. ODM File CF 370/95/04, 1964–1966, item 1, letter and enclosure of 14 Apr 1964.

212. Ibid., item 9, CDC Press Release of 29 July 1965 announcing the agreement to provide the capital for the three factories.

213. Treasury file 2FD 36/01, Part A, letter of 21 May 1963 from the President of IBRD to the Chancellor of the Exchequer.

214. Ibid., letter of 27 June 1963 from the Chancellor of the Exchequer to the President of IBRD.

215. Ibid., letter of 25 July 1963 from the Chairman to the President.

216. Ibid., minute of 2 Aug 1963 by the Permanent Secretary to the Treasury, Sir W. Armstrong.

217. Ibid., minute of 12 Sep 1963 by the Permanent Secretary to the Treasury, Sir W. Armstrong.

218. D.P. (64)23, 26 June 1964.

219. DP (64) 9th Meeting, 9 July 1964.

220. EP (64) 23rd Meeting, 27 May 1964.

221. DP (64) 27th Meeting, 7 July 1964 Terms of Aid Loans: Note by the Treasury, para. 26.

222. Treasury File 2FD 36/01, Part B, minute of 8 Oct 1964.

223. Ibid., minute of 3 Nov 1964.

224. Ibid., minutes of 2 and 11 Nov 1964. In its Memorandum to the Official Committee on Overseas Development (WPL(65) 1 Revise, 26 Jan 1965) it was stated that the suggestion of equity capital 'need not be seriously considered, nor do the CDC expect this'.

225. Secret file of ODM Finance Department CF 370/819/01, Part B, 1964–1966, item 91, letter of 17 Aug 1965.

226. Secret file of ODM Finance Department CF 370/819/01, Part B, 1964–1966, item 40, WPL(65)1 Revise, 26 Jan 1965 which became DVO(O)(65)12, 11 Apr 1965.

227. DVO(O)(65)12, paras 14–15. In Cmnd 2736, *Overseas Development: The Work of the New Ministry*, 3 Aug 1965, it was stated that: 'The CDC has a unique part to play in development by pioneering new patterns of co-operation with local enterprise. . . . It can, in effect, provide for selected projects the combination of financial help and technical management expertise which is characteristic of the best forms of private enterprise' (para. 109).

228. DVO(65)3 – the paper submitted to the Ministerial Committee by the Chairman of the Official Committee.

229. DVO(o)(65)12, para. 16.

230. Idem, para. 17.

231. CDC: Report and Accounts, 1965, p. 4.

232. Idem, pp. 3–4.

233. Secret ODM file CF 370/819/01, Part B, item 95, letter of 28 Sep 1965 from the Chief Secretary to the Treasury to the Minister of Overseas Development – quoted in Chapter 6, Section vi, above.

234. CDC: Annual Report and Statement of Accounts, year ended 31 Dec 1968, p. 16.

235. Ibid., p. 17.

Appendix
The Colonial Office,
1924–1967

1924, 23 January	Rt Hon. J. H. Thomas
1924, 7 November	Rt Hon. L. C. M. S. Amery, CH
1929, 8 June	Rt Hon. Lord Passfield
1931, 26 August	Rt Hon. J. H. Thomas
1931, 9 November	Rt Hon. Sir Philip Cunliffe-Lister, GBE, MC (later Viscount Swinton, CH)
1935, 7 June	Rt Hon. Malcolm MacDonald
1935, 27 November	Rt Hon. J. H. Thomas
1936, 29 May	Rt Hon. W. G. A. Ormsby-Gore (later Lord Harlech, KG, GCMG)
1938, 16 May	Rt Hon. Malcolm MacDonald
1940, 13 May	Rt Hon. Lord Lloyd, GCSI, GCIE, DSO
1941, 8 February	Rt Hon. Lord Moyne, DSO
1942, 23 February	Rt Hon. Viscount Cranborne (later Marquess of Salisbury, KG)
1942, 24 November	Rt Hon. O. F. G. Stanley, MC
1945, 3 August	Rt Hon. G. H. Hall (later Viscount Hall)
1946, 7 October	Rt Hon. A. Creech Jones
1950, 2 March	Rt Hon. James Griffiths
1951, 27 October	Rt Hon. Oliver Lyttelton, DSO MC (afterwards Viscount Chandos)
1954, 30 July	Rt Hon. Alan T. Lennox-Boyd, CH (afterwards Viscount Boyd of Merton)
1959, 19 October	Rt Hon. Iain Macleod
1961, 16 October	Rt Hon. Reginald Maudling
1962, 17 July	Rt Hon. Duncan Sandys (later Lord Duncan-Sandys)
1964, 17 October	Rt Hon. Anthony Greenwood (later Lord Greenwood of Rossendale)
1965, 23 December	Rt Hon. The Earl of Longford

1966, 6 April   Rt Hon. Frederick Lee (later Lord Lee of Newton)

MINISTERS OF STATE FOR COLONIAL AFFAIRS (1948–1963)

1948, 5 January	Rt Hon. The Earl of Listowel, GCMG
1950, 2 March	Rt Hon. John Dugdale
1951, 2 November	Rt Hon. Alan T. Lennox-Boyd, CH (afterwards Viscount Boyd of Merton)
1952, 8 May	Rt Hon. Henry Hopkinson, CMG (afterwards Lord Colyton)
1955, 20 December	The Hon. John H. Hare, OBE (afterwards Viscount Blakenham)
1956, 19 October	Rt Hon. John Maclay, CH, CMG (afterwards Viscount Muirshiel)
1957, 17 January	Rt Hon. The Earl of Perth
1962, 19 April	The Most Hon. The Marquess of Lansdowne, PC

MINISTERS OF STATE FOR COMMONWEALTH RELATIONS AND FOR THE COLONIES (1963–1964)

1963, October   The Most Hon. The Marquess of Lansdowne, PC

His Grace the Duke of Devonshire, PC, MC

PARLIAMENTARY UNDER-SECRETARIES OF STATE FOR THE COLONIES

1924, January	Lord Arnold
1924, November	Rt Hon. W. G. A. Ormsby-Gore (later Lord Harlech, KG, GCMG)
1929, June	Mr W. Lunn
1929, December	Sir Drummond Shiels, MC
1931	Sir Robert Hamilton
1932	Rt Hon. The Earl of Plymouth
1936	Rt Hon. Earl De La Warr, GBE
1937	The Marquess of Dufferin and Ava
1940	Rt Hon. G. H. Hall (later Viscount Hall)
1942	Rt Hon. Harold Macmillan
1943	His Grace the Duke of Devonshire, KG, MBE
1945	Rt Hon. A. Creech Jones
1946	Mr Ivor Thomas (later Bulmer-Thomas)

1947, 8 October	Mr D. R. Rees-Williams, TD (afterwards Rt Hon. Lord Ogmore)
1950, 2 March	Mr T. F. Cook
1951, 5 November	Rt Hon. The Earl of Munster, KBE
1954, 18 October	Rt Hon. Lord Lloyd, MBE
1957, 19 January	Mr J. D. Profumo, OBE
1958, 1 December	Rt Hon. Julian Amery
1960, 31 October	Hon. Hugh Fraser, MBE
1962, 17 July– October 1963	Mr (later Sir Nigel) Fisher, MC
1964, 21 October	Mrs Eirene White, later Baroness White
1966, 6 April	Mr John Stonehouse

PARLIAMENTARY UNDER-SECRETARIES OF STATE FOR
COMMONWEALTH RELATIONS AND FOR THE COLONIES FROM 1963

1963, October	Mr (later Sir Nigel) Fisher, MC
	Mr John Tilney, TD
	Mr Richard Hornby
1964, October	Lord Taylor
1965, October	Lord Beswick

PERMANENT UNDER-SECRETARIES OF STATE FOR THE COLONIES

1925	Brig.-Gen. Sir Samuel H. Wilson, GCMG, KCB, KBE
1933	Sir John Maffey (afterwards Lord Rugby of Rugby), GCMG, KCB, KCVO, CSI, CIE
1937, 2 July	Sir Cosmo Parkinson, GCMG, KCB, OBE
1940, 1 February	Sir George Gater, GCMG, KCB, DSO
1940, 28 May	Sir Cosmo Parkinson, GCMG, KCB, OBE
1942, 13 April	Sir George Gater, GCMG, KCB, DSO
1947, 1 February	Sir Thomas Lloyd, GCMG, KCB
1956, 20 August	Sir John Macpherson, GCMG
1959, 20 August	Sir Hilton Poynton, GCMG

DEPUTY PERMANENT UNDER-SECRETARIES OF STATE

1931, 15 August	Sir John E. Shuckburgh, KCMG, CB
1942, 18 March	Sir William Battershill, KCMG
1945, 13 April	Sir Arthur Dawe, KCMG, OBE
1947, 1 February	Sir Sydney Caine, KCMG ⎫
1947, 6 April	Sir Charles Jeffries, KCMG, OBE ⎭ Joint

	Sir Charles Jeffries, KCMG, OBE	Joint
1948, 5 August	Sir Hilton Poynton, KCMG	
	Sir Hilton Poynton, KCMG	Joint
1956, 1 July	Sir John Martin, KCMG, CB, CVO	
	Sir John Martin, KCMG, CB, CVO	Joint
1959, 20 August	Sir William Gorell Barnes, KCMG, CB	
1963, 1 June	Sir John Martin, KCMG, CB, CVO	
1965, 26 January	Mr (later Sir Arthur) Galsworthy, KCMG	

The Colonial Office was combined with the Department of Commonwealth Affairs on 1 July 1966 and discontinued on 7 January 1967. When the Commonwealth Office was merged with the Foreign Office to form the present Foreign and Commonwealth Office, the Secretary of State for Foreign and Commonwealth Affairs became ultimately responsible for the remaining Colonial territories. A Minister of State was deputed to deal with affairs on a day-to-day basis. At the official level, the Permanent Under-Secretary of State was ultimately responsible but normally a Superintending Deputy Under-Secretary dealt with the matter arising. Sir Arthur Galsworthy held the position until 1969 when he was succeeded by Sir Leslie Monson, who retired in 1972.

Index